THE GERMAN LAW OF UNJUSTIFIED ENRICHMENT AND RESTITUTION

A Comparative Introduction

The German Law of Unjustified Enrichment and Restitution

A Comparative Introduction

GERHARD DANNEMANN

OXFORD
UNIVERSITY PRESS

This book has been printed digitally and produced in a standard specification in order to ensure its continuing availability

OXFORD
UNIVERSITY PRESS

Great Clarendon Street, Oxford OX2 6DP
United Kingdom

Oxford University Press is a department of the University of Oxford. It furthers the University's objective of excellence in research, scholarship, and education by publishing worldwide. Oxford is a registered trade mark of Oxford University Press in the UK and in certain other countries

First published 2009
Reprinted 2012

British Library Cataloguing in Publication Data
Data available

Library of Congress Cataloging in Publication Data
Data available

ISBN 978-0-19-953311-4

Preface

The story of this book goes back fifteen years. In summer 1994, when I was about to join the Oxford law faculty, I met the Regius Professor of English Law, Peter Birks, to discuss my tasks. He asked me to join his restitution course and to give a series of lectures on the German law of unjustified enrichment. I ended up giving those lectures for the eight years which followed, and with a lasting fascination for the comparative law in this area.

An early version of my lecture notes was published in 1997.[1] The present book draws on the latest version as well as a number of articles which have resulted from my encounter with unjust(ified) enrichment.[2] It owes much to all students and fellow convenors who contributed to the discussion in the Oxford BCL Restitution Seminar, arguably the best testing ground for any ideas one might have on this subject.

The book is divided into three parts. Part I (Chapters 1–7) explains the German law of unjustified enrichment in the context of other models of restitutionary liability. Part II (Chapters 8 and 9) looks at the wider comparative perspective. Chapter 8 discusses issues of scope, taxonomy, and approach towards unjust(ified) enrichment, and explains why English and German law have much more in common than first meets the eye. Chapter 9 looks at lessons which German and English law might learn from each other. Particular attention is paid to the suggestion by the late Peter Birks that English law should switch from an unjust factor approach to a German style absence of basis approach.[3] Part III contains translations of leading German cases (Chapter 10) and of provisions of the German Civil Code (Chapter 11) which relate to unjustified enrichment and restitution. These should enable readers without

[1] Basil Markesinis, Werner Lorenz, and Gerhard Dannemann, *The German Law of Obligations, Vol. I: The Law of Contracts and Restitution: a Comparative Introduction* (1997), 710–816.

[2] 'Restitution for Termination of Contract in German Law', in: *Failure of Contracts: Contractual, Restitutionary and Proprietary Consequences*, ed. by Francis Rose (1997), 129–153; 'Illegality as a Defence' (2000) Oxford U Comparative Law Forum 4; 'Unjust Enrichment by Transfer: Some Comparative Remarks', in: 79 Texas Law Review (2001), 1837–1867; 'Unjust Enrichment as Absence of Basis: Can English Law Cope?', in: *Mapping the Law*, 363–377. For the use of 'unjust' or 'unjustified', see p. 37.

[3] Birks, *Unjust Enrichment*, Ch 5.

knowledge of the German language to familiarize themselves with the primary sources, and allow them to draw their own comparisons.

This reliance on primary sources is also a methodological feature of the book. While it engages in Part I in an asymmetrical comparison by using English law as a contrast foil or point of reference for explaining German law (rather than presenting German and English law in the same detail), it nevertheless treats both on an equal footing in terms of using legal sources. The book seeks to keep an equal distance from the strong focus on restating existing case law which is traditional for English textbooks (although not for most of the recent English literature on unjust enrichment) and the equally strong focus on doctrinal issues which is traditional for German textbooks. As a consequence, primary sources take pride of place when it comes to stating what the law is, and scholarly writing is given more prominence when it comes to explaining how the law functions and what it should look like. English and German law are also given equal attention in the more comprehensive comparative analysis in Part II.

The book thus aims to represent German law in such a way that it can be more easily understood by readers trained in the common law, but not less accurately than a classical German textbook. It seeks to explain authentic rather than anglicized German law. I hope that it may provide new insights not only to common law readers, but also to those from other jurisdictions, perhaps even German lawyers.

Next to those who have been mentioned above, I owe thanks to the Texas Law Review and Hart Publishing for their kind permission to reproduce or otherwise draw on materials in which they have copyright,[4] to Joy Ruskin-Tompkins for her careful editing of the manuscript, to Corinna Radke, Irene Maier, and Nico Köppel for their painstaking editorial work on Chapter 10, to Nico Köppel also for having compiled the table of cases, and to all student assistants at the Centre for British Studies, Humboldt-Universität for their help in borrowing books and copying articles.

The law is stated as of 1 January 2009.

Gerhard Dannemann
Berlin, February 2009

[4] Gerhard Dannemann, 'Unjust Enrichment by Transfer: Some Comparative Remarks', in: 79 Texas Law Review (2001), 1837–1867. Chapter 10 contains English translations of three cases which were first published in *Cases, Materials and Texts on Unjustified Enrichment*, ed. by Jack Beatson and Eltjo Schrage.

Contents—Summary

Contents

Table of Cases

COMMONWEALTH AND UK

GERMANY

Bundesverfassungsgericht

Reichsgericht

Bundesgerichtshof

Other Courts

OTHER COUNTRIES

Austria

France

United States

PART I
UNJUSTIFIED ENRICHMENT AND RESTITUTION IN GERMAN LAW

1

Introduction

This book aims to make the German law of unjustified enrichment and restitution familiar to readers who are trained in the common law, and also to contribute to an ongoing comparative debate. The comparative perspective of this book draws significantly on the different ways in which the German and English laws of unjust(ified) enrichment have evolved.[1]

It is sometimes forgotten that unjust enrichment has a long tradition in English law. Bracton mentions both *condictio indebiti* and *negotiorum gestio*.[2] *Slade's Case* established an action in debt without need for a contractual promise more than 400 years ago.[3] In 1760, in *Moses v Macferlan*, Lord Mansfield laid the foundations for a comprehensive analysis of unjust enrichment.[4] In 1802 the first publication of a modern scholarly treatment of the English law of unjust enrichment was seen.[5] Moreover, comparisons between the German and English laws of unjust(ified) enrichment have been made for at least seventy years.[6]

This long tradition is easily overlooked because unjust enrichment was for long neglected by courts and academics as an area of English law in its own right. It was barely if at all taught in universities and

[1] See below, Chapter 2, section 6.1, for an explanation of the difference between unjustified and unjust enrichment.

[2] Henry de Bracton, *De legibus et consuetudinibus Angliae* (c. 1220–1250), makes a brief mention of the *condictio indebiti* and *negotiorum gestio* in the chapter *De Actionibus* under the heading *De obligationibus quæ quasi ex contractu nascuntur*.

[3] *Slade's Case* (1602) 4 Coke Rep 91.

[4] *Moses v Macferlan* (1760) 2 Burr 1005.

[5] Sir William Evans, *An Essay on the Action for Money Had and Received* (1802).

[6] See in particular the contributions by W Friedmann and Dawson; an important contribution to an Anglo-French debate was made by Gutteridge and David (all as indicated in the Select Bibliography).

unfamiliar to most legal practitioners. This has changed. Preceded and assisted by scholarly work,[7] English courts have unfrozen the law of unjust enrichment and have, in less than one decade, achieved a rapid development which in other areas of the law might have taken a century.[8] At the same time, a rich comparative debate has unfolded,[9] which has gained a new focus by the proposition made by the late Peter Birks that English law should abandon its present unjust factor approach in favour of a German-style absence of basis approach to unjust enrichment.[10] By contrast, unjustified enrichment has maintained an established position in the *Bürgerliches Gesetzbuch* (BGB, German Civil Code) for more than a century, during which time it has always formed part of the undergraduate syllabus at German law faculties. In German legal learning and practice, unjustified enrichment has for long been as well established as contract and tort. Moreover, the German law of unjustified enrichment appears well settled, as the last phase of major development occurred some forty years ago.

Taking a closer look at the German law of unjustified enrichment from the perspective of English law can therefore be very useful. It can reveal whether English law is capable of switching to an absence of basis approach, and whether the advantages would outweigh the disadvantages which go hand in hand with such a shift. It can also show us where German law, which may have become somewhat complacent over the last decades, can learn from the recent English experience.

[7] Many have contributed to this debate. Three milestones will be mentioned: the American Law Institute's *Restatement of the Law of Restitution, Quasi Contracts and Constructive Trusts* (1937) by Austin W Scott and Warren A Seavey; Robert Goff and Gareth Jones, *The Law of Restitution*, 1st edn (1966); P Birks, *An Introduction to the Law of Restitution* (1985).

[8] The most rapid development occurred between 1991 and 1999: *Lipkin Gorman v Karpnale Ltd* [1991] 2 AC 548 (HL); *Woolwich Equitable Building Society v Inland Revenue Commissioners* [1993] AC 70 (HL); *Barclays Bank plc v O'Brien* [1994] 1 AC 180 (HL); *Westdeutsche Landesbank Girozentrale v Islington London Borough Council* [1996] AC 669 (HL); *Kleinwort Benson Ltd v Lincoln City Council* [1999] 2 AC 349 (HL). However, cases such as *Royal Bank of Scotland v Etridge* [2001] UKHL 44, *Deutsche Morgan Grenfell Group Plc v Her Majesty's Commissioners of Inland Revenue* [2006] UKHL 49, and *Yeoman's Row Management Limited and another v Cobbe* [2008] UKHL 55 show that the phase of development continues.

[9] The reader is referred to the numerous comparative works indicated in the Select Bibliography.

[10] Birks, *Unjust Enrichment*, Ch. 5.

Part I (Chapters 1–7) presents the German law of unjustified enrichment to common law readers by using English law as a contrast foil which serves to illustrate connecting points, similarities, and differences.[11] This comparison is asymmetric[12] in the sense that English law is not explained in the same detail as German law. Chapters 1–7 are also based on the structure of the German law of unjustified enrichment, which is shown in the context of other restitutionary remedies available under German law. As far as sources of law are concerned, the comparison aims at symmetry between English and German law. The traditional German fondness for dogmatic dispute at the expense of the law as practised by the courts finds as little reflection in this book as does the traditional English focus on case law at the expense of scholarly debate, a debate which has been and continues to be a driving force for change in the law of unjust enrichment. The book aims to take the middle ground, by explaining how primary sources (statutes and case law) have interacted with secondary sources (academic writing) to the degree that it is difficult to understand one without the other. It is left to the readers whether they will agree that this methodological set-up is equally beneficial for both English and German law.

Part II (Chapters 8 and 9) presents a more comprehensive comparative analysis on the basis of Part I. A closer inspection of issues of classification (scope, taxonomy, and general approach) will reveal unexpected similarities between English and German law, forming the basis for the discussion in Chapter 9 concerning what the English law of unjust enrichment and the German law of unjustified enrichment can learn from each other. In particular, Chapter 9 discusses whether English law should switch to a German-style absence of basis approach as proposed by Birks.

Part III makes some important German primary sources on the law of unjustified enrichment and restitution accessible to anglophone readers. Chapter 10 contains English translations of 17 key German judgments (referred to throughout this book as, for example,

[11] See Gerhard Dannemann, 'Comparative Law: Study of Similarities or Differences?', in: *The Oxford Handbook of Comparative Law*, ed. by Mathias Reimann and Reinhard Zimmermann (2006), 383–419.

[12] On symmetric and asymmetric comparisons, see Jürgen Osterhammel, 'Sozialgeschichte im Zivilisationsvergleich', Geschichte und Gesellschaft (1996), 143ff, 157.

'case no. 12'), and Chapter 11 translations of key provisions of the German Civil Code.

1. The law of unjustified enrichment within the German Civil Code

When an area as vast as civil law is codified it is first necessary to develop a relatively clear concept of how the different component parts of this area of law relate to each other. If nothing more, the basic need to number provisions in a code entails the necessity for an internal order. This structure generally reveals underlying issues, and this is certainly true for the German law of unjustified enrichment.

At its core, the German law of unjustified enrichment consists of 11 sections in the German Civil Code, §§ 812–822 BGB, which are placed in the second book of the BGB, the law of obligations, between contract and tort. Book 3 (§§ 854–1296 BGB) regulates the law of property (*Sachenrecht*). Family law (*Familienrecht*) is treated in Book 4 (§§ 1297–1921). The fifth book (§§ 1922–2385) covers inheritance law (*Erbrecht*).

Within the second book, there is a general part on obligations (sections 1–7). This covers a number of areas which were classified as being common to all obligations, such as rules on performance of obligations, set-off, and assignment. Some are in fact common only to contract and tort law (in particular the rules on damages, §§ 249–254), and a large part is mostly or exclusively concerned with contract law (in particular rules on irregularities and remedies).

Section 8 of the second book governs particular obligations, starting with various types of contracts such as sale, rent and lease, contracts for works and services, but also including provisions for *negotiorum gestio* (§§ 677–687) which in German law is not considered part of the law of unjustified enrichment.[13] Unjustified enrichment is placed between contracts and torts. It is not regulated within contracts because German law did not go down the impasse which English law adopted for some time by treating restitution as claims under an

[13] Below, section 4.2.

implied contract.[14] Like the Roman god Janus, unjustified enrichment has two heads, which are positioned back to back. One head is looking backwards to contract, where restitution under unjustified enrichment will frequently be required to mop up what contract law has spilled. The other head, for a similar purpose, looks onward to torts, and beyond torts to the third book on property law.

The fact that the German law of unjustified enrichment is part of the law of obligations reveals one substantial difference with English law. German unjustified enrichment rules will give rise only to obligations, never to rights *in rem*. This means that they are granted to the claimant as a person, rather than being attached to a particular property. It is important to keep in mind that the distinction between obligations and rights *in rem* relates to the claimant, rather than to the object of the claim. If we look at the object of unjust(ified) enrichment claims, we can observe the reverse situation: while English unjust enrichment rights *in rem* will usually result in a claim for money only, German unjustified enrichment claims can be for the surrender of chattels or property—but only as a personal obligation, not as a matter of proprietary rights.[15]

For the moment, we also need to consider the first book of the BGB (§§ 1–240), the so-called General Part (*Allgemeiner Teil*). One distinct feature of German law is the systematic way and the extent to which general rules governing civil law have been extracted and are dealt with separately. These are to be found in the General Part and include rules which render transactions void on the grounds of mistake, deceit, duress, illegality, and immorality. As a consequence, the rules on mistake, deceit, duress, illegality, and immorality are essentially the same throughout the law of contract, unjustified enrichment, tort, and property. It is therefore only logical that contract and unjustified enrichment run in tandem: with few exceptions, performance made on a void contract can be claimed back. This is also

[14] Goff and Jones, 1–002 to 1–011. Under quasi-contract, unjust enrichment claims were based on an implied contract whereby the defendant was to pay money to the claimant. The high-water mark of this approach was marked by *Sinclair v Brougham* [1914] AC 398 (HL). German scholars embraced the Roman law-based notion of restitution as quasi-contract during the seventeenth and eighteenth centuries, but never agreed on an implied contract as being the basis for such a claim. See Schäfer, 96–100.

[15] See below, Chapter 6, section 1.

true in reverse: an enrichment is generally not considered unjustified if based on a valid contract.

2. From Roman *condictiones* to a general unjustified enrichment clause

German civil law finds its roots in Roman law.[16] In the area of unjust(ified) enrichment and restitution, Roman law offered a number of so-called *condictiones.* These were actions which could generally be used to enforce an obligation with a specific content (such as payment of a sum of money, or the surrender of, for example, a horse) without having to indicate the basis for this obligation.[17] This approach somewhat resembles the old English action on a promise (*assumpsit*) as applied after *Slade's Case.*[18] These *condictiones* could be used for restitution and were indeed employed for this purpose in the German *ius commune* or Common law, which applied in some parts of Germany until the end of the nineteenth century.[19]

It was mainly the work of nineteenth-century jurists and in particular the German scholar Friedrich Carl von Savigny to extract from these various *condictiones* a general principle, namely that they concerned situations in which one person's assets were increased by a decrease in the assets of another, whereby this shift of wealth is not justified by a valid legal ground (*causa*).[20] Savigny saw this as a common denominator for a variety of rather different situations. For him, this common denominator served as a description of what unjustified enrichment is all about. This is very similar to the position which English law adopted towards the end of the twentieth century.[21]

16 For a specifically detailed historical account of German law, see Schäfer, 84–312; for a comparative history: Schrage, *Unjust enrichment: the comparative legal history of the law of restitution.*

17 See Zimmermann, *The Law of Obligations*, 835–836.

18 *Slade's Case* (1602) 4 Coke Rep 91, 76 ER 1074.

19 Schäfer, 84–222.

20 Friedrich Carl von Savigny, *System des heutigen römischen Rechts*, Vol. 5 (1841), Kap. VIII, 503ff, at 525; similar Schäfer 145–155. For a different reading of von Savigny, see Zimmermann and du Plessis (1994) Rest L Rev 14, at 17.

21 Birks, *Introduction*, 21; *Lipkin Gorman v Karpnale Ltd* [1991] 2 AC 548 (HL).

For German lawyers today, however, this is not merely a description of an area of law, but rather defines who is entitled to restitution. Nearly 60 years after von Savigny's discovery, on 1 January 1900, the German Civil Code entered into force. It contained a general unjustified enrichment clause, which was garnished with a number of surviving Roman law-based specific enrichment regulations. The general clause on unjustified enrichment was added to the BGB rather late in the process as a grand, but largely untested, design, and some of the smaller *condictiones* may have been kept on board in the event that this grand design did turn out not to function as well as was hoped.[22]

While Roman law has played a very important role in the development of both French and German law and has also influenced the shape of the English law of restitution,[23] there are nevertheless striking differences between the approaches which these three systems have taken towards unjustified enrichment. From the English perspective, perhaps the most important of these is the employment of this general unjustified enrichment clause by German law, i.e. § 812 para. 1 sent. 1 BGB, which states:

> A person who obtains something by performance by another person or in another way at the expense of this person without legal ground is bound to give it up to him.[24]

While it is still disputed in German law whether this is really one general clause, or rather two,[25] the comparative context reveals that, in any event, the clause is very general. The French *Code civil*, on the other hand, which is renowned for its audacious general clause on tortious liability (Art. 1382), contains nothing more general on restitution than Art. 1376 on liability for what might in old English terminology be called an action for money had and received—i.e. a restitutionary claim for money which the claimant has paid to the defendant, for example under a mistake. The *Code civil* elaborates on this liability to some small degree in Arts 1377–1381, but has no clear

[22] For a detailed account of the drafting history of §§ 812–822 BGB, see Schäfer 279–312.

[23] This is particularly evident in Sir William Evans, *An Essay on the Action for Money Had and Received* (1802).

[24] See below, Chapter 11, for an English translation of BGB provisions which are relevant for unjustified enrichment.

[25] Schäfer, 429–493.

provision to cover restitution where services or goods were supplied without being due, claims which in old English terminology were for a *quantum meruit* or *quantum valebant*. The *Code civil* is equally silent on restitution for wrongs. It was, rather, the highest French court, the *Cour de Cassation*, which more than a century ago developed a general enrichment claim in the *Boudier* case.[26]

The traditional English position had been formulated by Lord Diplock in *Orakpo v Manson Investments Ltd*:[27]

> My Lords, there is no general doctrine of unjust enrichment recognised in English law. What it does is to provide specific remedies in particular cases of what might be classified as unjust enrichment in a legal system that is based upon the civil law.

English law has since reduced its distance from the German position,[28] and could come even closer if English courts were to adopt the dramatic turnaround which Peter Birks proposed, namely that English law should also generally reverse enrichments which lack a legal basis.[29] The German experience can assist those trained in the common law to understand better the difference between the old and the current approach, and the one proposed by Birks. Much of this book will be devoted to that task. Suffice it to say at this stage, that general rules are all very well for including cases which might otherwise have been ignored, but they also tend to cover more than might have been bargained for.[30]

[26] Cass. req. 15.6.1892, S. 1893.1.281; see Zweigert and Kötz, 547–8.

[27] *Orakpo v Manson Investments Ltd* [1978] AC 95, 104 (HL). Lord Diplock may not have been aware of the fact that this case—which concerned subrogation—would not actually have been an enrichment case 'in a legal system that is based upon the civil law' because a *cessio legis* (see section 4.6) would have prevented any enrichment.

[28] The essence of this principle is that it is unjust for a person to retain a benefit which he has received at the expense of another, without any legal ground to justify its retention, which that other person did not intend him to receive. This has been the basis for the law of unjust enrichment as it has developed both in the civilian system and in Scotland, which has a mixed system—partly civilian and partly common law. On the whole, now that the common law systems see their law of restitution as being based upon this principle, one would expect them to apply it, broadly speaking, in the same way and to reach results which, broadly speaking, were similar. . . (Lord Hope in *Kleinwort Benson Ltd v Lincoln City Council* [1999] 2 AC 349 (HL).)

[29] Birks, *Unjust Enrichment*, Ch. 5.

[30] See below, Chapter 2, section 1 and Chapter 9, section 3.2.

3. The unjustified enrichment model of restitution

It has been discussed in English law for some time whether 'unjust enrichment' and 'restitution' have an exclusive relationship, whereby all claims for restitution are based on unjust enrichment, and restitution is the only remedy available for unjust enrichment.[31] In German law, on the other hand, it is beyond dispute that the relationship is far from being exclusive. Unjustified enrichment is only one amongst several models that allow restitution as a remedy. Conversely, in a limited number of situations there can be claims based on unjustified enrichment which are not for restitution of an enrichment held by the defendant, but for recovery of expenditure regardless of whether this corresponds with an enrichment, or even a claim for damages.[32]

1. Unjustified enrichment in a nutshell

If we take a cursory glance at §§ 812–822 BGB, we are able to distinguish grounds of unjustified enrichment (is the claimant entitled to claim restitution from the defendant?) in §§ 812–817 BGB from rules on the measure of restitution (what and how much can the claimant claim?) in §§ 818–820. In short, the grounds of restitution are as follows. If the claimant, by an intentional act of performance, enriches the defendant without a valid legal ground, restitution is permitted under § 812 para. 1 sent. 1 alt. 1 BGB.[33] Defences against this type of claim are (1) the claimant knew there was no valid legal ground, (2) there was not a legal, but a moral obligation (both § 814 BGB), and (3) the claimant's own wrongdoing was the reason why the underlying contract was void (§ 817 BGB).[34] If the defendant acquired an enrichment other than by performance by the claimant, restitution occurs under § 812 para. 1 sent. 1 alt. 2 BGB. This provision covers in particular what in English law is wrongs-based restitution, but

[31] In favour of such an exclusive relationship: Birks, *Introduction*, 26, 40; Burrows, 5–7; against: Birks, *Unjust Enrichment*, 25–27; Mitchell, in: *English Private Law*, 18.04; Virgo, 6ff.

[32] Below, section 5.

[33] Below, Chapter 2, section 1.

[34] Below, Chapter 4.

additionally serves to fill the gaps left by any other situation which calls for restitution.[35]

The measure of restitution under §§ 818–820 BGB can be summarized as follows: restitution in kind can be claimed, if this is possible, or otherwise the monetary value of the enrichment.[36] This is generally measured as the benefit which survives in the hands of the defendant, thus excluding, for example, money which the defendant has since lost. What in English law is called the defence of change of position (or disenrichment) is thus considered within assessment (all § 818 BGB). Stricter rules operate once the claim for restitution is pending, or once the defendant is *mala fide* (§§ 818 para. 3, 819 BGB).[37] In these situations, the defendant is no longer liable under the unjustified enrichment model of measuring restitution, but must answer under the stricter general rules which govern the legal relationship between the owner of personal or real property and the unauthorized possessor (or owner/possessor model for short, §§ 818 para. 4, 292, 987ff. BGB). This implies, *inter alia*, that the defendant may be liable in damages (this being an example of damages being granted as a remedy for unjustified enrichment) and can no longer rely on disenrichment.

2. Applications of the unjustified enrichment model outside §§ 812–822 BGB

This example shows that unjustified enrichment is not the only model of restitution within the German Civil Code. But just as unjustified enrichment refers to the owner/possessor model, for example for the measure of restitution from a *mala fide* defendant, there are numerous provisions throughout the *Bürgerliches Gesetzbuch* which refer to the unjustified enrichment model of measuring restitution in § 818 BGB.

An example can be taken from inheritance law. Under German (and also French) law, surviving spouses and children have statutory minimum rights to inherit (*Pflichtteil* in German, *reserve* in French law). Let us assume that a dying person makes generous gifts to friends in

35 Below, Chapter 5.
36 Below, Chapter 6.
37 Below, Chapter 6, section 6.

order to circumvent those rights. After death, the surviving spouse or children may be permitted under the law of succession (§ 2329 BGB) to claim back some or all of those gifts. Rather than creating separate rules on how the surviving value is to be calculated in this situation, the law of succession will simply refer to the unjustified enrichment model of calculation in § 818 BGB.

To summarize, the *Bürgerliches Gesetzbuch* contains several different grounds for restitution-type relief, among which unjustified enrichment figures most prominently. Similarly, there are several models for the consequences of restitutionary liability.[38] These models for the measure of restitution are principally employed in tandem with a particular ground of restitution-type relief, but the law will also borrow these for certain other situations by operation of a cross-reference. It is important to remember that this is not a coincidental overlap between different areas of the law which have grown in different ways, as might easily have happened in English law, but, on the contrary, it is the product of careful design. To use a metaphor, it is a complicated clock mechanism rather than a pile of scrap metal. Superficial criticism would see chaos; more justified criticism would state that the most complicated clocks are not necessarily the most accurate.

4. Six other models of restitution

The six other models of restitution which German law offers are: (1) the termination of contract model, (2) the *negotiorum gestio* model, (3) the tort model, (4) the owner/possessor model, (5) the substitution model, and (6) the *cessio legis* model. They all cover some of the ground which, at least arguably, belongs to the English law of unjust enrichment, and they therefore deserve to be covered in turn.

1. The termination of contract model

If a contract is terminated, this will frequently entitle the parties to claim back what they have already performed, i.e. restitution. As will be explained below, the consequences of termination of contract are

[38] Below, sections 4 and 5.

governed by specific contractual rules in §§ 346ff BGB.[39] This is in contrast with English law, which treats this as a case of unjust enrichment (in the form of failure of consideration).

2. The *negotiorum gestio* model

Sometimes a party will act in the interest of another party without having been instructed to do so, for example in order to save another person's life, limb, or property in an emergency. In German law, this is not governed by unjustified enrichment, but rather by the rules on *negotiorum gestio* or *Geschäftsführung ohne Auftrag* (§§ 677–687 BGB). In sum, the party who was justified to act in the interest of another party can recover from the latter expenses which were reasonably incurred, while the other party can claim from the intervener any enrichment which the intervener gained from the exercise of the other party's interests. More will be said about this below.[40] This model will frequently be invoked by other models of restitutionary liability, in particular for the recovery of unauthorized expenditure. The same model is also employed for disgorgement of profits if the defendant wilfully infringed a right of the claimant (cases of unjustified *negotiorum gestio*, § 687 para. 2 BGB).[41]

3. The tort model

It has been debated in English law for some time whether wrongs-based restitution forms part of unjust enrichment or, rather, belongs to tort law.[42] No similar debate can be observed amongst German lawyers. This is largely due to the fact that restitutionary damages are not generally recognized as a measure of damages in German law.[43] Nevertheless, the enrichment of the defendant will serve as a measure

[39] Below, Chapter 3, section 3.

[40] Below, Chapter 5, section 3.2. For a comparative analysis, see Kortmann, *Altruism in Private Law*.

[41] Below, Chapter 5, section 2.3.

[42] See e.g. Birks, *Unjust Enrichment*, 11–16; Mitchell, in: *English Private Law*, 18.04; Virgo, 6–17 (not part of unjust enrichment). The opposite view is taken by for example Burrows 5–7, Goff and Jones, 1050–1051; Tettenborn, 17.

[43] See Hans Stoll, *Haftungsfolgen im bürgerlichen Recht* (1993), nos 33–36 and 196–235.

of damages in some areas where other methods are unsatisfactory because of the difficulty of proving loss, or in order to ensure that tort does not pay. This is in particular true for intellectual property rights. The case law of the *Bundesgerichtshof* gives the claimant a choice between three different measures of damages, namely (a) to prove and claim his or her loss, (b) to claim a reasonable licence fee, and (c) to claim the profit which the defendant has gained from the violation of the claimant's intellectual property right.[44] The third measure, which is undoubtedly restitutionary, is generally available 'in lieu of damages' for negligent or intentional copyright violations under § 97 para. 1 sent. 2 *Urheberrechtsgesetz* (Copyright Act).[45] We will return to this issue in the context of wrongs-based restitution.[46]

4. The owner/possessor model

The legal relationship between owner and possessor (*Eigentümer-Besitzer-Verhältnis*) concerns situations where corporeal property (i.e. chattels or land) is in the possession of a party who is not entitled to such possession against the owner. This covers, for example, a person living in a house without having title, a valid lease, or tenancy contract with the owner.

Of the claims arising under the owner/possessor model, three are of a restitution-type nature. First, the vindication claim itself, that is, the claim to restore the property to the owner under § 985 BGB. This is a purely proprietary claim and need not concern us any further in this context. Secondly, the owner's claim for the benefit which the possessor has gained from using the property, for example by living in the house. Thirdly, the possessor's counterclaim for unauthorized expenditure on the property.

The owner/possessor model will be covered below in more detail.[47] Its significance extends beyond situations governed by property law. As has been mentioned above, this model is invoked by the

44 BGH 16.2.1973, BGHZ 60, 206.

45 The German original of this provision reads: 'An Stelle des Schadenersatzes kann der Verletzte die Herausgabe des Gewinns, den der Verletzer durch die Verletzung des Rechts erzielt hat, und Rechnungslegung über diesen Gewinn verlangen.'

46 Below, Chapter 5, section 2.2.

47 At Chapter 5, section 2.1.

provisions on unjustified enrichment in order to increase liability once the enriched person is not acting *bona fide* or has been sued in court.

5. The substitution model

Another restitution-type remedy which can be available within the entire German law of obligations, is substitution. If a claim lies against a defendant, and the initial object of this claim is destroyed, been damaged, taken or given away by the defendant, the claimant is entitled to receive anything which the defendant has obtained on the basis of such destruction, damage, taking or giving away. The initial object of the claim is thus substituted with another object. Under § 285 BGB, whenever the defendant is excused from performing on the ground that performance is impossible, the claimant 'may demand surrender of what has been received as substitute or an assignment of the substitute claim'.

This can be illustrated by the following example. A advertises his used car and agrees with B a price of €10,000. Before B collects the car and hands over the money, C approaches A and offers €11,000. A sells the car to C and pockets the €11,000. A initially owed (specific) performance of the sales contract to B. This became impossible for A, as A no longer owns the car. Due to this impossibility, A no longer owes specific performance of the sales contract under § 275 BGB, but has to surrender under § 285 what he has received as a result of this impossibility—namely the €11,000. A can counterclaim from B the purchase price of €10,000, but as either party can declare set-off, the ultimate result is that B can cream off the extra €1,000 which A has made by his breach of contract with B.

Thus, substitution can serve as a gains-based remedy. German courts will, however, scrutinize not only the causal link between the impossibility and the defendant's receipt of value, but also whether the second object has really replaced the first. For example, if B had rented rather than bought the car from A, B will not be allowed to claim the purchase price, because that has not replaced the rental value of the car. In what is terminologically a slight overstatement, German courts require the second object to be identical to the object which it replaces (*Identität zwischen geschuldetem und ersetztem Gegenstand*).[48] Section 818 para. (1) contains a specific rule on substitution for unjustified enrichment claims, about which more will be said below.[49]

6. The *cessio legis* model

Some situations which in English law may call for restitution are instead covered by *cessio legis* in German law. This is an assignment which operates by virtue of the law and which is not merely imputed. For example, if a guarantor pays instead of the principal debtor, § 774 BGB transfers the creditor's claim onto the guarantor who can use this claim to proceed against the debtor.[50] Similar provisions apply, for example, to insurers who can recover from a tortfeasor for damage caused to the insured person.[51] *Cessio legis* also occurs if an absconding parent fails to pay maintenance for his or her child and another relative steps in; the relative can recover from the parent by virtue of *cessio legis* under § 1607 para. 2 or 3 BGB. Similarly, § 426 BGB allows joint and several debtors to recover from each other for what they have paid to the creditor in excess of their own share. And § 268 para. 3 BGB allows a creditor with a secured claim to save his or her securities by paying another creditor with privileged securities who has a claim against the same debtor. The same person can then recover from the debtor, by *cessio legis* of the claim which the privileged creditor has against the debtor. We notice here a difference in the scope of English and German unjust(ified) enrichment law. For English law, these would be cases of either subrogation[52] or legal compulsion. For German law, this is not an unjustified enrichment case: because

[48] See BGH 23.12.1966, BGHZ 46, 260. The registration of an emolument stipulated in favour of the claimant became impossible when the defendant sold the property to a third party. The claimant was not allowed to recover in substitution the difference between the purchase price and the lower price which the property would have attracted with a registered emolument. The *Bundesgerichtshof* argued that the purchase price replaced the property, rather than a contractual right to have an emolument registered.

[49] At Chapter 6, section 2.2.

[50] For a comparative analysis, see Jens Kuhlmann, *Rückgriffsgrundlagen bei Gesamtschuld, Bürgschaft und Schadensversicherung in Deutschland, England und Schweden* (2005).

[51] Section 67 *Versicherungsvertragsgesetz* (Insurance Contract Act) transfers the victim's claim to the insurer.

[52] See Charles Mitchell and Stephen Watterson, *Subrogation Law and Practice* (2007).

the claim is assigned by operation of the law, the debtor is not enriched but remains liable under the original claim.

This also explains why *cessio legis* is the only solitary restitution-type model. It does not borrow from others, and neither is it borrowed by other models of restitution-type relief.

5. Conclusions

To some extent, German and English law share a similar historical development in how unjust(ified) enrichment cases have been approached. Both have historically resorted to unspecific claims or actions which could, amongst other things, be used for what we now see as unjust(ified) enrichment claims, namely Roman law-type *condictiones* for German common law,[53] and *assumpsit* for English law. Both German and English law have subsequently turned unjust(ified) enrichment into a recognised area of law with individual grounds of enrichment, namely *condictiones* as first developed by von Savigny for German law, and unjust enrichment based on individual unjust factors for English law. On the other hand, unlike English law, German law never attempted to push unjust(ified) enrichment into 'quasi-contract'. Furthermore, German law moved in 1900 to a general unjustified enrichment clause for intentional transfers, whereby a shift of wealth is generally to be reversed if this is not justified by a legal ground, a proposition which has only recently been made for English law.

As regards the scope of unjust enrichment and restitution, English law operates with a relatively simple model. Restitution is invariably the remedy for unjust enrichment. While it is subject to dispute whether restitution as a remedy is limited to unjust enrichment-based claims, or whether notably wrongs-based restitution occurs outside unjust enrichment,[54] German law has adopted a much more complicated combination of various models of restitution-type remedies with various grounds which may give rise to those remedies. If we look at what is covered by unjust(ified) enrichment, we can observe the following:

(1) Unjustified enrichment in German law covers the majority of the central ground, namely the reversal of unjust(ified)

[53] See Schäfer, 95–104.

[54] See above, section 4.3.

intentional transfers from the claimant to the defendant. There is one exception: the reversal of transfers made under a valid contract which was subsequently terminated is governed by German contract law, rather than being considered to be a case of unjustified enrichment.

(2) For situations in which the claimant has paid a debt which the defendant owed to a third party, *cessio legis* will frequently prevent any enrichment of the defendant, so that unjustified enrichment will have to deal only with some residual cases.

(3) As concerns improvements to the defendant's property and other cases of unauthorized expenditure, this is mainly covered by either the owner/possessor model, or *negotiorum gestio*, with unjustified enrichment playing no more than a marginal role.

(4) With regard to wrongs-based restitution, German law leaves this largely to unjustified enrichment, with the primary exception of claims between owners and unauthorized possesors, which are covered by the owner/possessor model.

As to the measure of restitution, Gėrman law distinguishes between the following, partially overlapping models:

(1) surviving enrichment, initially corresponding to the claimant's disenrichment (basic measure);
(2) initial enrichment of the defendant corresponding with the claimant's disenrichment (*mala fide* defendant, or claim pending);
(3) benefits derived from the initial enrichment, and substitutes; these may exceed the claimant's disenrichment;

and additionally for cases where enrichment and disenrichment are not initially identical:

(4) the claimant's disenrichment, even if this is larger than the defendant's enrichment (recovery of expenditure under *negotiorum gestio*);
(5) the defendant's entire gain, even where that exceeds the claimant's disenrichment and/or defendant's initial enrichment (available under unjustified *negotiorum gestio* and § 816, disputed for interference cases in unjustified enrichment).

This more complicated German model has some benefits, the most obvious one being that it allows for refined solutions. For example, English law has long struggled with mistaken improvements and other unauthorized expenditure, and finds it difficult to measure how exactly the defendant may be enriched. The German solution is to treat this partially outside unjustified enrichment and allow recovery based on expenditure incurred by the claimant, rather than on any increase in the defendant's assets.

On the other hand, the interaction between the different models can also demonstrate how the German Civil Code has exaggerated with its use of cross-references, as is illustrated by the following example.

Let us assume that A keeps a bicycle which A reasonably believes he has inherited from C. When it transpires that C has instead left his entire estate to B, B requires A to hand over the bicycle. Before doing so, A repairs a puncture and claims from B the cost of parts and for his (A's) labour. In order to solve this relatively simple case, we have to start our journey in the law of succession (the fifth book), and in particular § 2021, which refers to unjustified enrichment in the second book. Since A knew of B's right to the bicycle when A repaired the puncture, § 819 BGB will invoke 'the general provisions', which means § 292, which in turn refers to the law of property (the third book) and in particular to §§ 989 and 994 para. (2). The latter provision invokes the law of *negotiorum gestio* to discover whether A was entitled to repair the puncture. That is the case if B's consent could be presumed, as we will assume here. *Negotiorum gestio* in turn calls the law of mandate (a gratuitous contract of service) to find out what A can claim from B in this instance. After a journey through three books and the laws of inheritance, unjustified enrichment, obligations in general, property, and *negotiorum gestio*, we finally arrive at specific contracts and § 670 BGB to learn that A can claim for parts, but not for his labour. Surely there must be a simpler way to arrive at this unspectacular result.

2

The Undoing of Performance: Basics

1. The performance/non-performance divide

While there is broad agreement in English law that not all unjust enrichment cases are to be treated in the same way, no agreement currently exists on the most important distinctions to be made. One obvious default line is between wrongs-based restitution on the one hand, which for some does not form part of unjust enrichment, and what is called autonomous unjust enrichment on the other.[1] Another important distinction is between subtractive enrichment (i.e. an enrichment of the defendant which is identical to a correspondent reduction in the assets of the claimant as, for example, in cases of mistaken payment, but also of theft) and non-subtractive enrichment (for example by copyright violation).[2] This overlaps only partially with the distinction proposed by Birks between participatory enrichment (in which the claimant was involved, be it voluntarily or involuntarily) and non-participatory enrichment.[3] Outside restitution for wrongs, Goff and Jones distinguish between benefits which the defendant has acquired from or by the act of the claimant, and benefits which the defendant has acquired from a third party but for which he must account to the claimant.[4]

The crucial distinction which German law draws is between unjustified enrichment caused by the claimant's performance (*Leistung*) and any other type of enrichment. The performance/non-performance

[1] Birks, *Introduction*, 6. Goff and Jones, section 3, 'Where the Defendant has Acquired a Benefit Through his own Wrongful Act'.

[2] See e.g. Burrows, 25–31.

[3] Birks, *Unjust Enrichment*, 129; Andrew Burrows, 'Absence of Basis: The New Birksian Scheme', in: *Mapping the Law*, 34.

[4] Goff and Jones, sections 1 and 2.

dichotomy has a sure footing in the wording of § 812 BGB '. . . by performance by another person or in another way at the expense of this person' and throughout §§ 812-822 BGB. '*Leisten*' and its derivatives make a total of 21 appearances within these 11 sections. Nevertheless, it took the work of, in particular, one Austrian and one German scholar to exploit the full consequence of this distinction, namely Walter Wilburg and Ernst von Caemmerer.[5] The breakthrough for the performance/non-performance divide is more than merely legal history. It illustrates the advantages, but also the pitfalls, of using general clauses, to ensure that they do not cover more than the legislator has bargained for.

When German courts and academics attempted to control restitutionary liability under the new general unjustified enrichment clause in § 812 BGB, they initially somewhat neglected much of the wording of §§ 812–822 and instead resorted to an unwritten requirement of 'directness'—a move which the great comparative scholar Dawson once called 'ingenious'.[6] So restitution was allowed if there was a direct shift of wealth from the claimant to the defendant, regardless of whether it was the claimant who gave or the defendant who took. This interpretation made the general clause even more general, and it might as well have read 'whoever obtains something directly at the expense of another without a legal ground must give it up to that person', which, incidentally, comes quite close to the wording of the Swiss general clause on unjustified enrichment (Art. 62 para. 1 *Obligationenrecht*).

But this generality was bought at the expense of precision and certainty, and equitable considerations had to play a greater role in defining the boundaries of unjustified enrichment.[7] In other words: in this generality, the clause took German law back to the times of von Savigny, by describing what unjustified enrichment is about rather than defining who is entitled to restitution. It might as well have read:

(1) Restitution is about an enrichment which one person has received at the direct expense of another.

[5] von Caemmerer, 'Bereicherung und unerlaubte Handlung'; Wilburg, *Die Lehre von der ungerechtfertigten Bereicherung nach österreichischem und deutschem Recht.*

[6] Dawson, 121.

[7] See Zimmermann and du Plessis, 24ff.

(2) If there is no legal ground for the enrichment, it must be given up.
(3) The case law of the courts will define groups of cases in which enrichment has occurred 'without a legal ground'.

In this reading, the general clause serves predominantly as a description of an area of case law rather than as a definition of a claim, and the case law of the courts will produce types or groups of cases where enrichment seems unjustified, bringing it closer to an unjust factor approach. The general clause is not what it seems.[8] Some resemblance can be found to the position of modern Canadian law with its requirement of a 'juristic reason', albeit with the difference that Canadian law does not insist on the enrichment being direct.[9]

In German law, this situation was perceived as unsatisfactory. It was overcome because Wilburg and von Caemmerer succeeded in convincing their colleagues and the courts that one must clearly distinguish between the two alternatives of § 812 para. 1 sent. 1 BGB, thus making *Leistung* (performance, or transfer) the watershed in restitution.[10]

The first and foremost purpose of this distinction is this: by allowing a claimant to recover for benefits which he or she conferred intentionally on a defendant and with a particular obligation in mind, but without a valid legal ground, German law has described the largest possible coherent group of enrichment cases where restitution is required without having to resort to an examination of more specific requirements, such as unjust factors, or of equity. The general *Leistungskondiktion* simply leaves it to other areas of law to decide whether the enrichment is unjustified. By this *Leistungskondiktion*, German law has covered the majority of what in English law is mistake, duress, undue influence, and failure of consideration, as well as many cases of illegality, legal compulsion, and incapacity. At the same time, the *Leistungskondiktion* avoids being overly generous in allowing restitution.

[8] See von Caemmerer 337ff; Staudinger-Lorenz § 812 no. 1.

[9] *Pettkus v Becker* [1980] 2 SCR 824, confirmed in *Peter v Beblow* [1993] 1 SCR 980. See generally L Smith, 45 Can Bus Law J (2007), 281ff.

[10] The *Bundesgerichthof* adopted the performance/non-performance divide in BGH 31.10.1963, BGHZ 40, 272; below, Chapter 10, section 4 (translation).

The second purpose of the performance concept is to define who can claim restitution from whom in situations involving three or more parties, whereas most English unjust factors will define only one of the parties (usually the claimant). We will have the opportunity to look at some of these complicated situations in more detail below.[11] The concept of *Leistung* serves as a compass in this territory. Once we are aware of who has performed towards whom, we will generally know who can claim restitution from whom.

There is, of course, a price for this to pay. While the *Leistungskondiktion* is generally not too wide, it is, in spite of its generality, sometimes too narrow. It does not cover restitution for wrongs. Neither does it cover situations where one person unintentionally shifts wealth to another person, for example if a caretaker mistakenly uses his own fuel to heat a communal building.[12]

But the *Leistungskondiktion* can also be too narrow in situations where there is a performance. In particular, in situations involving more than two parties it is possible that a transfer, although based on a valid legal ground, nevertheless amounts to an unjustified shift of wealth between two of the parties. For example, if the main shareholder pays her company's fiscal debt in the mistaken belief that she is jointly and severally liable for the debt, she cannot recover from the tax authorities because the fiscal debt provides the valid legal ground, and neither can she recover from the company under the *Leistungskondiktion*, since she intentionally and purposefully performed what she thought was her own obligation towards the tax authorities not towards the company.[13] German writers and courts believe that the performance/non-performance divide entails that these cases must be resolved under the second alternative of the general enrichment clause, i.e. the enrichment in another way at the expense of the claimant, which includes the recovery for payment of the defendant's debt towards a third party.[14]

[11] At Chapter 3, section 2.

[12] von Caemmerer, 351. This is to be distinguished from the 'rising heat' example discussed by Birks, *Unjust Enrichment*, 158–159, see below, Chapter 9, section 3.2.A.

[13] Variation of an example given by Fikentscher and Heinemann, no. 1486.

[14] Below, Chapter 5, section 4.4.

This has some disadvantages. First, extremely different cases are bundled together into what appears to be an amorphous group covering 'non-performance-based enrichment'.

Secondly, cases which belong together (as in our last example) are treated under different headings and with different requirements. In this context, it may be helpful for the German lawyer to look to the English approach where mistake is at the core of many of these situations.

Additionally, there is one imperfection in the performance/non-performance divide which is not based on a flaw in the system, but, rather, because German law allows the Roman *condictiones* to rule from the grave, or has actually failed to bury them. In particular, the *condictio causa data causa non secuta* fails to run in tandem with the law of contract. These matters will be considered further below.[15]

In summary, the *Leistungskondition* provides a simple solution for the majority of all unjustified enrichment cases, but leaves a residue of situations which have to be covered by the 'enrichment in another way' provision and where, in English law terminology, another 'unjust factor' must be found.

2. Enrichment of the defendant

The way in which the *Leistungskondiktion* functions will usually indicate whether the defendant has been enriched. Not only is *Leistung* (1) a particular type of enrichment, but (2) it can also serve to connect the right claimant with the right defendant.

1. Enrichment

Bereicherung (enrichment) is mentioned in the heading of §§ 812–822 BGB, and in the provisions on the measure of enrichment (§§ 818–820), but interestingly not in § 812 para. 1. Rather, that provision requires that the defendant has 'obtained something'. We can conclude from § 818, however, that this refers to the initial enrichment.

[15] At Chapter 3, section 1.1.

Within performance-based unjustified enrichment, the question whether the defendant is enriched makes an additional appearance in the definition of 'performance'. Performance is understood to be an intentional and purpose-oriented enlargement of another person's assets.[16] Performance has therefore incorporated enrichment by requiring this 'enlargement of another person's assets' (*Vermehrung fremden Vermögens*).

This definition of enrichment suggests an economic, objective analysis. This is certainly true for money as 'the very measure of enrichment'.[17] If A receives a mistaken payment of €1,000, he will not be heard with the defence that his interests lie beyond the material and that therefore money is of no value to him; on the contrary, such an argument simply adds to the reasons why A should surrender the money. But as regards other assets, unjustified enrichment has adopted a model which first broadens the scope of enrichment (i.e., whether the defendant has received a benefit) and then narrows the scope of restitution (i.e., what the defendant must surrender to the claimant).

The scope of enrichment is broadened by the view which looks towards other areas of the law, and in particular contracts, in order to define enrichment. Since the *Leistungskondiktion* aims to undo a performance which was not actually due, it is consistent logically that anything which can be the object of an obligation can amount to an enrichment; and no other area of the law allows as much ingenuity in creating obligations as contract does. Consequently, the assignment of a right or a claim amounts to an enrichment, as does the mere delivery of possession in chattels or real property. Therefore, if a charity sends out a collection of ten particularly tasteless Christmas cards in the hope that recipients might be willing to buy them, the recipients are enriched. If the charity then claims back the cards from those recipients who are unwilling to buy them, it is irrelevant that those recipients have not acquired anything of economic value and certainly no title to the cards. It is also irrelevant whether the charity has title to the cards, for example because its suppliers have retained title. Nor is it relevant that there is no contract between the recipients

[16] BGH 24.2.1972, BGHZ 58, 184, 188: 'bewußte und *zweckgerichtete* Vermehrung fremden Vermögens'.

[17] Birks, *Introduction*, 109.

and the charity. The recipients are enriched by the mere possession of the cards.[18] It should be noted, though, that the claim will ultimately be unsuccessful. The defence of § 814 BGB rushes to the aid of the recipients, since the charity was plainly aware that they were under no obligation to perform.[19] More recently, § 241a has been added to the BGB, based on Art. 9 Distance Sales Directive. This provides that no statutory claims (including those based on unjustified enrichment) can arise from the delivery of unsolicited goods to a consumer.

This wide concept of enrichment is generally employed where the enrichment is capable of being returned in kind, as return in kind is the primary object of restitution in German law.[20] The claimant's performance (and thus the defendant's enrichment) can be of no or very limited commercial value, for example if the claimant has issued to the defendant an inaccurate receipt or IOU, or has consented to what turns out to be an inaccurate change in the land register in favour of the defendant.[21] Having what is shown to be an inaccurate receipt, inaccurate IOU, or inaccurate position in the land register, is naturally an enrichment which most honest people would not bargain for. These are enrichments which any defendant would find extremely difficult to convert into money. We need to look for a moment at the consequences of restitution in order to understand why these situations should nevertheless constitute an enrichment: because the law will provide for restitution in kind, i.e. surrender of the incorrect receipt or IOU, and enforcing or replacing the defendant's consent to amend the land register. Restitution will thus prevent the situation from becoming worse.

But what if performance and enrichment cannot be returned in kind? A price must then be placed on an enrichment, and that will generally favour a more objective view. Thus, if the enrichment has no commercial value and restitution in kind is impossible, the wide concept of restitution becomes somewhat theoretic. If A signs a tenancy contract with B which prohibits A from playing the piano and a court later declares this clause void, A will find it difficult to claim back the

[18] For a discussion of mere possession as an enrichment under English law, see Robert Stevens, 'Three Enrichment Issues', in: *Mapping The Law*, 49ff, 62ff.

[19] Below, Chapter 4, section 1.

[20] Below, Chapter 6, section 1.

[21] BGH 12.1.1973, NJW 1973, 613.

value of having complied, even if B lives in the same building and has greatly enjoyed her quiet Sunday afternoons while A was suffering under the unlawful restriction. Likewise, it is at the least problematic to claim in restitution the value of having been mistakenly allowed to inspect books or documents under a void contract, or under a pretended other right.[22]

If a benefit which cannot be returned in kind has a commercial value, this will usually qualify as enrichment. For example, if a person cleans the windows of another person's house, this will not necessarily increase the owner's wealth, but the owner can nevertheless be enriched.[23] This can still be constructed as an economic asset, in particular if the owner would otherwise have paid for the same service. The saving of the expense is undeniably a benefit in the German law of unjustified enrichment.[24]

The situation becomes more difficult if the defendant neither saved any expense nor experienced any other increase of assets by the claimant's performance. This is illustrated by the following celebrated case.

In this case decided by the *Bundesgerichtshof* in 1971 (case no. 7), the defendant was a minor who had booked a flight from Munich to Hamburg.[25] At Hamburg airport, he managed to join the passengers embarking on the same plane for its onward flight to New York, where he was refused entry by the immigration authorities. The claimant (the flight operator) took the minor back to Germany on the return flight. The *Bundesgerichtshof* found it difficult to argue why the defendant had been enriched by the flight to New York. He had certainly not saved any expenditure. For lack of both capacity and funds, he would not have been able to obtain a ticket. The court took refuge in § 819 BGB which bars the defence of disenrichment to a *mala fide* defendant.[26] The *Bundesgerichtshof's* insistence that enrichment

[22] Section 810 BGB gives such rights under rather restricted circumstances.

[23] This example has been much debated in English law in a different context, namely whether 'free acceptance' should be recognized as an unjust factor. In support of this view are e.g. Goff and Jones, 1–019 to 1–022, Birks, *Introduction*, 265; against Burrows 402–407.

[24] See e.g. Schlechtriem, *Schuldrecht BT*, no. 724. But see the different position adopted by the majority in *Phillips v Homfray* (1883) 24 Ch D 439, 454–455, which, however, did not concern performance.

[25] BGH 7.1.1971, NJW 1971, 609; below, Chapter 10, section 7 (translation).

[26] See below, Chapter 6, section 6.2.

requires 'a true increase of assets'[27] is understandable as an attempt to avoid opening the floodgates, but certainly does not square with the above-mentioned judgment according to which something as worthless as an inaccurate land registry entry is an enrichment.[28] It seems that the English doctrine of free acceptance, while controversial as 'unjust factor',[29] could nevertheless better explain why there should be an enrichment in this case, namely because the defendant had through his action shown that he wished to have that particular performance. It is a separate problem altogether under both German and English law that a minor should thus be made to pay for a performance for which he had no contractual capacity to bargain.[30] It should also be noted that the potentially very wide scope of enrichment in German law is narrowed down again later in the process of measuring enrichment, i.e. by the rules relating to subjective devaluation, substitution, and disenrichment. These will be considered below.[31]

2. Of the defendant

A second function of the principle of *Leistung* is to define who is enriched by the performance and is therefore the correct defendant. This can be illustrated by the following example from von Caemmerer.[32] A tenant has a window repaired by a glazier, and the contract is void on the ground of, say, mistake. On an economic analysis of assets, it is the landlord who becomes the owner of the new window and benefits from the labour, and who is thus enriched at least as much as the tenant. Should the glazier be allowed to recover directly from the landlord? Probably not, for a number of reasons which we will have an opportunity to consider below in the context of restitution involving three or more parties.[33] The principle of *Leistung* indicates that the tenant is the correct defendant, as this was clearly a performance which the glazier undertook towards the tenant, who approached

27 At 610.
28 BGH 12.1.1973, NJW 1973, 613; below, Chapter 10, section 7 (translation).
29 Goff and Jones, 1–019 to 1–022; Tettenborn 16–17; critical Burrows 402–407.
30 See below, Chapter 9, section 2.2.C.
31 At Chapter 6.
32 von Caemmerer, 351.
33 See below, Chapter 3, section 2.

him, not towards the landlord; the glazier might not even have known that the tenant was not the owner of the house.

The example of the glazier soon became a celebrated *Kathederfall* (a case invented for teaching rather than one obtained from practice) in Germany. It proved to be an academic example with a sense of prophecy. Thirty-six years later, an actual case involving a glazier, a tenant, and a landlord was decided by the *Landgericht* Bonn.[34] The glazier was the claimant and the landlord the defendant. The case concerned a prospective (rather than an actual) tenant, who had negotiated with the landlord over a possible lease of the property, a pub with residential flat. The would-be tenant and the landlord agreed that the former could use the flat prior to any formal agreement on the lease, and should in return carry out minor renovation work to the property. For this purpose, the landlord even paid a small sum of money to the would-be tenant, who was without any financial means. The would-be tenant then instructed the glazier to replace 14 windows. The *Amtsgericht* as first instance court awarded the glazier a claim against the landlord for unjustified enrichment. The judges at the *Landgericht* apparently had a better recall of the lectures on unjustified enrichment, and allowed the landlord's appeal. The glazier was performing towards the would-be tenant, not towards the landlord, and could therefore not claim under performance-based enrichment against the landlord.[35]

3. At the expense of the claimant

1. Expense

Since the entire law of restitution appears to be concerned with benefits which the defendant acquired at the expense of the claimant, it may come as a surprise that in German law the predominant view is that within the *Leistungskondiktion* it is not a requirement that the benefit must have accrued to the defendant at the claimant's expense.[36]

[34] LG Bonn 3.12.1990, NJW 1991, 1360.

[35] See below, section 3.2 (principle of subsidiarity).

[36] Schlechtriem, *Schuldrecht BT*, no. 725; Larenz and Canaris, 131 (against); Lieb in *Münchener Kommentar* § 812 no. 10–13 sees a role for 'at the expense of the claimant' in

The wording of § 812 para. 1 sent. 1 BGB is somewhat ambiguous and the meaning depends on where the reader includes a pause. If one were to distinguish the alternatives by assigning to them them separate lines, this could be done in one of two ways:

'A person who obtains something
 – by performance by another person or
 – in another way at the expense of this
  person . . .'.

'A person who obtains something
 – by performance by another person or
 – in another way at the expense of this
  person . . .'.

This discussion has revealed few, if any, practical consequences. The *Leistungskondiktion* is concerned only with undoing performance and thus applies only in situations in which the claimant has intentionally provided the defendant with a benefit by way of performance. It is difficult to see how this can occur without the loss of any assets, labour, or other disadvantage on the side of the claimant. It has been stated for English law that the requirement 'at his expense' covers cases which are not simply giving back,[37] and *Leistungskondiktion* is concerned with precisely that. In the end, the entire question may be terminological. If 'at the expense of the claimant' receives as wide a definition as 'benefit', i.e. including anything which can be the object of an obligation, then 'at the expense of the claimant' becomes identical to 'by performance by the claimant'.

2. Of the claimant

Of more importance is the person who has been disenriched. Within performance-based unjustified enrichment, this is the person who performed. Was that indeed the claimant, or was it someone else? Let us return to the example of the glazier and assume that it was the glazier's apprentice who carried out the work. Should the glazier or the apprentice be the claimant as regards the value of the work? All parties involved would agree that it was the glazier and not the apprentice who attempted to discharge an obligation towards the tenant. Therefore the concept of performance serves to find not only the right

cases of performance involving three or more parties. For the minority view, see Palandt *Bürgerliches Gesetzbuch*, 59th edn (2000), § 812 nos 32ff (Thomas), no longer maintained in the 68th edn (2009), § 812 nos 5, 20 (sprav).

[37] Birks, *Introduction*, 12.

defendant, but also the right claimant from four possible restitutionary situations: glazier–landlord, glazier–tenant, apprentice–landlord, and apprentice–tenant. It is the glazier who can sue the tenant for restitution under the *Leistungskondiktion*.

Under current English law, most unjust factors (mistake, compulsion,[38] ignorance, etc.) have built-in mechanisms for finding the correct claimant, i.e. the person who was mistaken or was forced to shift wealth, or was ignorant of his or her wealth being shifted. On the other hand, these unjust factors are arguably less helpful in finding the right defendant: the fact that a glazier was mistaken in repairing a window does not tell us whether the glazier should sue the tenant or the landlord. For this reason, a mistake-based analysis finds it more difficult in multiparty enrichment situations to address the issue of which of these parties should sue which other party.[39] Furthermore, within subtractive enrichment, those unjust factors which denote the defendant (such as free acceptance or unconscientious receipt) are not only controversial,[40] but can also be equally unhelpful in determining who is the correct claimant. Failure of consideration may be the best example for an unjust factor which links a particular claimant (as the party who gave something expecting a consideration) with a particular defendant (as the party who failed to provide this consideration).

But what happens in German law if, say, the apprentice sues the landlord under the enrichment in another-way option? Surely the landlord is enriched by the apprentice's labour, and there is no legal ground for this enrichment. In order to prevent the enrichment in another-way option from interfering with the *Leistungskondiktion* in this fashion, courts and the majority of academics agree that the latter takes precedence over the former. In other words: in a given situation of enrichment, enrichment in another way is subsidiary to enrichment by performance (principle of subsidiarity). This prevents the

[38] Within compulsion, duress can be named as an unjust factor which, at least normally, links claimant and defendant. Undue influence, on the other hand, is frequently relied on against defendants who have not themselves exerted undue influence, notably banks.

[39] See e.g. *Barclays Bank Ltd v WJ Simms, Son & Cooke (Southern) Ltd* [1980] QB 677 (QBD).

[40] Free acceptance: Goff and Jones, 1–019 to 1–022; Tettenborn 16–17; critical Burrows 402–407; unconscientous receipt: Burrows, Ch. 7 (exploitation of weakness).

apprentice from suing either the landlord or the tenant, and the glazier from suing the landlord. And, indeed, subsidiarity was the explanation given by the court in the real glazier case for disallowing this claimant from suing the landlord under enrichment in another way.[41] We will return to this issue below in the context of performance-based unjustified enrichment involving three or more parties.[42]

4. Must the shift be direct?

It has been mentioned above that the controlling element of unjustified enrichment in German law used to be the requirement that the shift of wealth must be direct. This requirement was eventually abandoned. Let us assume in our example that the glazier had subcontracted, that the subcontractor sent an apprentice to carry out the work, and that again the contract is void. As far as the value of the work is concerned, it was the apprentice who created and shifted this wealth. Indirectly, it was the subcontractor, who paid and used the apprentice as an agent, who shifted the wealth onto the tenant. Even more indirectly, it was the glazier as the tenant's contractual partner who shifted this wealth and who paid and used the subcontractor as an agent. So where is the direct shift of wealth from the glazier to the tenant? Similar issues arise if banks are used for payment. Let us assume that the tenant pays by bank transfer, and mistakenly pays too much. The tenant's bank transfers the payment to the glazier's bank. The glazier is in debit and has exhausted his agreed overdraft. If the tenant sues the glazier for the excess amount, where is the direct shift of wealth from the tenant to the glazier? Surely it can be no answer to the tenant's claim that the glazier was in debit and that the bank therefore kept the money?

The concept that the sun and the other planets revolve around the earth had to be renounced because the constructed movements of all other planets around the earth had become excessively complicated as a result. The concept of quasi-contract was renounced in English law because the constructions which this requires show a similar degree

[41] LG Bonn 3.12.1990, NJW 1991, 1360.

[42] At Chapter 3, section 2.

of artificiality and complexity.[43] Likewise, 'direct shift of wealth' in situations involving payment and receipt of payment through banks and within chains of performance could be maintained only at the expense of constructions such as 'immediate shift of wealth through indirect bestowal (indirect performance)'.[44] This provides strong competition with terminological delicacies such as 'pseudo-quasi-contract'[45] and 'constructive quasi-trust' which have made appearances in the Common Law literature.[46] Nowadays within the *Leistungskondiktion*, it is sufficient that the claimant performed towards the defendant, regardless of whether intermediaries were involved in the process. Experience has shown that 'directness' is of virtually no assistance in defining remoteness of damage in tort.[47] The German experience has shown that it is equally ineffective to employ 'directness' for the purpose of unjustified enrichment.

5. Intent and purpose

The concept of performance requires that the claimant enriched the defendant intentionally and with a specific obligation in mind (even if no such obligation existed). For example, in *Kelly v Solari*, the insurers intentionally paid money to the widow in order to discharge what they thought was their obligation under an insurance contract.[48] Admittedly, the notion of 'intentionally' and 'obligation in mind' can become rather stretched if performance is carried out at gunpoint. Nevertheless, claimants are able to recover under performance-based restitution even in extreme cases of duress, as long as the claimant was

[43] *Lipkin Gorman v Karpnale Ltd* [1991] 2 AC 548 (HL); *Westdeutsche Landesbank Girozentrale v Islington LBC* [1996] 2 WLR 808, 833.

[44] Ludwig Enneccerus and Heinrich Lehmann, *Lehrbuch des bürgerlichen Rechts, Band 2: Recht der Schuldverhältnisse*, 15th edn (1958), 880.

[45] Percy Winfield, *The Province of the Law of Tort* (1931), 148: 'The phrase is barbarous, but we can think of no other.'

[46] R H Maudsley, 'Proprietary Remedies for the Recovery of Money' (1959) 75 LQR 235, 245, criticized by Birks, *Introduction*, 22.

[47] *Overseas Tankship (UK) v Morts Dock and Engineering Co (The Wagon Mound)*, [1961] AC 388 (PC), overruling the directness requirement adopted in *In Re Poelemis* [1921] 3 KB 560 (CA).

[48] *Kelly v Solari* (1841) 9 M&W 54.

forced to agree to a contract, and paid under this voidable contract, as for example in the Australian case of *Barton v Armstrong*, which concerned the sale of shares under threath of death.[49]

If, however, this was simply a case of robbery, no specific obligation was considered by the victim when handing over the cash. And if the robber took the money from the victim's pocket, the transfer of assets was not even intentional. No performance-based claim will therefore lie in robbery cases. Nevertheless, the victim can recover, namely under wrongs-based restitution (and also under tort and property law).

Regarding cases which in English law would be covered by ignorance as unjust factor, these will regularly be catered for either by restitution for wrongs, or by the specific regulations in § 816 BGB on dispositions made by an unauthorized person which are effective against the entitled person. These will be considered below.[50]

6. 'Without legal ground': absence of basis

1. Functions of legal ground

The notion of 'legal ground' requires some clarification. From a comparative perspective, we can distinguish three different functions which 'legal ground'—*causa* in Latin, *cause* in French—can assume within the law of unjust(ified) enrichment.

The first function is negative: no claim in unjust(ified) enrichment will lie for a benefit which the defendant is entitled to obtain from the claimant.

The second function is positive, i.e. that of a main controlling element in a claim for unjustified enrichment. An enrichment which the defendant has received at the claimant's expense must be given up if there is no legal ground which entitles the defendant to keep it. Here, the legal ground is not only a bar to recovery, but the device through which most considerations must be channelled which considerations ultimately decide whether a claim in unjustified enrichment lies.

[49] *Barton v Armstrong* [1976] AC 104 (PC). For a comparative treatment of the English law of duress, see Schindler, *Rechtsgeschäftliche Entscheidungsfreiheit und Drohung*.

[50] Below, Chapter 5, section 2.4.

The third function is the most subtle: transfers of benefits for which there never was a legal ground are treated differently from transfers of benefits made for a legal ground in the form of an agreement which is surrounded by circumstances which may render this agreement void, voidable, or subject to termination by one party. We will return to this issue below.[51]

The first and the third functions are essential for any law of unjust enrichment. They are covered by both German and English law, the latter with some exceptions.[52] This is not to say that it is necessary to cover these functions with an explicit use of 'legal ground' (or 'legal basis') in the formulation of requirements to be met for a claim in unjust enrichment, or with a defence against such a claim. It is essential, though, that these functions are indeed covered.

The second function, on the other hand, is only one amongst several available options for setting up a law of unjust(ified) enrichment. German law makes use of the second function. It also applies in English law, but only for claims against public authorities under *Woolwich Equitable Building Society v Inland Revenue Commissioners*, whereby money paid under an *ultra vires* demand by a public authority must be returned regardless of whether one of the usual unjust factors (mistake, compulsion, etc.) is present.[53] However, to date English courts—unlike their Scottish counterparts—have not embraced the second function for all other cases which do not concern the reversal of payments made on demand by a public authority.[54] The main thrust

[51] Below, Chapter 9, section 3.1.C.

[52] Below, Chapter 9, section 3.1.C.

[53] *Woolwich Equitable Building Society v Inland Revenue Commissioners* [1993] AC 70 (HL).

[54] The door was left open for future development in *Deutsche Morgan Grenfell Group Plc v Her Majesty's Commissioners of Inland Revenue* [2006] UKHL 49 by Lord Hoffmann at 21: 'at any rate for the moment, . . . unlike civilian systems, English law has no general principle that to retain money paid without any legal basis (such as debt, gift, compromise, etc) is unjust enrichment.' See also Häcker, (2007) LQR 177. When Scots law unified its fragmented law of restitution in favour of an absence of basis approach in *Shilliday v Smith* 1998 SLT 976 (per Lord President Rodger), approved by *Dollar Land (Cumbernauld) Ltd v CIN Properties Ltd* [1998] UKHL 53, it also made a terminological shift from 'unjust' (Shilliday) to 'unjustified' enrichment (*Dollar Land*, per Lord Hope). See also MacQueen, 2–5.

of Peter Birks' last book was that English law should generally adopt the second function of legal ground.[55]

Using 'legal ground' within this second meaning is reflected in German terminology. *Ungerechtfertigte Bereicherung* translates as unjustified enrichment, rather than unjust enrichment, which would be *ungerechte Bereicherung.*[56] This terminological choice already makes it clear that this is not a question of 'whatever moral and political values might best suit a party's case', a fear which Birks at one time thought might be evoked in English judges by the term 'unjust enrichment'.[57] This choice of words is telling of a conceptual difference between German and English law—in terms of *Leistungskondiktion*, any transfer of wealth requires justification, otherwise it can be claimed back. By this mechanism, unjustified enrichment and contract law run in tandem. Whenever it transpires that a contract has not been concluded, made void, or rescinded, whatever has been performed under this contract can, in principle, be claimed back. There is no need to resort to any unjust factors.

2. Embedding legal ground in German civil law

Those who drafted the BGB did not turn a blind eye to unjustified enrichment when formulating the provisions on contract law. On the contrary, many provisions in contract law were designed with a view towards unjustified enrichment. These features are of crucial importance for a system of unjustified enrichment which relies on other areas of law for the question whether an enrichment may be retained.

A. Gratuitous contracts

German contract law provides for legal grounds which allow a recipient to retain a gratuitous performance. For practically every standard contract under which performances are exchanged, there is a gratuitous version which obliges only one of the parties to perform.

[55] Birks, *Unjust Enrichment.*

[56] It is interesting from a comparative viewpoint that French law is reported to have borrowed from German law when inventing the term *enrichissement sans cause* (enrichment without a cause), Zweigert and Kötz, 548.

[57] Birks, *Introduction*, 19.

Schenkung (donation, or gift, §§ 516–534) is a contract under which the donor promises to transfer assets to the donee, but the donee makes no promise in return. Three contracts are available where one party promises gratuitous use, rather than transfer of assets. The first is called *Leihe* (§§ 598–606) and concerns the gratuitous lending of chattels or real property, perhaps comparable with some forms of bailment (which, however, is not a contract in English law).[58] Under a contract of *Darlehen* (loan, §§ 488–498), one party promises to make a sum of money available to the other which eventually has to be returned. The other party will normally have to pay interest, but the same agreement can also be stipulated as gratuitous loan. A similar arrangement is made for the loan of fungible goods or *Sachdarlehen* (§§ 607–609).

Similarly, several contracts are available where one party promises to provide some service (in the broad sense) without expecting anything in return. *Auftrag* (mandate), a contract whereby one person promises to look after another's business or affairs, is presumed to be gratuitous unless a remuneration has been stipulated. This type of contract is normally used for agency agreements. In a contract for services (*Dienstvertrag*, §§ 611–630) or for works (*Werkvertrag*, §§ 631–651), on the other hand, it is presumed that a remuneration is due for the services or works provided (§§ 612 and 632, respectively), but both can also be stipulated as gratuitous contracts.

As a consequence, a person who agrees to make a gift, to allow someone else the use of his or her property free of charge, or to provide a gratuitous service, cannot claim back the performance or its value on the ground that he or she received nothing in exchange. The contract under which this performance was made provides the cause which allows the recipient to retain the enrichment.

B. *Requirements of form*

In German law requirements of form also dovetail with unjustified enrichment. Generally, lack of a required form makes a contract void (§ 125), with the effect that this void contract cannot provide any cause, so that anything which has been performed under it can be

[58] See below, Chapter 9, section 2.3.B for bailment and its relevance to unjust enrichment.

claimed back. However, a number of provisions can be found which expressly state that once the contract has been executed, the lack of form is healed and the agreement becomes valid. An offer to provide a guarantee must be made in writing (§ 766 sent. 1),[59] but once the guarantor has paid, the lack of form is healed (§ 766 sent. 3). A contract for the sale of real property must be drafted, written, and sealed by a notary (§ 311b sent. 1), but once property has passed when the new owner has been entered into the land register, the lack of form is healed (§ 311b sent. 3). The same is true for a contract of donation (§ 518). A promise to pay a legal practitioner a fee which exceeds that provided by the official fee scale must be made in writing (§ 4 RVG), but once an orally stipulated fee has been paid, the lack of form is healed—provided, as § 4 RVG further specifies, that the client paid voluntarily and without reservation.

These provisions have in common that they aim to protect a party against having to perform under a contract without being first afforded the clarity or perhaps even warning which is associated with a particular form. However, once this party has carried out performance in full, the protective purpose is not strong enough to require unwinding of the contract by way of restitution of performance. The lack of form is healed by performance, and the contract stands.

It should be noted, though, that it is not the task of the courts to decide in which cases lack of form should be healed and in which they should not. This is generally a decision to be taken by the legislator, who is clearly expected to have unjustified enrichment in mind when establishing requirements of contractual form. Healing a lack of form by way of execution of a contract is limited to those situations where this effect is expressly provided for by statute. The rule remains therefore that contracts which lack a required form do not provide a cause which would allow a recipient to retain a benefit received under such a contract.[60] In some cases, however, a party may be stopped from relying on lack of a form requirement, with the effect that restitution will not be allowed.[61]

[59] This is somewhat similar to Sec. 4, Statute of Frauds, see below, Chapter 9, section 2.2.B. However, the German provision does not apply to commercial transactions.

[60] BGH 2.2.1967, NJW 1967, 1128 (contract for sale of a share in an inheritance).

[61] BGH 3.12.1958, BGHZ 29, 6. The claimant, a prospective seller of real property, had the sales contract notarized at a stage when she had no intention of signing, as she

C. Limitation of claims

Rules on limitation of claims provide that once a certain period of time has lapsed, a claimant is no longer entitled to receive what was once due to him or her. These rules aim to provide certainty and closure after that time, and an incentive for claimants not to sleep on their rights. However, they do not aim to prevent performance of time-barred claims. This is specifically provided for in § 214 para. 2 BGB: 'Performance made in satisfaction of a claim that has become time-barred may not be reclaimed, even if made without knowledge of the time-bar'.

D. Gaming and betting

The German Civil Code covers gaming and betting in a subsection on 'incomplete obligations'. Section 762 para. 1 BGB provides:

> Gaming and betting do not create obligations. What has been performed on the basis of the game or the bet cannot be claimed back on the ground that the obligation did not exist.

This is similar to the position in English law before s 335 of the Gambling Act 2005 made all lawful gambling agreements enforceable. The construction is slightly different: rather than providing for a 'soft' or 'natural' obligation which is not enforceable, § 762 BGB provides that those agreements do not create any obligations. The purpose of this provision, however, does not extend to restitution. There are some similarities to limitation of claims. However, § 762 falls short of making such agreements valid once the bets have been paid out, which would perhaps be the tidiest solution.

was expecting higher offers; when ultimately she did sign, the notary failed to record this later date in the document, with the effect that the sales contract was not properly notarized. The actual transfer of property to the buyer (*Auflassung*) was also marred by a formal deficiency, so that no healing of the sales contract occurred when the buyer was entered into the land register. The buyer paid out existing debts relating to the property which, if not honoured, could have resulted in the loss of that property to the impecunious claimant. After those debts had been paid, the claimant required return of the property. The *Bundesgerichtshof* held that the principle of good faith prevented the claimant from relying on the lack of form which was caused by her late signature, and rejected her claim for restitution of the property.

E. Ground as purpose

The above are refinements of the principle that a benefit transferred under a contract can be reclaimed if the corresponding obligation did not exist or has lapsed. The principle remains the same: a valid obligation provides the legal ground which allows the recipient to retain the benefit.

In some situations, however, legal ground has a different meaning. Rather than pointing to the obligation which was to be fulfilled by the performance which constitutes the enrichment, legal ground refers to the purpose behind that obligation. It is, in particular, in two situations that German law uses 'legal ground' in this sense: recognitions of debt and the so-called *condictio causa data causa non secuta*.

Section 781 BGB regulates what is called an abstract recognition of the existence of a debt (*abstraktes Schuldanerkenntnis*), whereby 'abstract' indicates that such a contract provides no reason why the obligation in question should exist. This appears to be similar to an acknowledgment of indebtedness under English law. The difference is that the German version creates an obligation, whereas the main effect of the English version is to postpone limitation of actions.[62]

An abstract recognition of debt must be distinguished in particular from gifts, compromises, and guarantees:

A contract whereby A agrees to give B €1,000 as a present is a contract of donation; the understanding that this should be a present is the underlying reason, the *causa* behind the promise. This is not an abstract contract.

Nor is a contract of *Vergleich* (compromise, or settlement, § 779 BGB) considered an abstract recognition of debt. If there was a dispute between parties about the existence or the amount of an obligation, and if these parties have met somewhere in the middle, this is a valid contract of compromise. Not only does compromise create an obligation, but compromise also carries its own *causa*, i.e. the process of giving and taking, which under English law would be the consideration. Unlike an abstract recognition of debt, a valid compromise

[62] Sec. 29 Limitation of Actions Act 1980; *Bradford & Bingley plc v Rashid* [2006] UKHL 37; *Spencer v Hemmerde* [1922] 2 AC 507 (HL); see also *Chitty on Contracts*, 28–094 .

cannot be challenged on the ground that there was no legal ground behind the compromise.

The same is true for a contract of guarantee (*Bürgschaft*, § 765), whereby the guarantor (*Bürge*) becomes liable for what the principal debtor owes to the creditor.

On the other hand, a contract whereby A recognizes that she owes to B €1,000 without indicating expressly or impliedly that this is a gift, a guarantee, the result of a compromise, or is an outstanding payment under, say, a loan agreement, is an abstract recognition of a debt. Such a contract is valid and can be enforced. However, this promise can be claimed back in unjustified enrichment if no good reason can be found for this recognition, for example because parties were mistaken as to the existence of a debt. It is for this reason that § 812 para. 2 BGB states specifically: 'The recognition or denial of the existence of an obligation by way of contract is also considered as performance.' Thus, this 'performance' must be backed up by a legal ground outside the act of recognition (or denial). This could be either an existing obligation (for example, the outstanding payment under a loan agreement), or a 'legal ground' in the sense of a purpose of this recognition.

Literally speaking, the beneficiary of either recognition or denial is required by § 812 para. 2 BGB to 'give up' that recognition or denial. The reader may wonder how this could possibly be done. The answer is that unjustified enrichment will be used as a defence against a claim for performance under an abstract recognition of debt. Such a defence is expressly provided in § 821: 'A person who undertakes an obligation without legal ground can refuse performance even if the claim for release from this obligation is time-barred.'

Section 821 also reveals the different meaning that 'legal ground' takes in this context. Whereas normally any valid obligation provides a legal ground that entitles the recipient to keep an enrichment, under § 821 this is not the case. 'Legal ground' refers to circumstances outside this obligation. In the case of an abstract recognition of debt, this is either an existing obligation which is confirmed by the recognition, or else the purpose which, according to the parties, this recognition was to serve.

The practical implication of this complex construction is this: an abstract recognition of a debt, although creating an obligation, eventually does little more than shift the burden of pleading and proof onto the debtor, who must show that there was no cause to support the promise.[63]

The above can be illustrated by two cases in which money had been embezzled, and in which relatives of the tortfeasor promised to make good the damage in order to prevent him or her from being exposed to criminal prosecution. In one case, this promise was formulated as a guarantee, and in the other as a recognition of debt.

In a case decided by the *Bundesgerichtshof* in 1988, the tortfeasor had embezzled more than DM 1 million (approx. €500,000) from the counter-claimant, and the tortfeasor's wife, mother, and mother-in-law (the counter-defendants) had provided guarantees for the payment of the tortfeasor's debt on the counter-claimants' demand and in fear that their relative would otherwise be prosecuted.[64] As this was a contract of guarantee rather than a recognition of debt, the money could not be claimed back under § 812 para. 2 BGB. The only hope for the relatives lay in contract law, rather than unjustified enrichment, namely by relying on the contract being void or voidable. They argued that the guarantee was voidable on the ground of duress (*widerrechtliche Drohung*, § 123 BGB), or void under § 138 para. 2 BGB for exploitation of a predicament (somewhat similar to undue influence in English law). The *Bundesgerichtshof*, however, refused to entertain either argument. It held that the facts amounted to no more than that the counter-claimant was in a position to report the tortfeasor to the police, that the counter-defendants wanted to save the tortfeasor from this fate, and that all participants were aware of these facts. And while the exploitation of a predicament could make the contracts of guarantee void under § 138 BGB, this was not necessarily the case. The facts established by the Appeal Court did not warrant the conclusion that the contract was void under § 138 BGB. Therefore the promise of the relatives to make good the damage caused by the tortfeasor remained valid.

The second case was decided by the same court two years later (case no. 11). The claimant was the husband of a cashier employed by the defendant. When it transpired that his wife had embezzled

[63] See Hüffer in *Münchener Kommentar*, § 780 no. 48.

[64] BGH 7.6.1988, NJW 1988, 2599; for an English translation, see Markesinis, Lorenz, and Dannemann, *The German Law of Contracts and Restitution: A Comparative Introduction* (1997), case no. 32.

large sums of money, the claimant signed a notarized deed by which he acknowledged that he owed the defendant some DM 175,000 (approx. €87,500), submitted to immediate execution, and created a mortgage over this amount on his property.[65] Both parties were in agreement that the husband did this in order to prevent his wife from being reported to the police. The defendant nevertheless reported the wife to the police, and was then sued by the husband who wanted the court to set aside this notarized deed.

This case differs from the previous one in one important aspect: this was an abstract recognition of a debt rather than a contract of guarantee. A contract of guarantee, as we have seen above, provides a complete cause. On the other hand, an abstract recognition of a debt provides a valid claim, but constitutes an unjustified enrichment and can thus be claimed back under § 812 para. 2, para. 1 BGB if there is no separate legal ground for this recognition of debt. It is submitted in this case that this cause was an understanding between the claimant and the defendant that the claimant would pay his wife's debt in exchange for the defendant not reporting the wife to the police, and that this cause had failed due to the conduct of the defendant.

The *Bundesgerichtshof* arrived at the same result using a different approach, namely by relying on § 812 para. 1 sent. 2 2nd alt. BGB, the *condictio causa data causa non secuta*, which will be covered in the following chapter.

[65] BGH 23.2.1990, NJW-RR 1990, 827; below, Chapter 10, section 11 (translation).

3

The Undoing of Performance: Refinements

1. Specific *condictiones* based on performance

The BGB contains some specific conditiones which are meant to complement the general clause in § 812 para. 1 sent. 1 BGB. We will begin with the one which the *Bundesgerichtshof* applied in the above case.

1. *Condictio causa data causa non secuta*

Under § 812 para. 1 sent. 2 2nd alt. BGB, performance can be claimed back 'if the result does not occur which the performance had been aimed at to produce according to the content of the legal transaction'. This is the *condictio causa data causa non secuta,* which is also called *condictio ob causam datorum*, or *condictio ob rem,* a legacy from Roman law which was designed for Roman law contracts which do not exist in German law. To be precise, the contracts for which this *condictio* was designed had reportedly ceased to exist at the times of Justinian, and this *condictio* found its way into the *codex iuris civilis* for the purposes of tradition rather than practical need.[1] It was maintained in § 812 para. 1 sent. 2 BGB more than a millenium later on similar grounds, because the draftsmen were uncertain about whether there would be a need for this *condictio.*

Today, this *condictio* has a narrow field of application. It relates to situations where the claimant has provided performance to the defendant not in exchange for counter-performance of another obligation, but for another purpose, and where both parties have agreed that this purpose was the reason for the performance. From an English

[1] Reuter and Martinek, 148; see also von Caemmerer, 346.

perspective, it could be said that this *condictio* concerns failure of consideration outside contracts. Even under German law with its wide notion of contracts, including in particular gratuitous contracts,[2] failure of consideration outside contracts can arise, in particular in situations where the expected event consists in an act of the defendant which cannot be made the subject of a valid contractual obligation. In one such case, a farmer transferred his farm and all his other assets to his estranged wife in order to encourage her to return to him; when she did not return, the farmer was allowed to rely on § 812 para. 1 sent. 2 BGB.[3]

As mentioned above, the same *condictio* was also employed by the court in case no. 11, involving a cashier who had embezzled large amounts of money, and whose husband (the claimant) had signed a recognition of debt according to which he owed the defendant (the victim) some DM 175,000 (approx. €87,500), submitted to immediate execution, and created a mortgage over this amount on his property.[4] The *Bundesgerichtshof* reiterated that, in order for § 812 para. 1 sent. 2 to apply, there must be an agreement between the parties as regards the purpose, and that in this case the defendant had required securities for a specified purpose which had not been fulfilled, with the effect that the defendant could not enforce the recognition of debt. This appears to be a classical application of the *condictio causa data causa non secuta*, but the same result is achieved by the general *Leistungskondiktion* in conjunction with § 812 para. 2 BGB.[5] The husband's promise was an abstract recognition of debt, which was open to an enrichment claim for want of a legal ground from the moment the wife was reported to the police.

Some academics have also taken the view that the *condictio causa data causa non secuta*, rather than the general *Leistungskondiktion*, should apply in cases where the parties have performed in anticipation of a contract which is never concluded,[6] perhaps because one or both parties have changed their minds. A party may likewise have performed under a contract which it knows to be void for lack of form,

[2] Above, Chapter 2, section 6.2.A.
[3] RG 18.1.1923, SeuffArch 78 (1924) n. 124.
[4] BGH 23.2.1990, NJW-RR 1990, 827; below, Chapter 10, section 11 (translation).
[5] See above, Chapter 2, section 6.2.E.
[6] Reuter and Martinek, 151ff.

expecting this lack to be healed by complete performance.[7] This could concern, in particular, contracts for the sale of land where parties have indicated a lower sales price in the notarized contract in order to save on stamp duty and notary costs.[8] If the buyer is unwise enough to pay in advance, and the seller then refuses to transfer the title, the seller could under § 814 BGB rely on the fact that the buyer was fully aware of the lack of an existing obligation and thus defeat the buyer's enrichment claim. In practice, this is unlikely to happen, because the notary is bound to ensure that payment and title change hands at the same time.

Some see the *condictio causa data causa no secuta* as a way of circumventing § 814. Section 815 BGB provides a separate defence for cases of failure of purpose. This defence is based on a particular lack of mistake, namely the knowledge that the purpose could not be achieved.[9] Section 815 is therefore no bar to recovery if a person performs in anticipation of a contract which is never concluded.

This view, however, makes sense only if § 815 is understood as the more specific provision, with the effect that § 814 does not apply to any case within the ambit of § 815. However, if § 815 BGB does indeed take precedence as the more specific regulation, there appears to be no reason why it should not serve the same function for the general *Leistungskondiktion*. Moreover, the courts have adopted the view that, regardless of whether the restitutionary claim figures under *Leistungskondiktion*[10] or under *condictio causa data causa non secuta*,[11] the defence of § 814 BGB does not apply if both parties were aware that the contract on which they were performing was void for lack of form, provided that they expected the form requirement to be 'healed' by full performance. The same defences are therefore available, regardless of whether a claim falls under the general *Leistungskondiktion* or under the *condictio causa data causa non secuta*.

[7] See above, Chapter 2, section 6.2.B.

[8] BGH 26.10.1979, NJW 1980, 451. In this situation, the documented agreement with the lower purchase price is a sham transaction and void under § 117 BGB, whereas the intended agreement is void for lack of form under §§ 125, 311b sent. 1 BGB.

[9] Below, Chapter 4.

[10] BGH 26.9.1975, NJW 1976, 237.

[11] BGH 26.10.1979, NJW 1980, 451.

This leads to a more general point. It seems that whenever *condictio causa data causa non secuta* raises its head, it causes more problems than it solves. After a flirtatious period, the *Bundesgerichtshof* gave up employing this *condictio* for resolving marital property disputes in divorce in cases where spouses had agreed to keep their property completely separate, but had nevertheless used mixed funds to acquire property which rested only in one of the spouses.[12] In these and in other situations the courts discovered that the doctrine of frustration of contract (*Wegfall der Geschäftsgrundlage*), which now is enshrined in § 313 BGB, offered a far more flexible solution than the 'all or nothing' approach of the *condictio causa data causa non secuta*, and that there is little if any difference between this and frustration of the purpose of a contract (*Zweckvereitelung*).

Nevertheless, 2008 saw another U-turn by the *Bundesgerichtshof* in a case in which unmarried partners had pooled their savings for building a family home registered in the name of only one of them (case no. 17, a 'non-marital property' dispute).[13] The *Bundesgerichtshof* allowed an appeal by the disappointed partner who had invested his life savings and some 1,000 hours of work and instructed the *Oberlandesgericht* Jena to examine more closely whether this investment had been made with the communicated and accepted purpose (*Zweckabrede*) of obtaining a lifelong right to live in the home. At the same time, however, the *Bundesgerichtshof* instructed the *Oberlandesgericht* to also consider restitution claims following frustration of contract under § 313 BGB, *Wegfall der Geschäftsgrundlage*. The *Bundesgerichtshof* remained silent on the issue of which of those claims should take precedence.

[12] See Staudinger-Lorenz § 812 nos 100ff. Interestingly, this occurred at about the same time that the Canadian Supreme Court in *Pettkus v Becker* [1980] 2 SCR 834 began to do just that. See Lionel Smith, 'The Mystery of 'Juristic Reason' (2000) 12 Supreme Ct L Rev 2nd Series, 211–244.

[13] BGH 9.7.2008, NJW 2008, 3277; below, Chapter 10, section 17 (translation). The facts of this case appear to resemble *Tinsley v Milligan* [1994] 1 AC 340 (HL), with, however, one major difference. The purpose of registering the home in the name of only one of the partners was not social benefit fraud, as in *Tinsley v Milligan*, but rather to prevent the children of the unregistered partner from acquiring rights against the registered partner. In the closely related Scottish case of *Shilliday v Smith* 1998 SLT 976, the pursuer improved the defender's house in the expectation that they would marry. See MacQueen, 33–35; Sheehan (2008) Oxford U Comparative L Forum 1, text adjacent to note 154.

This illustrates a general problem for any possible remaining applications of the *condictio causa data causa non secuta*. This appendix amongst the *condictiones* distorts the harmony between contract and unjustified enrichment by allowing a person to claim back what was performed under a valid obligation. It is incapable of being reconciled with the first function of the notion of 'legal ground' in unjust(ified) enrichment.[14] The nearly 1,500 years which have passed since it was included in Justinian's code because the drafters were unsure if it still might have a use and the more than one hundred years which have elapsed since it was incorporated in the German Civil Code for the same reason, should surely have allowed sufficient time for an evaluation to conclude that there was, after all, simply no necessity for this *condictio* alongside the general unjustified enrichment clause in § 812 para. 1 BGB. As a minimum, the *causa data causa non secuta* should no longer be allowed for a claim in unjustified enrichment where the enrichment is supported by a valid legal ground.

2. *Condictio ob causam finitam*

The *condictio ob causam finitam*, expressed in § 812 para. 1 sent. 2 1st alt. BGB, allows recovery of performance in situations where there was a legal ground when performance was made, but where this cause later lapsed. A paradigmatic example are payments for lost or stolen objects under insurance contracts, where the insurance company can reclaim their payment under this *condictio* if the lost or stolen object is later found and returned to its owner.[15] There are similar common law cases of insured cargo which was mistakenly believed to be lost or damaged.[16] In *Napier and Ettrick v Hunter*, an equitable lien was granted in favour of the insurer over monies received by an insured after indemnification.[17] Similarly, case no. 14 concerns maintenance

[14] See above, Chapter 2, section 6.1.

[15] RG 4.3.1924, RGZ 108, 110, 112; Staudinger-Lorenz § 812 no. 96.

[16] *Norwich Union Fire Insurance Society Ltd v W H Price Ltd* [1934] AC 455 (PC), where the insured lemons had been sold because they were ripe, and the insurer had mistakenly believed that they had been damaged.

[17] *Napier and Ettrick v Hunter* [1993] AC 713 (HL).

payments made under an interim court regulation, which later turned out to amount to an overpayment.[18]

The *condictio ob causam finitam* is straightforward and largely unproblematic. Within the German law of unjustified enrichment, it serves as an explanatory rule to the general *Leistungskondiktion*: hindsight will determine whether there was a legal ground for performance.

3. Performance in spite of defence

Section 813 para. 1 BGB allows a person to recover for performance made under an obligation which existed in principle, but which was barred by a permanent defence. Such a permanent defence can arise, *inter alia*, under unjustified enrichment rules. As explained above, § 821 BGB provides a defence against a claim under an abstract recognition of debt which lacked a supporting *causa*.[19] In tort law, § 853 BGB can provide a similar defence, for example if the claimant has performed an obligation which the defendant had fraudulently obtained by way of assignment. The majority of the case law, however, concerns cases where the defence was not permanent so that no claim could lie under § 813 para. 1. It seems that there is little application of this rule.

2. Performance between three or more parties

As mentioned, one of the main functions of performance-based unjustified enrichment is to find a satisfactory solution for tri- or multipartite enrichment situations such as in the example of the glazier, his apprentice, the tenant, and his landlord.[20] This does indeed work rather well provided that all parties are aware of who is performing within which contractual relationship. Performance-based unjustified enrichment becomes more problematic, though, if the parties concerned have differing views about who has performed towards whom,

[18] BGH 17.6.1992, BGHZ 118, 383; below, Chapter 10, section 14 (translation).
[19] At Chapter 2, section 6.2.E.
[20] Above, Chapter 2, sections 2.2 and 3.2.

or whether the enrichment was actually based on performance. In consequence, performance-based restitution between three or more parties has become one of the most controversial areas of the German laws of obligation. Interestingly, the controversy is not so much about how leading cases should have been decided, but focused more on the reasoning behind these decisions.

Restitution of performance between three or more parties bears some resemblance to what Goff and Jones refer to as a benefit which the defendant has acquired from a third party for which he must account to the claimant, as well as with what Burrows calls 'benefits conferred by third parties' and shows some overlap with what Birks termed 'interceptive subtraction'.[21] On a comparative note, French law, with its *action directe en paiement*, uses a contractual approach to deal with similar problems.[22]

In German law, courts with the support of the majority of academics use the following concept as a framework:

Disenriched party perspective rule. The first rule is that if there was a shift of wealth and one of the parties believed this to be performance while another did not, it is the view of the disenriched party that will decide whether this is a case of performance. We will call this the 'disenriched party perspective rule'.

Case no. 5 serves as an illustration.[23] A thief steals two young bulls belonging to the claimant and sells them to the *bona fide* defendant, who converts them into meat and sausages. As the defendant could not acquire *bona fide* title in the stolen bulls (§ 935 BGB), he acquired property only when the bulls were converted into food (§ 950 BGB, based on the Roman law *specificatio*).[24] From the defendant's view, it could be argued that he acquired this enrichment under his contract with the thief (although the thief was not actually in a position to perform). But the claimant as the person who lost the property did not perform, therefore this is a case of enrichment in another way.

[21] Goff and Jones, section 2; Burrows 31–41; Birks, *Introduction*, 133–139; Birks, *Unjust Enrichment*, 75–77; Virgo, 108–112.

[22] See Simon Whittaker, 'Privity of Contract and the Law of Tort: the French Experience', 1995 OJLS 327–370, in particular 357–361.

[23] BGH 11.1.1971, BGHZ 55, 176, below, Chapter 10, section 5 (translation).

[24] Below, Chapter 6, section 2.1.

It should be noted, however, that in this case, the *Bundesgerichtshof* failed to mention either *Leistungskondiktion* or subsidiarity of enrichment in another way.

Recipient perspective rule. The second rule is that if there has been performance, it is the view of the enriched party that decides which of the various parties performed.[25] Therefore, if goods are sold in a chain of contracts, and the producer, on the instruction of the distributor, delivers directly to the ultimate buyer, that party is not answerable to an unjustified enrichment claim from the producer because, from the buyer's perspective, this was performance by the distributor. We will call this the 'recipient perspective rule'.

For both rules, it is not the subjective beliefs of the parties concerned which matter, but rather the view which an objective person would take from the perspective of that party, and in particular based on the information available to that party.

The result is that a *Leistungskondiktion* is available to a claimant who was disenriched without legal ground through what, from the perspective of that party, objectively looked like the claimant's performance, against a defendant from whose perspective the enrichment objectively looked like having been provided by the claimant.

Subsidiarity of enrichment in another way. Furthermore, if the enrichment occurred as a result of a performance, no restitution is allowed between the other parties under the enrichment in another-way option of § 812 para. 1 sent. 1 BGB (this is the so-called subsidiarity of 'enrichment in another way').

The case in which the *Bundesgerichtshof* embraced the performance/non-performance taxonomy (case no. 4) serves as a further illustration.[26] The claimant delivered electrical appliances which were installed in buildings owned by the defendant. The claimant allegedly believed he was acting under a contract with the defendant. In fact, however, there was no such contract. Rather, the defendant

[25] See e.g. Fikentscher and Heinemann, no. 1431.

[26] BGH 31.10.1963, BGHZ 40, 272, below, Chapter 10, section 4 (translation), confirmed in BGH 20.4.2001, BGHZ 147, 269. While this judgment is widely supported by academic writing, it has been criticized by Schall, *Leistungskondiktion*, 92ff, who would abandon the subsidiarity principle and treat claimant and third party as joint creditors in this case. This is an interesting solution, but is prone to shifting insolvency risks.

had instructed a third party, who had subcontracted to the claimant. It was the claimant's perspective that decided that there was performance in this case, and the defendant's perspective which decided that this was performance by the third party which employed the claimant as a subcontractor. The claim was disallowed.

Rule against leapfrogging. This is the general rule which can be taken from this and similar cases involving chains of performance: if any of the contracts within the chain of performance is imperfect, restitution must occur between adjoining parties in the chain, and no leapfrog restitution is allowed between a supplier and a remote recipient.[27]

The reasons for this restriction are as much economic as they are legal. Canaris has formulated these reasons into the following three principles:[28]

(1) In any situation of an imperfect obligation between two parties, neither party should be deprived of its defences against the other. (In our case, the defendant had already paid the third party for the appliances and could still rely on this fact.)

(2) On the other hand, both parties should be protected against defences that the other party has acquired from legal relationships with third parties.

(3) Parties must bear no more and no less than the risk of insolvency of a party which they have chosen to be their contractual partner. Unjustified enrichment must not create new defendants when the claimant's contractual partner becomes insolvent.[29] (In our case, if the third party had become insolvent, allowing a leapfrog claim from the supplier to the defendant would have moved the risk of the third party's insolvency to the defendant.) Moreover, unjustified enrichment should not serve to replace a solvent defendant with an insolvent defendant if the claimant had not chosen to bargain with the insolvent defendant.

[27] For similar cases, see BGH 14.3.1974, NJW 1974, 1132; LG Bonn 3.12.1990, NJW 1981, 1360; but see also below, Chapter 5, section 4.4 for exceptions allowed under the *Rückgriffskondiktion*.

[28] Canaris, 'Bereicherungsausgleich'; Larenz and Canaris, 204ff.

[29] Similar von Caemmerer, 370.

Interestingly, though, Canaris is a leading critique of employing the concept of *Leistung* for finding the right claimant and the right defendant in cases involving three or more parties.[30] But if it was said before that the concept of performance serves as a compass for this task, it may be suggested that these three principles provide the map; and compass and map are usually complementary rather than irreconcilable methods for finding the correct course. In our case, Canaris has explained the policy which is served by adopting the two above-mentioned rules, the 'disenriched party perspective rule' for deciding whether a case falls under performance-based unjustified enrichment, and the 'recipient perspective rule' for deciding who is the right claimant.

Bank cases. The most difficult category of multipartite relationships are arguably those between two account holders and their respective banks when an error has occurred with a payment made from the account of one to the account of the other. Having said this, there is one category of cases which is so straightforward that they are not even perceived as multipartite cases: if both banks have correctly made the transfer and the problem is simply that the receiving account holder was not entitled to the payment made by the other account holder, this is treated as a case involving two parties. The fact that wealth is shifted to the final recipient by the receipient's bank, and to the recipient's bank by the sender's bank is entirely ignored for the purposes of unjustified enrichment in this situation. The banks have done no more than move the funds between the two parties concerned.

However, matters become more complicated if one of the two banks, usually the sender's bank, does not comply with the sender's instructions. This will turn the situation into a tripartite case—again, the recipient's bank is ignored for the purposes of unjustified enrichment unless an error has also occurred on the recipient's side.

Cases such as these have troubled English and German courts alike. The detailed comparative study by Solomon identified several serious difficulties which these cases present for an unjust factor-based approach in which claimants have to rely on mistake.[31] These cases

[30] Larenz and Canaris, 199ff and 248ff.

[31] Solomon, *Der Bereicherungsausgleich in Anweisungsfällen*. See also Schall (2004) Rest L Rev 110–131 (discovering communality between English and German law, whereby a failure of purpose oriented approach could help both to overcome existing problems).

show that the previous notion of 'liability mistake' will not work, in particular because banks are usually not liable to the recipients.[32] However, the competing notion of a 'simple mistake' is entirely unhelpful for separating the deserving from the undeserving cases, and for identifying the right claimant and the right defendant.[33] This task was increasingly left to the defence that the payment was received for 'good consideration', which therefore in this area of English law is used for functions which are similar to those of 'with legal ground' in the German law of unjustified enrichment.[34]

Has the performance-based approach been more successful in sorting out tri- or multipartite cases involving banks which have failed to comply with their instructions? Case no. 8 provides an example. A tenant (a brewery) had cancelled a standing order after a quarrel with its landlord (the defendant) over deficiencies which allegedly prevented the premises from being used by the brewery as a pub, and had announced to the defendant that they were no longer willing to pay the rent.[35] The bank (the claimant in the action) overlooked the cancellation and paid for another thirteen months. For some reason the tenant failed to notice the continued payments. Eventually the bank sued the defendant for return of the payments. This was clearly a case of performance, but was it the bank or the brewery who had performed? Under the 'recipient perspective rule', this was considered as performance between the tenant and the defendant. The landlord had every right to believe that the tenant had stopped short of realizing his threat. Thus, the landlord was exposed only to a claim by the tenant, which left the landlord with an opportunity to rely on the fact that there was a tenancy contract, which could thus provide the legal ground for the payment. To be on the safe side, however, the *Bundesgerichtshof* held that each case was to be decided on its own merits, and that the general concept was a guideline and not binding. The factual situation of this case resembles *Barclays Bank Ltd v W J Simms Son & Cooke (Southern) Ltd*, where, in that instance, the bank was allowed to recover from the recipient.[36]

32 Solomon, 155ff.
33 Solomon, 164ff.
34 Solomon, 171ff.
35 BGH 19.1.1984, BGHZ 89, 376; below, Chapter 10, section 8 (translation).
36 *Barclays Bank Ltd v W J Simms Son & Cooke (Southern) Ltd* [1980] 1 QB 677 (QBD).

There is, however, another case in which the *Bundesgerichtshof* allowed a bank to recover from the recipient of a mistaken payment.[37] As in the previous case, the bank had also ignored a cancellation (this time, of a cheque). It was, however, disputed between the parties whether the recipient was aware that the cheque had been cancelled. It is noteworthy that the bank was allowed to recover directly from the recipient on the assumption (made for the purpose of the appeal) that the recipient knew of the cancellation, even though the bank believed it was performing its banking contract towards its account holder, not towards the recipient. The result is different, but that does not necessarily indicate an exception to the 'recipient perspective rule'. This was a case of performance towards the recipient, and the only question was whether this was performance by the bank or by the account holder. As this is generally to be determined from the recipient's perspective, the bank should be the right claimant. If the recipient knew that the bank was mistaken, he also knew that the bank shifted its own and not the account holder's wealth onto him. It is true that this deprives the recipient from raising defences against the bank which might arise from his relationship with the account holder, but a recipient who knows that this is a mistaken payment under a cancelled cheque does not seem particularly worthy of such protection. On the other hand, it was certainly not helpful that the *Bundesgerichtshof* refused to state whether restitution should be allowed under the *Leistungskondiktion* or for enrichment in another way.[38]

Shifting cases out of performance-based unjustified enrichment. The *Bundesgerichtshof* has since resolved this question against the *Leistungskondiktion* and in favour of allowing restitution for enrichment in another way in cases where an instruction to the party who effectuates payment (in our last two cases, the bank) is lacking. In a relatively recent case (case no. 16), a credit broker had made a name

[37] BGH 16.6.1983, BGHZ 87, 393.

[38] See also BGH 25.9.1986, NJW 1987, 185. The defendant was to receive agent's commissions from his principal amounting to DM 1.499,60, and the principal instructed the bank accordingly. By mistake, the bank transferred the sum of DM 14,996. The *Bundesgerichtshof* allowed the bank to recover from the recipient, even though it was unclear whether the recipient knew that the bank was responsible for the mistake. It seems that the *Bundesgerichtshof* attaches more importance to whether the recipient was *mala fide* rather than to the person who was performing from the perspective of the recipient.

for himself by arranging short-term credit deals directly between local authorities. The idea behind this scheme was that by cutting out the banks as middlemen, the broker could offer to local authorities seeking to invest their money returns above market rates, while offering loans with interest rates below market rates to those authorities which were in need of credit.[39] However, the broker diverted several millions Deutschmarks to his own account and covered up the fraud by using new investments to repay old ones.

In one such instance, the credit broker first told the defendant, a county council (*Landkreis*), that the council would provide a loan worth more than DM 3.5 million (€1.75 million) to the city of P, a loan which in fact P had no intention of taking out. The defendant paid the sum to an account held by the credit broker, who used the money for himself. When repayment was due a few months later, the credit broker told a similar story to the claimant, a local authority, and instructed the claimant to make their payment for this fictitious loan to the account of the defendant, indicating as the reason for the transfer 'Redemption City of P'. On this information, the claimant transferred more than DM 3.5 million to the defendant's bank account. The *Bundesgerichtshof* allowed the claimant to recover this sum from the defendant not under the *Leistungskondiktion*, but under enrichment in another way.

On a performance analysis, the claimant thought it was performing a credit agreement with the city of P, which would later return the sum with interest. The defendant also believed he had a credit agreement with the city of P, and that they were receiving their due repayment from P.

The 'disenriched party perspective rule' will tell us that this is a case of performance (it is, also, from the defendant's perspective). The 'recipient perspective rule' will furthermore tell us that from the defendant's perspective, this was performance under their credit agreement with the city of P. The main problem, which also distinguishes this from

39 BGH 5.11.2002, BGHZ 152, 307; below, Chapter 10, section 16 (translation). The case shows some similarities to *Dextra Bank Trust v Bank of Jamaica* [2001] UKPC 50, where the payer was also led to believe it was repaying a loan, and the recipient believed it had received the money in return for a previous payment. The main difference is that in *Bank Trust*, the recipient had made its own payout not as part of a loan, but as a currency deal, and only very shortly before receiving the claimant's payment.

previous cases, is that both of the agreements under which the parties thought they were performing existed only in their imagination. The 'recipient perspective rule', which protects a party against being sued by the wrong party in tri- or multipartite performance situations, is justified where contracts are valid, void, voidable, or terminated, because it allows the recipient to rely on a valid defence which arises out of this valid, void, or failed relationship. However, preference of the recipient is difficult to justify if the entire situation which could or could not provide a legal ground for keeping the enrichment is purely fictitious, because a fictitious legal relationship cannot give rise to a valid defence. The defendant city council deserves no more protection in their reliance on a fictitious agreement than the claimant in their reliance on a similar fictitious agreement.

The outcome of the case, namely that the claimant was allowed to recover from the defendant, could be justified under the rule against shifting insolvency risks. Both parties had generally accepted the fictitious risk of the city of P becoming insolvent. The claimant might have taken on an additional risk by paying not to the city of P, but to the defendant, relying on the credit broker's information that this was done under the instruction of P. However, while the claimant may have assumed a risk that the payment could go to the wrong person, the only additional insolvency risk they could thereby have assumed is that the defendant might not have the money to repay them. The defendant, on the other hand, had allowed their payment to go to the credit broker's bank account, so they could be viewed as having accepted the risk that the credit broker would not pass the money on to the city of P and could become insolvent. Therefore the defendant might be considered as having accepted the risks associated with paying money to a fraudster and the unlikely possibility of being able to recover from this person, whereas this could not be said about the claimant.

However, by moving the case out of performance, the *Bundesgerichthof* has, it is submitted, thrown the proverbial baby out with the bathwater. This was clearly performance by the claimant—an intentional shift of assets, with a particular obligation in mind. If performance-based unjustified enrichment cannot handle clear cases of performance, what is it good for? All that is needed, it is suggested, is a refinement of the 'recipient perspective' rule, namely that this operates for void, imperfect, or otherwise failed obligations, but not for purely imaginary ones.

Purpose of performance and contractual capacity. While this decision has weakened a performance-based analysis by moving a problematic case out of performance, another judgment by the *Bundesgerichtshof* (case no. 13) has weakened a performance-based analysis from within.[40] This case involved a claimant who had lost the mental faculties required for legal capacity under German law, with the effect that both his credit agreement with the bank and his instruction that part of the credit should be paid directly to a third party were void (§§ 104, 105 BGB).[41] This lack of capacity became apparent at a later date, and a guardian was appointed who sought to recover the balance of the claimant's bank account. The bank declared set-off with a claim in unjustified enrichment for the amount which the bank had paid to the third party. The *Bundesgerichtshof* held that the bank had no such claim.

The normal analysis would have been that, between claimant and third party, this is performance by the claimant towards the third party and, at the same time, between bank and claimant, a case of performance of the bank towards the claimant. If unjustified enrichment claims are to be kept within failed contractual relationships, the bank should thus have been allowed to recover from the claimant, and the claimant to recover from the third party. However, the *Bundesgerichtshof* argued that legal capacity is required for a party to associate a performance with a particular purpose (*Zweckbestimmung*), as this association is similar to a legal transaction (*rechtsgeschäftliche Natur*).

With respect, the argument that contract rules should apply by analogy to the question whether a particular purpose has validly been attached to a performance can defeat the entire notion of performance-based restitution. If a contract is, for example, voidable on the ground of duress (§ 123 BGB), the claimant will almost certainly also have been pressurized into performing for this particular purpose. So this claimant's *Zweckbestimmung* is equally affected by duress and should, by the same logic, also be invalid. The absurd result would

[40] BGH 20.6.1990, BGHZ 111, 382; below, Chapter 10, section 13 (translation).
[41] Ibid.

be that such a claimant cannot recover this performance under the *Leistungskondiktion*.

This argument comes as close to circularity as that of the House of Lords in *Sinclair v Brougham* when the House held that if a bank contract was void on the ground of *ultra vires* (because building societies were not at that time permitted to act as banks), no claim for restitution could lie for customers seeking to recover their deposits because any fictitious promise to repay would have been equally void on the ground of *ultra vires*.[42] However, the judgment of the *Bundesgerichtshof* is correct as a matter of legal policy. Protection of those who lack judgement is a cause which can be more deserving than the protection of those economic interests in tripartite restitution situations which the 'recipient perspective rule' aims to protect. The case of incapacity should simply form a second exception to the 'recipient perspective rule'.

3. Termination of contract

We have seen above (Chapter 1, section 4.1) that restitution of performance after a contract has been terminated is not governed by unjustified enrichment rules under German law. The BGB contains in §§ 346–359 BGB (and thus at quite a distance from unjustified enrichment in §§ 812–822 BGB) specific contract law rules which define the mutual restitutionary claims which may arise after termination.[43] English law, in contrast, sees this as a case of unjust enrichment in which restitution may be required for failure of consideration. Another conceptual difference is that, according to the modern

[42] *Sinclair v Brougham* [1914] AC 398 (HL).

[43] It is interesting to note that several comparative lawyers with a German law background are critical of this division and would prefer a unified restitutionary system to apply to failed and terminated contracts alike: Coen, 49f; Hellwege, Ch. 3; S Maier, No Basis: A Comparative View, in: *Mapping the Law*, 343ff, 345; Schlechtriem, *Restitution und Bereicherungsausgleich*, Vol I 3 nos 1–2; Christiane Wendehorst, 'Die Leistungskondiktion und ihre Binnenstruktur', in: *Grundstrukturen eines europäischen Bereicherungsrechts*, 47, 82f. For the pre-reform law, see Dannemann, 'Restitution for Termination of Contract in German Law'; Reinhard Zimmermann, 'Restitution after Termination for Breach of Contract in German Law' (1997) Rest L Rev 13–26.

German view, the contract survives termination.[44] Rather than rendering a contract void *ex post*, termination will create a different set of contractual obligations.

This different construction has a number of consequences when compared with the unjust enrichment approach taken by English law, namely:

(1) Performances made under the terminated contract must be returned, regardless of whether the failure was total (the latter having traditionally been a requirement in English law).
(2) Impossibility of counter-restitution does not defeat restitution claims, in contrast with traditional English law.
(3) The price agreement remains valid for the purpose of valuing a performance that cannot be returned.
(4) Disenrichment is not available as a defence (although impossibility of returning the performance may defeat a claim for its restitution; see below).

An additional difference to English law, unrelated to the construction of these restitution claims as contractual, is that, with only one exception,[45] restitutionary liability and its extent do not depend on whether the claimant or the defendant was in breach of contract.

Sections 346–359 BGB have been reformulated and amended by the Act to Modernise the Law of Obligations, which entered into force on 1 January 2002. They now apply regardless of whether the contract was terminated in exercise of an express contractual right, or of a statutory right (normally: for breach of contract).[46]

[44] The BGB did not specify whether the contract ceases to exist or continues in a different form. The latter view was promoted by Heinrich Stoll, *Die Wirkungen des vertragsmäßigen Rücktritts* (1921), and is now generally accepted in Germany, see e.g. BGH 8.12.1989, NJW 1990, 2068, at 2069.

[45] Under the termination of contract model, an innocent recipient will in some situations be liable only for a reduced standard of care, see below, section 3.2.B.

[46] Previously, § 346 BGB applied to termination in exercise of a statutory right only *mutatis mutandis*, by reference to § 327 sent. 2 BGB (old version), a controversial provision which applied unjustified enrichment rules to claims against an innocent party who had terminated a contract. For the old law, see Gerhard Dannemann, 'Restitution for Termination of Contract in German Law', in: *Failure of Contracts: Contractual, Restitutionary and Proprietary Consequences*, ed. by Francis Rose (1997), 129–153.

1. Restitution in kind

Under the basic rule in § 346 para. 1, parties must return what they have received in performance of the terminated contract, and also 'benefits derived from such performance' (see below, section 3.3). As is usual in German law (see also below, Chapter 6, section 1), this claim aims at restitution in kind rather than restitution of value. Therefore any performance which is capable of being returned must be given back, including in particular goods and real property.

There is some disagreement concerning the place of performance for this obligation under § 346 para. 1, but it appears that if termination occurred as a remedy for breach of contract, the place where the object (for example, goods) is to be returned is the place where the object is situated according to the contract.[47] This will normally imply that the cost of returning defective goods will fall on the seller, unless provided otherwise by the contract, which can also define a place of performance for obligations after termination.

2. Restitution of value

Section 346 para. 2 BGB provides exceptions to the general rule that restitution must be made in kind. It also replaces restitution in kind by restitution for value (i.e. payment of a sum of money) for three situations in which restitution in kind is impossible.

First (§ 346 para. 2 no. 1), there are performances which are generally incapable of being returned, as is the case for most services, but also for construction contracts. If a builder agrees to renovate A's bathroom and removes the old tiles and then no longer arrives for work, there is nothing A can do after termination of the contract to return the work to the builder. If the builder has laid the new tiles but not got as far as installing, or even ordering, the new shower and mirror, A could of course rip out the new tiles and return the fragments to

[47] BGH 9.3.1983, BGHZ 87, 104. This judgment relates to the former § 462 BGB, a specific provision in sales law on termination as a remedy for defective goods (*Wandelung*), which now has been merged with the general notion of termination (*Rücktritt*), § 440 BGB.

the builder. But while this would have the effect of undoing this part of the work, it would still not return the builder's performance.[48]

Secondly (§ 346 para. 2 no. 2), the recipient may have 'consumed, transferred, encumbered, processed, or transformed' an object received under the contract, with the effect that the recipient cannot provide restitution in kind. This will frequently happen, for example, with food, goods in a supply chain, or building materials.

Thirdly (§ 346 para. 2 no. 3), an object received under the contract may have deteriorated or been destroyed. Although the recipient could, in principle, return any rubble or debris that might be left, restitution in kind is excluded in this situation and replaced by restitution of value.

A. *Contractual price as yardstick*

Section 346 para. 2 sent. 2 BGB provides: 'If the contract specifies a counter-performance, such counter-performance is to be taken as a basis for calculation of the compensation for value.' Effectively, this means that any contractually stipulated price remains effective and will be used for determining the value of any goods or services provided under the (now terminated) contract. The new version is wider than its predecessor in the old § 346 sent. 2 BGB. First, the new version applies to all contractual performances, rather than being limited to calculating the value of a service or the use of an object. Secondly, the new provision no longer relates to contractual price agreements but extends to all types of 'counter-performance' (*Gegenleistung*), so that it would also apply to barter, where it could lead to unexpected results. If, as in the fairytale of the Brothers Grimm, *Hans im Glück* (*Hans in Luck*), Hans trades a head-sized lump of gold for a horse and then (unlike in the fairytale) terminates the contract on account of the horse being defective, he can require the horseman to give back the lump of gold. If, however, the horseman has lost, given away, or sold the lump of gold, the value which the horseman must provide to Hans in exchange for the returned horse is not the value of the lump of gold,

[48] But see below, section 3.3 for a situation where the claimant can request, as restitution in kind, the removal of an unauthorized building: BGH 21.12.1956, BGHZ 23, 61, below, Chapter 10, section 1 (translation).

but the value of the horse as owed under the contract—i.e. the value of a horse which is free from defects.

The German provision thus escapes a criticism which has occasionally been levelled against English law, namely that it allows a party to escape a bad bargain. This is illustrated by the well-known US case of *Boomer v Muir*, where the claimants were awarded an additional payment of nearly $258,000 for work involved in building a dam, even on the assumption that they had already been paid all but $20,000 of what they were owed under the contract.[49]

The two examples show that allowing a party to escape a bad bargain can be just as problematic as preventing it by keeping the contractual balance of values. However, some justification can be found for the German approach. If all benefits conferred under the contract can be returned (lump of gold against horse), the same situation exists as would have existed without the contract; this is the very purpose of termination of contract. However, if benefits cannot be returned due to their nature or because they are no longer in the hands of the recipient, the contract, although terminated, has irreversibly changed the parties' positions. Therefore, if the contract has this irreversible effect, it could at least serve to determine all the reversal that can be made, i.e. in money. The fact that in *Boomer v Muir* the defendant failed to pay in time for work provided by the claimant does not alter the fact that the parties have agreed on what the work is worth. The price agreement is not normally affected by the deficiency which leads to the termination of contract. Relying on the price agreement can also avoid lengthy arguments about the value of services provided, or about other benefits.

B. *Restitution without counter-restitution*

It may come as a surprise to readers trained in the common law that § 346 paras 2 and 3 BGB provide for a number of situations in which the recipient is not required to return anything, but is nevertheless entitled to claim back his or her performance, normally the payment

[49] *Boomer v Muir* 24 P2d 570 (1933). However, the court held that the contractual price would apply if provided specifically for portions of the work which had been fully performed and fully paid.

of the contractually stipulated price.[50] The original version of § 350 BGB made it possible for a recipient in whose hands an object (usually goods) received under the contract had accidentally been damaged or perished to proceed with termination and claim back his or her own performance (usually the purchase price) without having to compensate for the value of the received object. This provision was controversial as a matter of legal policy, in particular on the ground that it was not easily reconciled with the rule in sales law that the risk passes to the buyer on the transfer of possession (§ 446 BGB). When the provisions on termination were reformed as part of the Act to Modernise the Law of Obligations, the legislators reacted to this criticism not by reducing, but rather by extending, the situations in which a recipient is not liable for returning anything and may yet claim back for his or her own performance. Taken together, these cover the following five situations:

(1) The deterioration results from the 'proper use of the object for its intended purpose' (§ 346 para. 2 no. 3). A brand new car may lose 10 per cent of its value simply by being driven off the forecourt, but the disappointed buyer does not have to recompense the seller for this loss of value. The buyer will, however, have to return the car and pay for the value of its use (as a benefit derived from performance).[51]

(2) A defect which gives rise to a right to terminate the contract becomes apparent only when the recipient processes or transforms the defective object (§ 346 para. 3 no. 1). For example, if cement delivered to a building site fails to set properly, no restitution of value is due for the defective cement even if this could still have been put to some commercial use.

(3) The party who has supplied the object is responsible for its deterioration or destruction (§ 346 para. 3 no. 2). For example, a car dealer sells a car with serious safety defects, and these defects cause an accident in which the car is written-off. The buyer is under no obligation to provide restitution of value for the written-off car and may nevertheless claim back the purchase price.

[50] Impossibility of counter-restitution has traditionally been seen as a complete bar to recovery in the English law of unjust enrichment; see below, Chapter 6, section 5.2.

[51] See below, section 3.3.

(4) Under the same provision, the recipient of an object which is damaged or destroyed is exempt from liability if the damage would also have occurred if the objects had remained in the hands of the other party (the seller in a sales contract). In most situations, this will be difficult to prove. The provision could realistically be invoked if hidden defects cause further deterioration or destruction, a case which will often also be covered by the previous exception. The same provision could, however, also apply if a building is damaged or destroyed by a natural disaster (for example, lightning) which is not in any way linked to the breach of contract which gives rise to termination (for example, dry rot).

(5) Finally, the recipient need not provide restitution of value even if he or she negligently caused the deterioration or destruction, as long as 'he has taken the care which he usually takes in his own affairs' (§ 346 para. 3 no. 3). This provision applies only if the recipient has terminated the contract in exercise of a statutory right, normally for breach of contract by the other party. It has nevertheless been severely criticized for shifting the rules on passing the risk beyond what is reasonable. As Reinhard Zimmermann stated, 'the risk of the purchaser being a careless person has to be borne by the seller'.[52] Two recent judgments shed light on both this provision and the criticism of it.

A case decided by the *Oberlandesgericht* Hamm involved a car which, at the time it was handed over to the claimant, had a defective timing belt cover.[53] After a period of time this defect resulted in serious damage to the engine. The defendant, a car dealer, argued that the buyer was to blame for the deterioration. The buyer had failed to take the car for its regular service, at which time the defect would have been picked up. The court held that the buyer was under no obligation towards the seller to have his car regularly serviced in accordance with the recommendations of the manufacturer, and that he had not been in breach of the standard of care which he usually took in the conduct of his own affairs. Under § 346 para. 3 no. 3, the buyer was thus allowed to recover the purchase price against return of the car, without having to compensate for the value of the defective engine.

[52] Reinhard Zimmermann, 'Restitution after Termination of Contract: German Law After the Reform of 2002', in: *Mapping the Law*, 323, at 336.

[53] OLG Hamm 8.9.2005, Neue Zeitschrift für Verkehrsrecht 2006, 421–424.

The same provision was recently tested again in another interesting case involving the sale of a new motorcycle in 2003.[54] In 2005, in a rear-end collision, the buyer was injured and the front of the motorcycle damaged. The buyer could show that the motorcycle, although unused at the time of sale, had been manufactured in 1999 and imported to Europe in 2001. This defect allowed him to terminate the contract and reclaim the purchase price. With regard to the seller's counterclaim, the buyer relied on § 326 para. 3 no. 3. His lawyer argued that the fact that he had been injured in the accident showed that he had applied exactly the same standard of care to the motorcycle which he had applied to himself. While the logic of this argument was impeccable, it was nevertheless rejected by the *Oberlandesgericht* Karlsruhe. The court held that the dangers of road traffic did not make any allowance for individual carelessness or personal character traits.

With respect, this would be an effective answer if the buyer had raised the same defence against the car owner's claim for damages caused by the motorcyclist. However, the seller was not involved as a road user. Therefore the question whether the motorcyclist had to compensate the seller for the damage to the motorbike had nothing to do with public reliance on an objective standard of care by road users. Rather, this concerned the standard of care owed in a contractual relationship under § 346 para. 3 no. 3. The case therefore shows that some courts may share the sentiments of the critics of § 346 para. 3 no. 3 by giving a restrictive interpretation to the provision. In general, *diligentia quam in suis*, that is the level of care which a party normally takes in the conduct of his or her own affairs, is problematic as a yardstick for a party's conduct, because that party can tweak this measure to its own advantage by pleading his or her own carelessness.

C. *Remaining enrichment*

Section 346 para. 3 sent. 2 BGB contains a little corner of autonomous unjustified enrichment within termination of contract. The provision simply states: 'Any remaining enrichment must be given up.' This provision is meant to refer directly to the consequences of a claim in unjustified enrichment under § 818 BGB without having to go through the requirements of § 812.

[54] OLG Karlsruhe, 12.09.2007, OLGR Karlsruhe 2007, 1008–1011.

Section 346 para. 3 sent. 2 applies in all cases where a party is relieved from providing restitution of value under para. 3, that is to situations (2) to (5) above.[55] The provision has no direct predecessor in the pre-reform BGB, and it appears that it has not yet been tested in the courts. It should operate in situations (2) to (5) if the loss was insured, as in the case of the buyer having taken out insurance against the accidental destruction of goods.

This looks much like a case of substitution. However, the normal provisions on substitution do not operate in the context of § 346 para. 3 BGB. The general provision of § 285, whereby a claimant 'may demand surrender of what has been received as substitute or an assignment of the substitute claim' (see above, Chapter 1, section 4.5) applies only in cases of impossibility under § 275 paras 1 to 3 BGB. And the specific provision on substitution within unjustified enrichment (§ 818 para. 1 BGB, see below, Chapter 6, section 2.2) would not apply to termination of contract because this is not perceived as a case of unjustified enrichment in German law.

For this reason, § 346 para. 3 sent. 2 contains a separate catch-all provision which reverts to the other party any remaining enrichment in the hands of a party who, after termination of contract has occurred, is relieved from providing restitution for value. It is not limited to situations of substitution, but there is no other obvious example of a remaining enrichment in this situation.

As a matter of legal policy, it is doubted whether this provision fits equally well to all situations covered by § 346 para. 3. It may make sense that the seller of a house which is infested with dry rot can profit from the buyer's house insurance against lightning in situation (2) above. But why in situation (3) should the seller of a car with a serious safety defect benefit from a comprehensive car insurance policy taken out by the buyer? If the policy rationale is that the buyer should not be allowed to collect the insurance payment in addition to the restitution claim for the purchase price under § 346 BGB, then the car insurer would certainly be a more worthy recipient of what otherwise would be a windfall for the buyer.

[55] For situation (1), see below, section 3.3.

3. Benefits derived from performance

Section 346 para. 1 BGB extends the obligation to return any performance made under the terminated contract to 'benefits derived from such performance'. Such benefits are called *Nutzungen* and defined in § 100 BGB. They include the fruits of an object or a right, and also the advantage of using such an object or a right, for example the advantage of having lived in a house. This rule would cover, for example, the hire-charge which the defendants were forced to pay in the English case of *Strand Electric and Engineering Co Ltd v Brisford Entertainments Ltd.*[56] The existing German judgments largely predate the 2002 reform, but remain relevant as the same surrender of *Nutzungen* was previously owed under § 347 BGB.

If these benefits are capable of being surrendered in kind (for example, harvested fruits), then the recipient is obliged to do so. If the benefits consist of money, then the recipient is obliged to pay the sum which represents the benefit.[57]

If the terminated contract was for the sale of a business, this implies that the buyer of the business is liable for an account of profits. In one case, the claimant had sold a petrol station to the defendant company. Shortly thereafter the defendant became insolvent, with the bulk of the purchase price remaining unpaid. The seller terminated the contract, reclaimed the petrol station, and was also awarded a full account of profits. However, the *Bundesgerichtshof* affirmed that this would exclude any profits which were due to the particular skills of the new owner—which, however, were obviously lacking in this case.[58]

In practice, the majority of cases concern benefits which cannot be returned in kind, normally the use of goods. In this instance, the recipient must pay a sum which represents the value of having had the use of those goods. Most court decisions concern the use of vehicles,

56 *Strand Electric and Engineering Co Ltd v Brisford Entertainments Ltd* [1952] 2 QB 246; see Birks, *Introduction*, 330. In this case, the defendants continued to use the claimant's theatre lighting equipment for their theatre after a deal with a prospective buyer of the theatre, who had initially rented the theatre and obtained the equipment, had fallen through. This is, therefore, not a case of termination of contract. It is nevertheless interesting that the hire-charge was awarded as damages, not as restitution.

57 For interest, see below, section 3.5.

58 BGH 12.5.1978, NJW 1978, 1578.

where the use of a new car is generally taxed at 0.67 per cent of its value per 1,000 km driven (assuming the life of a car to be 150,000 km).[59]

Calculating the value of the use as representing the fraction of the expected normal life of the object which the recipient has used, is not limited to vehicles. In another pre-2002 case, a hotel terminated a contract under which it had bought 163 beds, after it found that they were defective. Because the seller initially refused return of the beds, they continued to be used in the hotel for a further eight months before they were finally returned. The hotel was allowed to claim back the purchase price of DM 47,116 (approx. €24,000) plus interest, but the seller was allowed to set-off with a counterclaim for use which amounted to DM 32,303, i.e. more than two-thirds of the purchase price.[60]

This case also illustrates that the recipient must pay the value of the use from the time when the party received the object, rather than from the time when the contract is terminated. The new wording of the heading of § 347 BGB could cast some doubt on this rule: 'Benefits and expenditure *after* termination' (emphasis added). As, since 2002, all BGB headings are official and form part of the statute, this could be taken to exclude any obligation to compensate for use (or to recover for expenditure made) before termination became effective. Apparently, however, this was not what was intended. A recent judgment by the *Bundesgerichtshof* allows for a different reading, namely that the new § 347 BGB is applicable exclusively to all benefits drawn and all expenditure made after termination, but can apply next to other provisions for benefits drawn and expenditure made between receipt of the object and termination.[61]

If this reading of the new § 347 BGB is ultimately adopted, it would imply another change. Under the old law, an innocent party was liable only for any use which it had actually made. If, for instance, the innocent party had obtained possession of a property under the contract which it subsequently terminated, it would have had to give up any rent it had collected from letting the property to a third party (after deducting reasonable expenses), §§ 327 sent. 2 (old version),

[59] See e.g. OLG Hamm 29.6.1993, MDR 1994, 138.
[60] BGH 26.6.1991, BGHZ 115, 47.
[61] BGH 20.7.2005, BGHZ 163, 381.

818 para. 1 BGB. But if the innocent party made no use of the property, it would not have been charged for having failed to use this opportunity prior to the contract being terminated.

The new § 347 BGB provides: 'If, contrary to the rules of proper management, the debtor has failed to derive benefits even though it would have been possible to do so, he must compensate the creditor for their value.' Therefore, if the heading of § 347 BGB is indeed interpreted as suggested above, the provision applies to all benefits which the recipient should have derived from the time of receipt (rather than the time of termination). The possible harshness of this is mitigated by sent. 2, whereby a party who terminates a contract in exercise of a statutory right (namely, for breach of contract) 'must display with regard to the benefits only the standard of care which he usually takes in his own affairs'. So, once again, the troublesome concept of *diligentia quam in suis* is used to relax rules on termination of contract—with the effect that in many cases, an innocent party will be able to plead that its failure to derive benefits corresponded with its own standard of care.

This different standard of care also marks the only distinction which the new § 347 BGB draws between rights of the innocent party and those of a party in breach. This marks a clear difference with English law, where the party in breach is not allowed to recover at all for such benefits in kind.[62] Similar claims were rejected in both *Sumpter v Hedges* and in *Bolton v Mahadeva*.[63] Both cases concerned construction contracts which were either only partially completed (*Sumpter*) or where the work was deficient (*Bolton*). The defendants terminated the contracts, and the claimants were denied any claim for *quantum meruit*. Under German law, the defendants would have been liable in both cases.[64]

62 Goff and Jones, 20–047.

63 *Sumpter v Hedges* [1898] 1 QB 673 (CA); *Bolton v Mahadeva* [1972] 1 WLR 1009 (CA).

64 Under the previous law, the innocent defendants would have been liable to the extent that there was a surviving benefit (§ 818 paras 2 and 3 BGB) at the time when the contract was terminated. This is in fact a solution which Burrows favoured in the first edition of *The Law of Restitution* (1992), 277–279, and which apparently is not mentioned in the second edition, 350–354.

However, the benefit must be of a kind that was bargained for. In one leading pre-2002 case (case no. 1),[65] the claimant took a lease of the defendant's agricultural property and erected a massive building without permission from the defendant, who then terminated the lease. The claimant sued the defendant for the value of the building. The building had been erected not in performance but in violation of the lease contract, and did therefore not fall under § 346 BGB. In addition, the *Bundesgerichtshof* disallowed the claim under the rules of unjustified enrichment, arguing that the building was imposed on the defendant against his will, and that the building could be put to commercial use only by incurring considerable additional expense. Rather than paying for the value of the enrichment, the defendant was entitled to remove the building or, if this was unreasonable because of the costs involved, to require the claimant to remove the building. The case also illustrates that subjective devaluation can be used as a defence in termination of contract cases only if it concerns a benefit which the recipient had not bargained for.

4. Interest

The previous law had a special provision on interest in § 347, according to which any money received was to be paid back with interest (at the statutory rate of 4 per cent, unless provided otherwise), accrued from the date of receipt.

The provision was dropped in the 2002 reform. This does not mean that interest is no longer due. Rather, interest forms part of, and follows the same rules, as the return of other benefits, including the above-mentioned rules on liability for benefits which the recipient failed to derive under § 347 BGB. The result is that a party who has terminated a contract on account of the other party's breach can refuse to pay interest on the ground that it did not gain any interest on the money received. The party in breach, on the other hand, will normally (and even more so in commercial situations) be expected to have gained interest under the 'rules of proper management' referred

[65] BGH 21.12.1956, BGHZ 23, 61, at 64–65; below, Chapter 10, section 1 (translation).

to in § 347 BGB. What exactly that means and which interest rate should be used has been left to the courts to decide.

5. Recovery of expenditure

A recipient who has incurred expenditure on an object received under the contract may be entitled to recover under § 347 BGB. A number of restrictions apply to such claims.

First, the right to recover expenditure is limited to three situations, namely that (1) the recipient returns the object, or (2) compensates the other party for its value, or (3) that the duty to compensate for value is excluded under § 346 para. 3, no. 1 or 2 (situations (2) to (4) above; section 3.2.B.

Secondly, the recipient is allowed to recover only for what is called 'necessary expenditure' or *notwendige Verwendungen*, a concept borrowed from the owner/possessor model, and which will be discussed below (Chapter 5, section 3.1). If the expenditure was unnecessary, the recipient may not recover for the amount of such expenditure, only for any remaining increase in value. (See above, Chapter 1, section 5 for different measures of restitution claims.)

An example of expenditure which is unnecessary can be found in a recent case decided by the *Bundesgerichtshof*. The buyer had fitted a new car, priced at some €27,000, with alloy wheels, a carphone, satellite navigation, and a few other extras totalling some €5,000 before discovering various defects in the vehicle, not all of which could be remedied by the seller. The buyer eventually terminated the contract and claimed for the costs of the additional extras. These were clearly unnecessary. Under § 347 BGB, the buyer was allowed to claim from the seller only the increase in the value of the car which was due to those additional extras, which would certainly have been well below €5,000. However, the *Bundesgerichtshof* found a way of allowing the buyer to recover on the basis of expenditure rather than of increase in value, namely under § 437 (remedies for defective goods) in conjunction with § 284 (reimbursement for wasted expenditure), the latter being a provision of the law of general obligation which allows a claimant to claim for expenditure actually incurred as an alternative to damages. The *Bundesgerichtshof* held that if § 347 para. 2 was meant to override those provisions, this could apply only to any expenditure incurred after termination and therefore not to the present case. Therefore the restrictions of § 347 para. 2 will ultimately prevent recovery of expenditure only if this has been incurred after termination—at least for sales contracts, which under German law include the sale of goods, real property, and rights. The same should apply to works contracts, as § 634 BGB contains a similar reference to § 284.

4

Defences Against Performance-based Claims

Two general defences can be raised against performance-based unjustified enrichment claims, both of which are contained in § 814 BGB. First and foremost, the defendant is relieved from liability if the claimant knew at the time of performance that there was no obligation to perform. Secondly, the defendant can rely on the fact that performance corresponded to a moral duty or to common decency.

In addition, § 815 BGB provides two defences against the *condictio causa data causa non secuta* (above Chapter 3, section 1.1). The first applies if the claimant knew that the intended result could not occur, and the second if the claimant prevented the occurrence of this result in a manner which violated good faith. The latter defence was discussed (but rejected) in the above-mentioned embezzlement case.[1] The same is true for the 'non-marital property' case discussed above (case no. 17).[2]

Section 817 BGB contains a troublesome provision which operates as a defence against a *condictio ob turpem vel iniustam causam*: if both claimant and defendant violated a statutory prohibition or offended against good morals by the performance, no claim lies in unjustified enrichment.

The three most important defences, i.e. those under §§ 814 and 817 BGB, will now be considered in turn.

[1] BGH 23.2.1990, NJW-RR 1990, 827; below, Chapter 10, section 11 (translation); discussed above, Chapter 2, section 6.2.E.

[2] BGH 9.7.2008, NJW 2008, 3277, below, Chapter 10, section 17 (translation); discussed above, Chapter 3, section 1.1.

1. Claimant's knowledge of lack of legal ground

Section 814 prevents restitution if the claimant knew at the time of performance that there was no obligation to perform. Therefore, what is a requirement for a large proportion of unjustified enrichment in English law (i.e., that the claimant was mistaken when shifting wealth to the defendant), rather functions as a defence in German law: a claimant will not succeed if he or she was not mistaken. Section 814 BGB is wider to a certain extent, as 'knowledge' is a bar to recovery for all performance-based restitution if § 814 BGB is to be understood in a literal sense.[3]

But is this really true, or is English law correct in reserving the question of mistake and knowledge to a certain group of cases? The defence does apply but is pointless in cases where there is no legal ground because the contract has been rescinded under the rules on mistake and deceit. Knowledge at the time of conclusion of contract defeats both mistake and deceit; if the claimant becomes aware of the mistake or deceit after the conclusion of the contract, performance in spite of this knowledge prevents rescission under §§ 142 para. 2, 144 BGB. On the other hand, the defence most certainly does not apply to duress, for the victim of duress will usually be aware that there is no legal obligation. The high regard for the protection of minors in German law makes it unlikely that the defence would apply to claims for restitution of that which a minor has performed under a contract which is void for lack of capacity, even if the minor were fully aware that the contract was not valid. The defence should apply in principle to cases of one-sided illegality (two-sided illegality being covered by the more specific rule of § 817 BGB), but there appears to be a paucity of cases in which it was thus applied, perhaps because one-sided illegality will often not render a contract void.[4] The defence is unlikely to apply to what is failure of consideration in English law: if performance

[3] For a comparative analysis of the link between mistake and lack of legal ground, see below, Chapter 8, section 2.5; and also Sheehan (2008) Oxford U Comparative L Forum 1.

[4] See e.g. BGH 22.9.1983, NJW 1984, 230; for an English translation, see Markesinis, Lorenz, and Dannemann, *The German Law of Contracts and Restitution*, case no. 29; similar *St John Shipping Corp v Joseph Rank Ltd* [1957] 1 QB 267 (QBD) 1932.

was made under a contract which subsequently was terminated, § 814 does not apply because of the specific contractual rules in §§ 346ff (see above, Chapter 3, section 3); if the failure occurs outside the scope of a contract, the more specific defence of § 815 could then defeat a restitutionary claim under the *condictio causa data causa non secuta* (see above, Chapter 3, section 1.1). Therefore the 'no mistake' defence in § 814 is mainly geared towards cases where there was no obligation to begin with. In particular, it appears that § 814 BGB would exclude most of what some consider to be the unjust factor of free acceptance in English law.[5]

However, German law has not chosen an approach which is based on individual unjust factors, and other mechanisms have been found in order to ensure that § 814 BGB does not defeat restitution in most situations of duress and imbalance of bargaining power. It has been held that the defence of knowledge applies only to performance which was made voluntarily, i.e. without pressure being applied, and for this reason will not defeat restitution in cases of compulsion. The *Bundesgerichtshof* has used the same argument of voluntariness in a case which concerned payment under reservation. The *Bundesgerichshof* held that the defence of knowledge could be excluded by a reservation which was made during performance and argued as follows:[6]

> . . . according to the legislative purpose of § 814, this provision is based on voluntary performance. By making the reservation the person who performs objects to an interpretation of his conduct to the effect that he was willing to perform without regard to the existence of an obligation.

Naturally, such a statement was warmly welcomed, in particular by insurance companies which were quick to introduce standard reservation clauses to their notifications of payment. However, this practice found little sympathy with the courts. In a case which concerned a payment made by an insurance company to the victim of a road traffic accident, the *Oberlandesgericht* Koblenz held that reservations must be made specifically for the payment in question. If they are made by virtue of a standard clause, they will not prevent the application of § 814 BGB.[7] Nevertheless, the German position is in clear contrast

[5] Goff and Jones, 1–019 to 1–022; Tettenborn 16–17; critical Burrows 402–407.
[6] BGH 17.2.1982, BGHZ 83, 278, 282.
[7] OLG Koblenz 20.9.1983, NJW 1984, 135.

with a string of English cases in which such reservations were considered to be without effect.[8]

The concept of voluntariness—which is not mentioned in § 814 BGB in any event—was also employed in a case where statutory pensions had been paid to the account of a deceased person which continued after the relatives had notified the pension fund of the death of the recipient. Recovery was allowed in spite of § 814 BGB on the following unusual ground: as the pensions were controlled by statute, the pension fund had no choice about whether to continue payment, and lack of choice implied that there was no voluntary aspect![9] Importance was attached to the fact that the heirs were fully aware that they could not rely on retaining the pension, and this is presumably the policy issue which lay behind the dubious argument of voluntariness in the case.

English law has traditionally resolved the problem by a different approach to mistake. In *Kelly v Solari*, it did not matter that someone in the company was at some point made aware of the facts which led to the policy having lapsed; what mattered was that those who paid out were at the time labouring under a mistake.[10]

It should be stressed that § 814 BGB relates to knowledge of lack of legal ground, not to knowledge of all the facts. If someone is aware of the facts but mistakenly believes they are obliged to perform, then § 814 BGB will be no bar to recovery.[11] Under an unjust factor approach, the same rule would state that an enrichment claim will not fail because the mistake was one of law—a position which now is shared by English law following *Kleinwort Benson Ltd v Lincoln City Council*.[12]

[8] *CTN Cash & Carry v Gallaher* [1994] 1 All ER 714 (CA); *Nurdin & Peacock v D B Ramsden & Co* [1999] 1 WLR 1249 (Ch); *Twyford v Manchester Corporation* [1946] Ch 236; see below, Chapter 9, section 3.2.C.

[9] OLG Karlsruhe 30.12.1987, NJW 1988, 1920. It is even possible to say that this is the reverse of the general rule in *Woolwich Equitable Building Society v Inland Revenue Commissioners* [1993] AC 70 (HL), whereby a private individual can generally recover for payments which were made but not due. In the case decided by the OLG Karlsruhe, public authorities were allowed to recover for payments which were made but not due, regardless of their knowledge.

[10] *Kelly v Solari* (1841) 9 M&W 54.

[11] See e.g. RG 27.2.1912, RGZ 78, 427; for an English translation, see Markesinis, Lorenz, and Dannemann, *The German Law of Contracts and Restitution*, case no. 69.

[12] *Kleinwort Benson Ltd v Lincoln City Council* [1999] 2 AC 349 (HL).

2. Claimant's moral obligation

Section 814 BGB also serves as a bar to recovery if the shift of wealth corresponds with a moral rather than a legal obligation, or with notions of common decency, and where it would therefore be awkward to allow restitution. This resembles the money 'payable in point of honor and honesty' which Lord Mansfield held to be unrecoverable in *Moses v Macferlan*.[13] In German law, as a contract of donation will often provide a legal ground for an enrichment which follows from a moral duty, the appliction of this defence is mainly limited to cases concerning mistake of law, i.e. where the claimant mistakenly believes he or she is obliged to perform. This concerns, in particular, maintenance payments made by those relatives who are not required to pay; they cannot reclaim maintenance support from the child.[14] However, § 814 BGB does not cover the situation where a man pays maintenance for a child, in the mistaken belief that he is the child's father.[15] On the other hand, § 814 BGB would prevent recovery if someone leaves a 10 per cent tip in a restaurant in the mistaken belief that tipping is compulsory.

3. Claimant's own wrongdoing

1. Introduction

Section 817 contains both a *condictio* and a defence for situations of illegality. The *condictio ob turpem vel iniustam causam* allows recovery if the recipient violated a statutory provision or offended against good morals by accepting performance. It is doubtful though whether there is scope for an independent application of this *condictio*, because the normal performance-based restitution under § 812 covers cases of performance under an agreement which is void for illegality. Section 817 BGB is therefore mostly reduced to the defence in § 817 sent. 2 BGB, the so-called *in pari turpitudine* rule which applies to all

[13] *Moses v Macferlan* (1760) 2 Burr 1005; see also below, Chapter 8, section 1.3.B.
[14] RG 8.1.1941, RGZ 165, 358, 362.
[15] Staudinger-Lorenz § 814 no. 20.

condictiones based on performance.[16] The rule states that there is no restitution if both parties acted unlawfully or immorally by providing and accepting performance. The German Latin *in pari turpitudine melior est causa possidentis* rule is, of course, a relative of the English Latin *in pari delicto potior est conditio defendentis* rule.[17] Conversely, German law has no direct equivalent to the sister rule on illegality in English law, namely *nemo auditur turpitudinem suam allgans*—no one will be heard pleading his own immoral conduct, or a claim must not be founded on an illegality.[18]

The defence of § 817 sent. 2 BGB is surrounded by many disputes and uncertainties. It has been called 'one of the most dreaded perils in the sea of legal doctrine'.[19] It may help if we first look at the purpose which this defence and the *nemo auditur* rule are to serve, using the following example:

An instigator pays £1,000 to a thug who in return beats up a victim. The instigator then seeks to recover his payment in unjust enrichment. German and English law agree that this claim must be disallowed. For this, we arc normally given at least one of the following reasons with English law tending to focus more on the first two, and German law on the third.

(1) No one must be allowed to found his action on his own illegal conduct.[20]

(2) Courts would be tainted if they were to assist one villain in his claim against another.[21]

(3) The claim must be disallowed in order to deter—or even punish—illegal or immoral conduct.[22]

[16] See also Zimmermann and du Plessis, 22ff.

[17] See Goff and Jones, 24–002.

[18] See *Tinsley v Milligan* [1994] 1 AC 340 (HL).

[19] Zimmermann, *The Law of Obligations*, 864; similar Reuter and Martinek, 199.

[20] This is the inherent reasoning of the *nemo auditur* rule.

[21] Zimmermann, *The Law of Obligations*, 846; OGH 10.2.1950, OGHZ 4, 57, at 60; Burrows 573; Tettenborn, 282; see also Zweigert and Kötz, 576.

[22] RG 8.11.1922, RGZ 105, 270, 271–272 argued that the defence was intended as a punishment and justified its operation even against a claimant who was of unsound mind and thus without contractual capacity, provided that the defendant could still be liable in tort under § 827 BGB); BGH 31.1.1963, BGHZ 39, 87, 91 ('Strafcharacter'); see Zweigert and Kötz, 576.

The victim in the example now sues the thug in tort for injuries suffered. In turn, the thug sues the instigator for contribution to his tortious liability towards the victim. This action can succeed only if the thug can show that he committed the tort in execution of his agreement with the instigator. The thug must therefore plead his own illegal conduct. Furthermore, in allowing the thug's action, the courts will assist one villain in his action against the other. Additionally, by reducing the thug's overall liability, contribution equally diminishes the deterrent effect of his tortious liability. Therefore all the above reasons why illegality can be raised against a claim in unjust enrichment should prevent a joint tortfeasor's claim in contribution. Yet German and English law agree that the action for contribution must be allowed.[23]

It appears, therefore, that our three explanations of the illegality defence do not stand up to scrutiny. At the very least, they are formulated too widely, so that there must be something which makes these arguments workable in a situation of enrichment, but not in one of tort. At the same time, these arguments must be of fundamental importance, as the very purpose of the law of unjust enrichment is to prevent losses from lying where they fall.

It has been suggested earlier that, when assessing the merit of the illegality defence, it is of paramount importance to have regard to the policy rationale behind those rules which make a particular contract, performance, or transaction illegal.[24] It is further suggested that this rationale could explain some cases in which German courts have reduced those general principles to their useful role for justifying illegality as a defence against an unjust enrichment claim.

The reason why a party should not be allowed to rely on its own illegal conduct is that people should not be rewarded for their own unlawful behaviour. This is why an unpaid thug cannot recover a

[23] German law: the instigator and the thug are considered joint tortfeasors under §§ 830, 840 BGB; whoever compensates the victim can sue any other joint tortfeasor for contribution using the victim's claim, which is assigned to the compensating tortfeasor by operation of the law under § 426 BGB. English law: ss 1 and 2 Civil Liability (Contribution) Act 1978.

[24] Dieter Fabricius, 'Einschränkung der Anwendung des § 817 S. 2 BGB durch den Zweck des Verbotsgesetzes?', Juristenzeitung 1963, 85–91; similar Reuter and Martinek, 209; König, 1522 (§ 1.1(2)(d) of a proposed legal reform act), p. 1542; Staudinger-Lorenz, § 817 no. 2.

quantum meruit from the instigator, but why the same unpaid thug could still sue the instigator for contribution to his tortious liability towards the victim.

The second argument, whereby courts would be tainted if they assisted one villain against another, is largely exaggerated. If this were true, courts would either have a terrible reputation or a substantially reduced case load. The law is not against divorcing 'couples from hell', does not prevent lawsuits between 'neighbours from hell', and does not prohibit litigation between legacy hunters or between rogues who meddle with company mergers to their own financial advantage. What could taint courts, though, is if they are forced to allow an action the success of which would offend against legal or public policy. To allow an action for a *quantum meruit* for having beaten up a victim would have the same effect as declaring that the agreement between the thug and the instigator is a valid contract. This is why courts would indeed jeopardize their reputation if they allowed such an action. To allow an action by the thug against the instigator for contribution, on the other hand, does not counteract the policy which makes such agreements void.

Finally, the deterrence argument needs some fine-tuning. In any lawsuit, whoever wins will feel encouraged, and whoever loses will feel discouraged. If both parties are to blame, we may have to consider carefully which party, if any, needs to be deterred more. It is easy to state in a lawsuit between two villains that the action must be disallowed because the claimant needs to be deterred from illegal conduct—just as easy, in fact, as it is to state the exact opposite, namely that the action must be allowed because the defendant needs to be deterred. Where both parties need to be deterred equally, deterrence as the justification for either outcome becomes meaningless. The tortious action for contribution, on the other hand, distributes the deterrence between the culprits, as both are made to pay for the consequences of their wrongdoing.

We will now turn to the practical application of § 817 sent. 2 BGB, and distinguish between situations where all performances can be returned in kind (see 2 below) and situations where that is not the case (see 3 below). Within the second group, we will look at (a) claims for a *quantum meruit*, and (b) for financial restitution. We will then look at possible explanations (see 4 below). Finally, we will briefly look at further restrictions and extensions of § 817 sent. 2 (5).

2. All performances can be returned in kind

The above reasons for the illegality defence can hardly be applied to mutual performances which can be returned in kind. On the contrary, allowing a restitutionary claim in kind may be the best or even the only way of enforcing the policy rationales which may prohibit certain currency deals, restrict trade with national heritage objects, endangered species, toxic substances, drugs or arms. The same is true for agreements for the illegal concealment of assets, as for instance in the English case of *Tribe v Tribe*.[25] This is where an application of the *in pari turpitudine* rule is likely to produce the most disastrous results. This author is not aware of any cases, though, in which German courts have used § 817 sent. 2 to this effect.

One sub-category of performances which can be returned in kind concerns enrichments which were meant to be temporary by both parties, in particular loans or securities. For loans, German courts have frequently avoided this result by ruling that it is not the money itself but rather the temporary use of the money which constitutes the enrichment, so that § 817 sent. 2 BGB would not prevent recovery after the stipulated time for the loan has elapsed.[26]

3. Not all performances can be returned in kind

A. *Recovery of* quantum meruit

More subtle distinctions are required for claims for the value of a performance under an illegal agreement, where the performance cannot be returned in kind. One such case involved a claim for payment for a series of advertisements for what was described as 'Die schönen Stunden zu zweit' (Those lovely hours *entre deux*), garnished with the additions 'just call me', 'habla español', and 'parla italiano'.[27]

[25] *Tribe v Tribe* [1995] 3 WLR 913 (CA).
[26] RG 30.6.1939, RGZ 161, 52, 57.
[27] BGH 5.5.1992, BGHZ 118, 182.

The reader may already have an idea of the nature of the services which were offered. The judgment by the *Bundesgerichtshof*, anxious to avoid any doubt on this point, illuminated the matter with a graphic reproduction of the offending article and probably made legal history by placing this particular advertisement in an official case report. The court explained at some length why this was indeed an advertisement for prostitution and thus—at the time[28]—amounted to a petty criminal offence, and why the contract was void in consequence. We find nearly three pages on why the defendant's reliance on illegality against the claim for the agreed price did not offend good faith, and only one paragraph on the defence in § 817 sent. 2 BGB, which was held to apply both in word and in spirit, in particular in order to deter publishers from offending. Deterrence of the client who ran the brothel was apparently not an issue.

This case was preceded by a much more controversial decision which concerned a builder who had claimed a *quantum meruit* for a job which parties had agreed to keep secret from the taxman (case no. 12).[29] The court held that this action should, in principle, be defeated by the *in pari turpitudine* rule, but set this rule aside on the ground of good faith. It is somewhat puzzling that the court held honour amongst thieves to be higher than a provision of the Civil Code, and the judgment has indeed been criticized by some commentators as being *contra legem*.[30] More particularly, however, the court argued that denying the claim was not strictly necessary for enforcing the relevant tax and social legislation, and that it was unjust that the client, who would normally have the stronger bargaining position, should be allowed to keep the windfall. The contractor was not allowed to claim in full for the normal price. Deductions were to be made for the fact that the contractor was not liable for defects, a fact which should also serve as a deterrent.

It could be debated, of course, why the same rationale was not applied to the publisher in the previously mentioned advertisement case. The *Bundesgerichtshof* ruled in the advertisement case that the

[28] Under the *Prostitutionsgesetz* (Prostitution Act) of 21 December 2001, prostitutes' agreements create enforceable obligations to pay (but not to specific performance). At the same time, most forms of advertising prostitution services became legal.

[29] BGH 31.5.1990, BGHZ 111, 308, 312; below, Chapter 10, section 12 (translation).

[30] Staudinger-Lorenz, § 817 no. 10; Larenz and Canaris, § 68 III 3 g.

builder case was to be distinguished, but unfortunately failed to indicate any grounds on which such a distinction could be made.

B. Recovery of payments

We now turn to cases where one party has paid in advance for an illegal performance which cannot be returned in kind. In one such case, a couple paid DM 15,000 (approx. €7,500) under an illegal adoption agreement whereby the defendant was to procure, within 2½ weeks, an unnamed child from the Philippines.[31] The *Oberlandesgericht* Oldenburg barely mentioned good faith and the purpose of the prohibitory norm to arrive at the conclusion that courts are not meant to resolve the consequences where both parties have acted immorally or unlawfully. And in a mirror case to *Parkinson v College of Ambulance Ltd and Harrison*,[32] the *Bundesgerichtshof* held that a claimant who had paid US$50,000 in order to obtain the title of honorary consul of Sierra Leone was barred from recovering when the title failed to materialize (case no. 15).[33]

4. Explanations

With the exception of the builder case, it is noteworthy that all these judgments devote comparatively little time to the *in pari turpitudine* rule itself. They rush to conclusion as though they are a little embarrassed to deny a claim on such a tedious ground.[34] It is also noteworthy that good faith, purpose of the prohibitory norm, and reliance on one's own illegal conduct are used to explain each other, and somewhat interchangeably. However, it is submitted that a common rationale can be found behind those judgments.

The main argument flows indeed from the prohibitory norm, and it is that no claim should lie for the *quantum meruit* of an act which is in itself illegal. Otherwise, restitution would ensure that illegal

[31] OLG Oldenburg 13.12.1990, NJW 1991, 2216.

[32] *Parkinson v College of Ambulance Ltd and Harrison* [1925] 2 KB 1.

[33] BGH 5.10.1993, NJW 1994, 187; below, Chapter 10, section 15 (translation). Unlike in *Parkinson*, though, the recipient was not a charitable institution so that the payment could hardly be classified as a gift.

[34] The same is not true for OGH 10.2.1950, OGHZ 4, 57, at 60ff, which contains a long discussion of § 817 sent. 2 BGB.

conduct pays. This clearly explains the advertisement case. Similarly, no claim should lie for the *quantum meruit* of an act which, although not illegal in itself, should not be linked with a counter-performance in money—because this would enforce via restitution the very link which the prohibitory norm attempts to prevent. This could explain, for example, why merchants in knighthoods are not allowed to claim a *quantum meruit* for their services.

On the other hand, the builder's work was not in itself illegal. Neither was it illegal to build for payment. What was illegal was that no tax or social insurance contributions were paid from these earnings. Going back to the wording (and perhaps the history)[35] of § 817 sent. 2 BGB, it should also be questioned whether in this case performance was indeed made for an illegal or immoral purpose.

It could be assumed that the purpose of the prohibitory norm will play the same role for advance payments as it does for *quantum meruit* claims. The client should therefore have been allowed to recover for an advance payment in the builder case if the builder had not shown up, but not in the advertisement case if the advertisement had not been placed.[36]

5. Further extensions and restrictions of § 817 sent. 2 BGB

A major flaw of § 817 sent. 2 BGB is that there is no restitution if both parties acted immorally or illegally, but nothing seems to prevent a claimant from relying on his or her own unlawful or immoral conduct when the defendant is not to blame, a deficiency which the courts have often remedied by way of interpretation.[37] Furthermore, the scope of § 138 BGB has been broadened considerably during the twentieth century, extending to cases of public policy and inequality of bargaining power. This broader scope may call for a more restrictive interpretation of § 817 sent. 2 BGB, which was probably not geared towards such a wide concept of immorality.

[35] For the history of the *in pari turpitudine* rule, see Zimmermann, *The Law of Obligations*, 846–847.

[36] On this question, see further Dannemann, 'Illegality as a Defence', text adjacent to note 42.

[37] But see also BGH 15.3.1990, ZIP 1990, 915, discussed below, Chapter 6, section 1.2.

5

Restitution Not Based on Performance

1. General observations

The second alternative of the general enrichment clause in § 812 para. 1 sent. 1 BGB is 'enrichment in another way at the expense of another'. This is a negative description and allows restitution in situations where the shift of wealth from the claimant to the defendant occurred in any way other than by performance.

Following von Caemmerer,[1] courts and the majority of academics subdivide enrichment in another way into three categories.

(1) The first concerns restitution for the interference with another's right (*Eingriffskondiktion,* below Chapter 5, section 2.2). This covers what in English law is restitution for wrongs, but also much of ignorance as an unjust factor.

(2) The second category concerns unauthorized expenditure on someone else's property. Most of these cases, however, are either covered by the owner/possessor model,[2] or by performance, or by *negotiorum gestio.*[3] Only in a few leftover cases lies the so-called *Verwendungskondiktion.*[4] It should be borne in mind that a contractual regime applies to recovery of unauthorized expenditure where the property was subject to a contract which was terminated.[5]

(3) The third category concerns cases where the claimant performs towards a third party in order to discharge the defendant's debt

[1] von Caemmerer, 352ff.
[2] Below, section 3.1.
[3] Below, section 3.2.
[4] Below, section 3.3.
[5] Above, Chapter 3, section 3.

> towards this party, and which are not covered either by *cessio legis*[6] or by performance towards the defendant. A claim under the so-called *Rückgriffskondiktion* may lie in these cases.[7]

Besides covering most of what is called 'restitution for wrongs' in English law, enrichment in another way thereby caters for those situations of subtractive enrichment (i.e. where the defendant's enrichment is identical with the disenrichment suffered by the claimant) which are not covered by performance, in particular because the shift of wealth was not intended or even caused by the claimant, or because the claimant shifted wealth without any particular obligation in mind. The same alternative is also occasionally used as a safety valve for cases in which the enrichment occurred by way of performance, but where it seems appropriate on the merits of the case to leave the strict performance pattern and exceptionally to grant restitution between parties other than the performing and the receiving sides. Just as unjustified enrichment is used to mop up what contract has spilled, enrichment in another way is employed to cater for the leftovers of performance-based restitution.

All these situations have in common that the simple model of 'without legal ground' does not operate (i.e., that wealth was not shifted in performance of a presumed obligation of the claimant towards the defendant),[8] and a specific unjust factor must be found which connects the claimant's loss with the defendant's gain. The German experience—namely that there are enrichment situations beyond wrongs-based restitution which cannot be adequately covered by the 'performance without legal ground' approach—raises interesting questions for the 'absence of basis' approach favoured by Birks, an issue to which we will return later (at Chapter 9).

2. Interference with claimant's rights

Two situations must be distinguished within restitution for wrongs in German law. Recovery for the unauthorized possession of a corporeal

[6] Below, section 4.1.
[7] Below, section 4.4.
[8] See von Caemmerer, 337.

object (chattels or real property) is not governed by the rules on unjustified enrichment, but rather by the owner/possessor model (see 1 below). Restitution for other wrongs, on the other hand, is covered by the *Eingriffskondiktion* (see 2 below). The distinction between subtractive and non-subtractive enrichment, which has become a focal point for classification in English law, is all but ignored. While both owner/possessor model and *Eingriffskondiktion* predominantly cater for situations of non-subtractive enrichment, they also apply to some cases where the enrichment is subtractive.

1. The owner/possessor model

As mentioned above,[9] the owner/possessor model (§§ 987ff BGB) is a complex system of claims and counterclaims for vindication, restitution, compensation, and reimbursement of expenditure, with different degrees of liability depending on the degree to which the possessor was at fault, if at all. The uniting factor of the owner/possessor legal relationship (*Eigentümer-Besitzer-Verhältnis*) is a situation where the owner of corporeal property (i.e. chattels or real property) can require the possessor to relinquish possession because the possessor has no right towards the owner to hold on to the property in question. In other words: these are cases of interference with property rights, whereby the interference consists in taking or keeping possession of the property. This covers, for example, a person who lives in a house without having title or a valid lease or tenancy contract with the owner.

Three types of claims arising under the owner/possessor model are for restitution. This concerns first the vindication claim, i.e. the claim to restore the property to the owner under § 985 BGB. This is a very straightforward proprietary claim under German law, and need not concern us further. Secondly, the owner can claim for the benefit which the possessor has gained from using the property, *Nutzungen* in German.[10] *Nutzungen* are defined in § 100 BGB and can perhaps be translated 'with benefits'. They include the mere advantage of using the property, for example living in a house, but also fruits

[9] Above, Chapter 1, section 4.4.

[10] See above, Chapter 3, section 3.3 for recovery of benefits received under a terminated contract.

(and thus a case of subtractive enrichment). Thirdly, the possessor may be allowed to recover from the owner for unauthorized expenditure on the property.[11]

To what extent the second (and also and the third) claim are allowed depends largely on how much the possessor is perceived to have been at fault. In particular, the owner/possessor model distinguishes between the *bona fide* possessor for value, the gratuitous *bona fide* possessor, the *mala fide* possessor, and the tortious possessor.

At the top of the scale is a *bona fide* possessor who has not (yet) been sued in court and who has paid for obtaining possession. This would cover, for example, a person who innocently buys stolen goods, or a person who has rented a flat from a third party without title. This is the so-called *redliche Besitzer* (§ 993 BGB, *bona fide* possessor for value). This possessor need not surrender any benefits, except those which were gained by excessive use of the property. It should be noted in this context that this rule, which protects the *bona fide* possessor for value, has no equivalent in unjustified enrichment claims based on interference. As a consequence, this *bona fide* possessor accounts for the only substantive difference between restitution rules in an owner/possessor situation on the one hand, and restitution rules for interference in an unjustified enrichment situation on the other. In the latter context, the enriched party would have to give up any surviving benefit of use.

On the other hand, a *bona fide* possessor who did not pay for obtaining possession (the gratuitous possessor or *unentgeltliche Besitzer*) is liable for restitution of benefits. Section 988 BGB refers to the unjustified enrichment model of calculating the surviving enrichment (so that there is no difference between owner/possesor and unjustified enrichment situations of interference). If C lives in a house believing that she is entitled to use it, and if C did not pay for this, at the end of the day, C will have to pay for this use to the owner under §§ 988, 818 BGB.

The picture changes again if the possessor is *mala fide* (*bösgläubig*), or if an action is pending (*rechtshängig*) against the possessor. Such a possessor must surrender or pay the value of any benefits gained. This concept is not alien to English law. In *Strand Electric and Engineering*

[11] This will be covered below, section 3.1.

Co Ltd v Brisford Entertainments Ltd,[12] the defendants continued to use the claimant's theatre lighting equipment for their theatre after a deal with a prospective buyer of the theatre, who had initially rented the theatre and obtained the equipment, had fallen through. The defendants were aware that they were not entitled to use the equipment and were held liable for the amount of the hire-charge. A German court would have decided the same way.[13] The same rule would also have applied in *Morris v Tarrant*.[14] After divorcing the claimant, the defendant husband stayed in the wife's house for several years without her consent. While the English High Court disallowed a restitutionary claim for an occupation rent, German law would have allowed recovery against this *mala fide* defendant.

In addition, such a possessor who is not *bona fide*, or against whom an action is pending, is liable for not having made any use of the property in a negligent way (§ 987 para. 2 BGB). If D learns that he has no title to the five acres of good farmland which D thought were his, and does not farm them until the lawsuit is settled, D will be liable to the owner for the harvest which D failed to reap. Since § 819 BGB refers to the owner/possessor model for defendants which are *mala fide*, or against which an action for restitution is pending, there is again no difference between owner/possessor and unjustified enrichment situations of interference.

At the bottom of the scale of possessors we find the person who has obtained possession by unlawful force or a criminal offence (§ 992, *deliktischer Besitzer*). Such a possessor is additionally exposed to concurrent liability in tort, as he or she would be in an unjustified enrichment situation of interference.

2. *Eingriffskondiktion*

As stated above, the *Eingriffskondiktion* covers those restitution for wrongs cases which are not governed by the owner/possessor model. In this context, the most difficult question is which wrongs do and

[12] *Strand Electric and Engineering Co Ltd v Brisford Entertainments Ltd* [1952] 2 QB 246 (CA).

[13] For another example, see BGH 25.3.1963, BGHZ 39, 186, below, Chapter 10, section 2 (translation), discussed below, section 3.1.

[14] *Morris v Tarrant* [1971] 2 QB 143.

which wrongs do not give rise to claims in unjustified enrichment—a question which need not be addressed in owner/possessor situations of interference. And whereas the owner/possessor model rules on restitution are treated within German property law, the *Eingriffskondiktion* is firmly within unjustified enrichment.

A. Wrong, Eingriff, *and attribution*

Unjustified enrichment and tort both aim for the protection of rights, but they differ both in the range and in the scope of the rights which are protected. The same can be said in English law, regardless of whether 'restitution for wrongs' is classified within unjust enrichment, or as a separate category which comprises tort law and some other areas.[15]

Different scopes of 'wrongs' and '*Eingriff*'. It is necessary to understand that the English notion of 'wrongs' is wider than the notion of an infringement which underlies the German *Eingriffskondiktion*. German law focuses on what it calls absolute rights, being rights which the owner enjoys against anyone (such as physical property, intellectual property, and personality rights), and on statutory prohibitions. By contrast, it ignores for the purpose of the *Eingriffskondiktion* relative rights which the owner has only against a particular person (such as contractual rights). That may well be a residual effect from the time when German law based this part of enrichment exclusively on *Rechtswidrigkeit*, a concept of unlawfulness which does not extend to breach of civil law obligations.[16] In English law, on the other hand, since *Attorney-General v Blake* it has been clear that a party may be allowed to claim restitution for the wrong of breach of contract.[17] However, restitution may nevertheless be allowed for breach of contract under German law, namely under the contractual remedy of substitution under § 285 BGB (see above, Chapter 1, section 4.5). Relief may also be available under what is called unjustified

[15] See Burrows, Ch. 14; Virgo, Ch. 15; Thomas Krebs, 'The Fallacy of Restitution for Wrongs', in: *Mapping the Law*, 379, 388ff.

[16] For a more detailed analysis of how German law deals with cases where the 'wrong' is a breach of contract, see Giglio (2001) Oxford U Comparative L Forum 6, text adjacent to note 124.

[17] *Attorney-General v Blake* [2001] 1 AC 268 (HL), Burrows 486.

negotiorum gestio, which allows for gain-based restitution if a person without justification intervenes in another person's affairs.[18]

Nonetheless, German law may leave some gaps. One possible example concerns services which are taken in secret rather than bargained for. If a stowaway hides on board a train or boat, performance-based unjustified enrichment will not operate for lack of any intentional shift of wealth, and some argument would have to be made why this would be an *Eingriff*. The easiest route—seeing this as an infringement in the right of the owner of the vehicle to its commercial use which gives rise to an *Eingriffskondiktion*—may become difficult if the travel operator is not the owner. A statutory provision which makes 'obtaining benefits by devious means' a criminal offence will offer a good prospect for an *Eingriffskondiktion* in the case of a stowaway, but does not cover each and every case of a service which was taken rather than given.[19] Such situations are less problematic under English law, which makes this a case of subtractive enrichment where ignorance is available as unjust factor, or, in the alternative model proposed by Birks, absence of basis for this shift of wealth suffices to call for restitution.[20]

Rights that give rise to restitution when infringed. German and English law have in common that not every wrong gives rise to restitutionary remedies. While restitution is generally available in situations of subtractive enrichment, i.e. if the gain caused to the defendant by the wrong or infringement corresponds exactly to the claimant's loss,[21] it is not necessarily available outside subtractive enrichment.

18 See below, section 2.3, and also Giglio, ibid.

19 Section 265a para. 1 of the German Criminal Code (Straftgesetzbuch, StGB) reads:

> Whoever obtains the performance of a vending machine or a publicly operating telecommunications network, transportation, or entry to an event or institution by devious means and with the intention of not paying the price, will be punished with imprisonment for not more than one year or a fine. . .

20 Birsk, *Unjust Enrichment*, 154ff.

21 As mentioned above, the distinction between subtractive and other enrichment is discussed to a lesser degree in this context in German law than it is in English law. The proprietary *vindicatio* under § 985 BGB (see above, section 2.1) deals with most subtractive infringements of property law. A somewhat disputed (and in most cases unnecessary) concurrent claim could lie under the *Eingriffskondiktion* if pure possession is seen as enrichment. The special *condictiones* based on interference in § 816 (see below, section 2.4) cover situations of subtractive enrichment by operation of law, including *bona fide* acquisition of title.

If A suffers injuries in a supermarket when A is submerged beneath a cascade of badly stacked tins, A can claim damages, but cannot claim the extra profit which the supermarket has made by a policy of cheap rather than safe storage. This gain of lower operational cost was made at the expense of A's health, but no claim will lie in unjustified enrichment under the *Eingriffskondiktion*, and it is unlikely that such a claim would succeed before an English court. On the other hand, both German and English law allow restitution and refuse to grant damages if someone innocently violates the copyright of another person. For English law, this follows from s 97 Copyright, Designs and Patent Act 1988, and for German law from § 97 *Urheberrechtsgesetz* and § 812 BGB.

But how should those rights which give rise to restitution if they are infringed be distinguished? Prior to von Caemmerer, the predominant view was that restitution should be granted if the interference with the claimant's right was unlawful. That view has become untenable in both German and English law.[22] Currently, the majority view in Germany is that unlawfulness in itself will often not indicate who should be entitled to an enrichment which was gained unlawfully. Courts and the majority of academics now apply Wilburg's and von Caemmerer's doctrine of attribution (*Zuweisungstheorie* or *Theorie vom Zuweisungsgehalt*) in order to distinguish wrongs which give rise to restitution from those which do not.[23] This theory links the gain which was made with the right which was interfered with. If the legal order attributes the gain in question to the owner of the right, restitution will be granted. On the other hand, if the right in question is not bestowed on the owner so that he or she can reap and keep this particular gain, there is no restitution.

Examples. The right to physical integrity is granted and protected for a number of reasons, but not in order to make a gain from

[22] It should be noted that some academic supporters of the once predominant 'unlawfulness' approach have come some way towards meeting the doctrine of attribution. See e.g. Lieb in *Münchener Kommentar*, § 812 nos 240–244. For English law and a comparison with German law, see e.g. T Krebs, 'The Fallacy of Restitution for Wrongs', in: *Mapping the Law*, 379, 389: 'The essence of the modern version is that wrongfulness is a necessary, but not a sufficient, reason for restitution'.

[23] Wilburg, 27ff; von Caemmerer, 353ff.

its infringement. On the other hand, gains to be made from the use of chattels and real property will generally be considered as attributable to their owners. Copyright is another obvious example of a right where the infringement calls for restitution. A main purpose of copyright is that the creator of a work should benefit from its use. The use of the author's work is therefore a gain which the legal order attributes to the author. The same is true for other intellectual property rights.[24]

In cases of infringements of intellectual property rights, restitution will normally be granted to the measure of an appropriate licence fee; gain-based restitution may alternatively be available under unjustified *negotiorum gestio* (see below, Chapter 5, section 2.3). Somewhat irritatingly, and certainly inconsistent with the general German law of damages, awards of the appropriate licence fee are frequently classified as damages in tort law rather than as restitution and account for the only instance of 'restitutionary damages' in German law. German courts give victims of intellectual property violations a choice between restitutionary damages and damages measured by their loss;[25] if the intellectual property right in question is linked to a personality right, the victim may alternatively also claim for non-pecuniary loss.[26]

There has been some debate as to whether infringement of personality (or privacy) rights will generally lead to restitutionary remedies. The view currently seems to prevail that this depends on the degree to which a particular personality right is capable of being commercialized, as is the case not only for the right to one's own image, but also the right to one's name and certain confidentiality rights.[27] Personality

[24] BGH 18.12.1986, BGHZ 99, 244 has made clear that this includes trademark violations, a question which had previously been disputed.

[25] This includes the unauthorized use of an image for advertising purposes as in BGH 8.5.1965, BGHZ 20, 345, a case involving the actor Paul Dahlke, where the court, however, also found a concurrent *Eingriffskondiktion*.

[26] BGB 14.2.1958, BGHZ 26, 249 (gentleman rider case); an English translation by F H Lawson and B Markesinis is available at the German Law Archive at <http://www.iuscomp.org/gla/judgments/tgcm/z580214.htm>. This judgment did not consider restitution.

[27] As systematically developed by P Schlechtriem, 'Bereicherung aus fremdem Persönlichkeitsrecht', in: *Strukturen und Entwicklungen im Handels-, Gesellschafts- und Wirtschaftsrecht (Festschrift für Wolfgang Hefermehl)*, ed. by Robert Fischer et al (1976), 445, 449ff; see also T Krebs, 'The Fallacy of Restitution for Wrongs', in: *Mapping the Law*, 379, 385–386; Lieb in *Münchener Kommentar*, § 812 nos 262–264.

rights therefore account for another application of the doctrine of attribution.

Interference in the form of breach of a statute may in some cases also give right to claims under the *Eingriffskondiktion*. In practice, this concerns frequent violations of competition and trade practice law. Under the doctrine of attribution, it should be noted that most of the regulatory provisions aim to establish a level playing field for all market participants rather than assigning particular gains to particular competitors. Where unjustified enrichment claims have succeeded in the courts, they relate to the breach of statutory provisions where a particular victim can easily be identified, as is the case in the prohibited exploitation of trade secrets and confidential information which fall outside the scope of patent law,[28] or in cases of slavish imitations which fall short of intellectual property law violations.[29]

Comparison with the English approach. Some similarities can be detected between the German doctrine of attribution and the corresponding duty-based approach which English law has predominantly taken. This has been formulated as follows by Birks:[30]

> The test proposed under this head supposes that some wrongs are, and some wrongs are not, recognised by the law for the purpose of preventing disapproved modes of enrichment. More accurately this means that the primary duties, of which the wrongs are breaches, either are or are not designed to prevent enrichment.

For the reasons indicated, German law is happy to go along with the following example given by Birks:[31]

> Suppose that A hits B and then, because both A and B were trying to win a lucrative contract, A gains because B is out of action with a broken jaw. There would be no question of B's getting A's gain, because battery is not an anti-enrichment wrong. It might be different if A could show that B's blow was a deliberate stratagem to get A out of the way on the crucial day. . .

[28] Sections 17 and 18 Gesetz gegen den unlauteren Wettbewerb (UWG, Act Against Unfair Competition); BGH 18.2.1977, NJW 1977, 1062 (business secrets). See Lieb in *Münchener Kommentar*, § 812 nos 257–259.

[29] BGH 8.10.1971, BGHZ 57, 116.

[30] Birks, *Introduction*, 328; see also Virgo, 432ff.

[31] Birks, *Introduction*, 329.

Tettenborn comes closer to the German approach by distinguishing tradable and non-tradable rights, whereby infringements of the former call for restitution. He maintains a duty-based approach for fiduciary duties ('obligations of loyalty').[32]

The overlap between Wilburg and von Caemmerer's *Zuweisungstheorie* and a duty-based distinction between anti-enrichment and other wrongs is considerable, but not complete. Basing this distinction on the violation of a duty could be described as an approach which brings this form of restitution closer to the tort of negligence. Wilburg and von Caemmerer look at interference and at the scope and the purpose of the right that has been infringed, rather than searching for a specific protective duty. Are these different sides of the same coin, or do the two approaches lead to different results? Perhaps three German cases can shed light on the question and at the same time the leeway which the *Zuweisungstheorie* leaves to the courts.

The first two cases concern the right of owners to use the image of their property. While it is generally understood that property in land and chattels gives the owner the exclusive right to use, draw gains from, or sell the property, it is debatable to what extent the ownership in a building entails the exclusive right to use the image of this building. There are two cases in which the owners sued defendants on the ground that they did not authorize the commercial use of such pictures. The *Bundesgerichtshof* allowed such a claim in 1974, where the picture for a postcard had been taken on the owner's premises and argued that it was 'the natural privilege of the owner . . . to claim for himself the commercial use which can be drawn from the property which is only accessible by his consent'.[33] In 1989, the same court refused a similar claim where the picture was taken from a spot which was accessible to the public at large.[34] The *Bundesgerichtshof* based its analysis on the attribution of property rights. Anyone can take pictures of buildings from a public space and make money from selling those pictures, but the commercial gain associated with pictures taken of buildings from private premises belongs to the owner.

32 Tettenborn, 240–242.

33 BGH 20.9.1974, NJW 1975, 778. This was, however, an action for enjoinment rather than for restitution under unjustified enrichment.

34 BGH 14.3.1989, NJW 1989, 2251. This was an action for enjoinment *and* restitution.

Another illustrative case (case no. 10) concerned a borderline area between copyright, patent, and competition law.[35] The claimant had obtained government authorization to produce a new herbicide. In the preparation of the application, the claimant conducted extensive research on the toxicity of two substances which the herbicide contained. When the defendant, a competitor, later applied for, and obtained, a similar authorization, the research findings of the claimant were relied on during the proceedings. The *Bundesgerichtshof* disallowed the action for unjustified enrichment by reliance on the claimant's findings, and quite rightly so. The claimant was protected against unauthorized copying, distribution, marketing, etc. of the report, but not against the use of the findings made in this report. The law does not attribute to the author the benefit which others obtain from reading the work in question and applying the content of that work to their own practical needs. If it did so, this would be welcome news to all academics who have written law books and articles on which successful claimants have relied. However, such restitutionary liability would make little sense and ultimately mean that barristers would stop citing the academic works they have consulted.

When comparing the German doctrine of attribution and its application by the courts with English approaches to restitution for wrongs, it may be helpful to distinguish once again between the different scopes of 'wrongs' and '*Eingriff*' on the one hand, and the different constructions through 'duty' and 'attribution' on the other, starting with the latter.

Finding the appropriate duty in the first of the two above-mentioned cases involving the photograph of a building might be a little more difficult. Tort-like notions of trespass or negligence will provide little help. In the first case the owner might have consented to the photographer walking and taking pictures on the premises, but not to the commercial use of the pictures. In fact, the court held that even the explicit permission to take pictures would be presumed not to amount to consent to the commercial exploitation of those pictures.[36] On this assumption, the notion of duty offers little explanatory force.

[35] BGH 9.3.1989, BGHZ 107, 117, below, Chapter 10, section 10 (translation); see also Schlechtriem, *Schuldrecht BT*, no. 751.

[36] BGH 20.9.1974, NJW 1975, 778, at 779. Quite independently, a similar result was achieved on the other side of the Atlantic in injunctive relief proceedings in *Rock & Roll*

Of course it is possible simply to state that the publication of the picture without the owner's consent violates a duty of care, but this seems to be the consequence which tort and restitution draw from the fact that the law attributes to the owner the right to the commercial exploitation of the image of the property when this image is taken from a point where the public has no access. On the other hand, Tettenborn's distinction between tradable and non-tradable rights could explain all three cases:[37] the right to take pictures from private premises is tradable, the right to take pictures from within the public sphere is not, and neither is the right to make good use of information which other people have placed in the public sphere.

It could therefore be said that the duty-based approach towards distinguishing enrichment-type wrongs from other wrongs is more susceptible to 'backward reasoning',[38] whereby courts first decide whether they want to give restitutionary relief, and then find a duty if that is the case. The attribution approach can be used (or abused) for the same purpose, but less easily, as it focuses on entire rights and their boundaries rather than particular situations. In turn, a duty-based approach can be said to offer more flexibility to do justice in particular situations. It is interesting to note that English law, which normally prefers certainty over flexibility, has on this occasion chosen the more flexible approach.

This leads to the second question. The flexible English approach can perhaps be linked to the above-mentioned wider notion which English law has of 'wrongs'. An approach which is based in infringement of rights and attribution of benefits derived from those rights may become unwieldy if this includes breach of contractual obligations, which nearly always have some economical purpose. The fact that the law protects economic interests through the enforcement of contractual promises cannot generally explain why restitution should be allowed for the breach of some contractual obligations but not for breach of others.

Hall of Fame & Museum Inc v Gentile Productions, 134 F.3d 749 (6th Cir. 1998). This decision focused on trademark law and did not discuss any restitutionary consequences.

[37] Tettenborn, 240.

[38] Patrick Atiyah, *Introduction to the Law of Contract*, 5th edn (1995), 58–59.

Krebs believes that the German doctrine of attribution can explain why restitution was allowed in *Attorney-General v Blake*.[39] He argues that this doctrine would 'ask whether the contractual right reserves to the claimant a sphere of economic activity from which the defendant is excluded', and would answer in the negative. This explanation is, in the view of Krebs, superior to the English duty-based approach.

Such an extension of the attribution theory to contractual rights would shift the perspective from the economic sphere of the claimant, for which it has been designed, to that of the defendant. It is indeed fairly easy to say that the defendant, Blake, a double agent who went on to tell his story, was excluded by his contract with the government from exploiting his experience for commercial gain. But could it equally be said that the right to tell the story of spies who turned on their own government has been granted to the government in order to increase public revenue? That is the question which the doctrine of attribution would normally ask.

A similar argument can be made about the recovery of bribes paid to civil servants as being allowed to the Crown in *Reading v Attorney-General*:[40] it is submitted here that this would be all but impossible under the doctrine of attribution, for it would have to be argued that the right to sell out the law against bribes vests in the Crown. However, the bribes would in any event have been forfeited under §§ 73ff *Strafgesetzbuch* (Criminal Code), or else could have been claimed under unjustified *negotiorum gestio*.[41]

If the attribution perspective were to be shifted away from the claimant and onto the bribed official, it would of course be possible to argue that the official was excluded from the commercial abuse of his position. But would that not come just as close to backward reasoning as does constructing duties in general or, as in *Attorney-General v Blake*, explaining that the claimant 'had a legitimate interest in preventing the defendant's profit-making activity'?[42] Shifting the perspective away from the claimant's right to the defendant's failure to

[39] Krebs, 'The Fallacy of Restitution for Wrongs', in: *Mapping the Law*, 397–398; *Attorney-General v Blake* [2001] 1 AC 268.

[40] *Reading v Attorney-General* [1951] AC 507 (HL). See also the similar case of *A-G for Hong Kong v Reid* [1994] 1 AC 324 (PC).

[41] RG 27.4.1920, RGZ 99, 31; see above, section 2.3.

[42] *Attorney-General v Blake* [2001] 1 AC 268 (HL), per Lord Nicholls.

be entitled to the gain removes much of the explanatory force of the doctrine of attribution. *Attorney-General v Blake* is also a case where dogmatic consistency may have been sacrificed in order to prevent a public outcry against the House of Lords for allowing one of the most hated personalities in the UK to make a late profit from having turned against his own government.[43]

It is interesting to note in this context that Friedmann and Jackman have postulated approaches based on infringement of property, both of which have been rejected by Virgo on the ground that it is unclear where the extension of 'property' for this purpose should end.[44] Virgo's argument may be stronger for English law than it would be for German law due to their different notions of *Eingriffskondiktion* and restitution based on wrongs. It would, however, be more difficult for English law to limit restitution for wrongs in the same way as German law limits the scope of the *Eingriffskondiktion*, as English law does not cater for the German restitutionary remedies in contract such as § 285 BGB or in unjustified *negotiorum gestio* which can cover other situations involving 'wrongs'.[45]

B. *Without legal ground*

There is a superficial similarity between *Leistungskondiktion* and *Eingriffskondiktion* as regards whether enrichment occurred 'without legal ground': again, this question is mainly left to other areas of the law. But the similarity ends rather quickly. While *Leistungskondiktion* and the law of contract run in tandem with only very few exceptions, *Eingriffskondiktion* and tort do not necessarily agree. As we have seen above, there are torts which do not give rise to unjustified enrichment claims. Similarly, a provision in property law allows for certain infringements on real property against payment of a reasonable fee (§ 906 BGB, '*Ausgleich*'), so that even lawful interference can lead to a monetary claim situated somewhere between compensation and restitution.

43 Similar Lord Hobhouse in his dissenting opinion.

44 Daniel Friedmann, 'Restitution of Benefits Obtained Through the Appropriation of Property or the Commission of a Wrong' 80 Columbia L Rev 504 (1980); Ian Jackman, 'Restitution for Wrongs' (1989) 48 CLJ 302, 305–311; Virgo, 433. See also generally Edelman, *Gain-based Damages*.

45 See above, section 2.3.

C. Enrichment without impoverishment

All claims based on 'enrichment in another way' under § 812 para. 1 sent. 2 2nd alternative, including those under the *Eingriffskondiktion*, require that the defendant's enrichment occurred at the claimant's expense. Is it sufficient for this purpose that the defendant infringed a right the use of which is attributed to the claimant, or need the claimant show any loss? The question was controversial in English law for some time, but it appears to have been settled now that the claimant need not show any loss. This has also been the position of German law for more than a hundred years.

In one case, the defendant used a railway track which ran through the claimant's property.[46] The claimant had authorized the use of the property for transport to two adjoining plots, but not to the defendant's factory. The claimant, who had suffered no loss, was allowed restitution for the value of the unauthorized use of the track.[47]

A claimant may even be entitled to restitution if the infringement has caused a simultaneous gain. This is well illustrated by a case decided by the *Reichsgericht* before the BGB entered into force.[48] This so-called Ariston case involved as the defendant a company which produced mechanical music players in which a rolling tape played different songs. One of these songs was composed by the claimant, who had made a name for himself in some circles as a composer, but who was not widely known. The song had been used without his consent. The great success of the Ariston players may well have increased the fame of the claimant, but the *Reichsgericht* held that the claimant need not show any loss in order to recover. This decision may have inspired von Caemmerer to the following textbook case, which is still

[46] RG 20.12.1919, RGZ 97, 310.

[47] From a comparative perspective, it is interesting to note that Gutteridge and David, 214–215 criticize a similar French case on the ground that a 'chain of causation' was required between enrichment and impoverishment. In this case, a 'landowner built a road on his land at considerable expense, and used it for the purpose of working a quarry on his land'. A competing quarry owner used same road. The Cour d'Appel Grenoble ordered him to pay one-third of the cost of constructing the road and for its upkeep: 25.6.1924, D.P. 1926.2.41 note Rouast. An English translation of this judgment can be found in *Cases, Materials and Texts on Unjustified Enrichment*, 4.F.3.

[48] RG 8.6.1895, RGZ 35, 63. For a comparative discussion, see Giglio (2001) Oxford U Comparative L Forum 6, text adjacent to note 76.

frequently used as an example.[49] A script, which the defendant uses for the production of a film, is based on a previous publication by the claimant, whose consent has not been obtained. The release of the film generates interest in the original work and leads to an increase in its sale. Nevertheless, the claimant is entitled to claim a reasonable licence fee under § 812 BGB.

D. Defences, passing on

Sections 812–822 contain no defence which is explicitly applicable to the *Eingriffskondiktion*. The defences in §§ 814, 815, and 817 (see above, Chapter 4) are all limited to enrichment by performance. The lively discussion of whether 'passing on' should be allowed as a defence in English law of unjustified enrichment[50] finds little equivalent in German writing and court practice. There is, however, an interesting case which pre-dates the BGB.

The defendant baker had agreed to bake bread from dough supplied by the claimant, a shop owner. For years, he secretly kept some of the dough for himself.[51] When the shop owner discovered this, he sued the baker for the value of the dough which the baker had misappropriated. Such a claim is difficult to phrase in terms of damages, because any loss which the shop owner might have suffered by having received undersized loaves had been passed on to his equally unsuspecting customers, who had paid the usual price for normally sized loaves. The court kept this case within contracts and awarded the claim in damages—a faint instance of restitutionary damages in German contract law, as Giglio has argued.[52] A modern unjustified enrichment analysis would see this case on the borderline between performance (as the bread was supplied under the contract) and *Eingriff*, but belonging to the sphere of the latter, as the enrichment did not occur *by* performance of the baker, but by his misappropriation of the dough. The fact that the claimant had no financial loss would be just as irrelevant as it was more than a hundred years ago.

49 von Caemmerer, 354.
50 See e.g. Burrows, 591ff.
51 OLG Braunschweig, 26.1.1891, Seufferts Archiv 46, no. 173, p. 272.
52 Giglio (2001) Oxford U Comparative L Forum 6, text adjacent to note 135.

3. Unjustified *negotiorum gestio*

There is yet another way of claiming restitution in situations where the defendant has interfered with the claimant's rights. A well-hidden provision in the BGB allows restitution in cases of unjustified *negotiorum gestio*. Section 687 para. 2 BGB (referring to §§ 681 sent. 2, 667 BGB) applies to an interferer who conducts someone else's business in the full knowledge that he or she is not entitled to do so. It gives the person whose business is conducted the right to claim anything which the interferer has obtained by conducting this business, in exchange for reimbursement of reasonable expenses.[53] The wording of §§ 687 para. 2, 684 sent. 1 BGB is somewhat oblique and seems to indicate that either party can claim restitution from the other. In practice, intentional infringements of the rights of others will regularly be considered to fall under § 687 para. 2 BGB and thus give a gain-based remedy in restitution.

The reader may wonder why it is necessary to resort to an opaque and at best peripheral provision when the *Eingriffskondiktion* already provides a remedy for cases of infringement. The reason why unjustified *negotiorum gestio* became an attractive option concerns its measure of restitution. As it entitles the claimant to anything which the interferer obtained by conducting the claimant's business, this remedy is gain-based. Therefore for intentional infringements, this provision puts beyond discussion whether the claimant is entitled to strip the defendant of any profits made (for example by advertising using the claimant's good name), or limited to restitution calculated according to the value of the use of the infringed right (for example the appropriate licence fee). We will deal further with this issue below. Suffice it to say in this context that unjustified enrichment, tort, and unjustified *negotiorum gestio*, taken together, can produce a three-tier system of remedies for the infringement of rights.

- On the first tier, (at least) the value attached to the use of the infringed right can be claimed under the *Eingriffskondiktion*.
- On the second tier, damages are available in delict under § 823 BGB for negligent infringements of this right.

[53] See e.g. Schlechtriem, *Schuldrecht BT*, nos 714–717.

- On the third tier, the defendant has to disgorge profits under unjustified *negotiorum gestio* for intentional infringements.

4. Interference by operation of the law

Just as the general *Leistungskondiktion* is supplemented by some specific performance-based *condictiones*, the *Eingriffskondiktion* is complemented by some specific *condictiones* which are based on the infringement of another's right. These specific *condictiones* cover cases where it is not the defendant who has infringed the claimant's right, but where the infringement operates by virtue of the law.

These *condictiones* provide exceptions to the general rule, namely that if a person loses a right due to a statutory provision, he or she cannot claim restitution from the person who acquired the right.

For example, if A keeps a book in possession for ten years which A believes to be his, but which actually belongs to B, A acquires title under § 937 BGB, and B cannot claim back the book under unjustified enrichment.

However, if the loss of property in chattels occurs by way of connection to real property, by way of mixing or processing, § 951 BGB keeps the door open for a restitutionary claim as long as the other requirements are met. This is why the farmer was allowed restitution for the two stolen young bulls which had been turned into meat and sausages in case no. 5 above.[54]

Section 816 BGB deals with a more difficult question, namely the unauthorized disposal of a right which, by virtue of the law, is effective against the owner of the right. The most obvious and important application of this provision concerns the loss of property which occurs by *bona fide* acquisition of chattels (which have not been lost or stolen) under §§ 932ff BGB. *Bona fide* acquisition of land is also possible under § 892 BGB to the extent that a purchaser relied on an inaccurate entry into the land register. Section 816 BGB can also apply to situations where a debtor innocently performs towards the previous creditor who previously assigned the claim to a new creditor. The debtor can then rely on this payment as a defence against the new

[54] Above, Chapter 3, section 2; BGH 11.1.1971, BGHZ 55, 176; below, Chapter 10, section 5 (translation).

creditor under § 407 BGB. All these dispositions are effective against the true owner and the new creditor.

However, the rationale behind these provisions is the protection of the innocent buyer or innocent debtor, who should not pay twice, and not the shifting of wealth. It is for this reason that § 816 para. 1 sent. 1 BGB allows the person who lost property by the *bona fide* acquisition to recover from the person who made the unauthorized disposition. This person must then give up what he or she obtained by the disposition. That is usually the purchase price.

It is only in this context that an equivalent to 'waiver of tort' comes into operation in German law. If C's chattels were lost or stolen, C is still the owner and therefore cannot recover under § 816 para. 1 sent. 1 BGB from any person who sold them to a third party, because there is no *bona fide* acquisition of lost or stolen goods (§ 935 BGB). However, C can ratify the transaction under § 185 BGB and thus render the failed transfer of property effective. Title thus passes to the buyer, and C can claim the purchase price from the vendor. This is similar to the outcome in *Lamine v Dorrell*,[55] and the mechanism is the same as the one which Birks described as 'extinctive ratification'.[56] This option would have been open to the farmer in the young bulls case mentioned above, if he had sued the thief instead of the butcher.[57] In addition, the courts have allowed claimants to make ratification conditional on payment of the purchase price.

It is in one situation only that restitution will ultimately make a *bona fide* acquisition of title relatively worthless to the acquirer, namely if the acquisition occurred gratuitously. In this case, § 816 para. 1 sent. 2 BGB will allow the previous owner to recover the chattels from the new owner. This is the German equivalent of the English rule that *bona fide* acquisition gives title only if it occurred against value. In German law property does pass but can be claimed back in unjustified enrichment if there is no value to support the acquisition.

Finally, § 816 para. 2 BGB resolves the triangular enrichment situation which arises if a debtor relies on having paid the assignor rather than the assignee: the assignee has a restitutionary claim against the assignor for the debtor's performance.

[55] *Lamine v Dorrell* (1701) 2 Ld Raym 1216.

[56] Birks, *Introduction*, 315.

[57] Above, Chapter 3, section 2; BGH 11.1.1971, BGHZ 55, 176; below, Chapter 10, section 5 (translation).

It is worth noting in this context that German law takes a strict and orderly approach towards property law issues. Property rights exist only in corporeal property such as lands and chattels, and to a certain degree in intellectual property rights. For all corporeal property, there is a *vindicatio* by which the owner can claim back the property from a possessor who has no right to possession. There is no property right which would entitle a party to receive value in lieu of the property. There is also no doubling of property rights. For example, when A steals a bicycle and swaps it for a television, the owner of the bicycle has precisely one property right, namely in the bicycle, and no property right in the television.[58] In this sense, German law keeps property law orderly and confines any muddle to the law of obligations.

3. Unauthorized expenditure

The *Eingriffskondiktion* covers situations where the defendant took an enrichment, the *condictiones* in § 816 BGB situations where the claimant was disenriched and the defendant enriched by operation of the law. In the present category of unauthorized expenditure, it is the claimant who has enriched the defendant—without having a particular obligation in mind, because that would be covered by performance-based restitution.

German law provides several mechanisms for the recovery of unauthorized expenditure. The owner/possessor model takes precedence where its requirements are fulfilled, that is if the claimant spent money on the defendant's property while keeping it in possession, but without being entitled to possession (see 1 below). Otherwise, recovery can be allowed under the rules of *negotiorum gestio* if the claimant was knowingly acting in the interest of the defendant (see 2 below). It has already been mentioned that recovery for unauthorized expenditure may be possible if a contract has been terminated, but German law applies a separate contractual regime for claims after termination of contract (above, Chapter 3, section 3.5). Finally, the *Verwendungskondiktion* can serve to allow restitution in rare cases which are neither covered by any of these models, nor by the *Leistungskondiktion* (see 3 below).

58 See also below, Chapter 6, section 2.1.

1. The owner/possessor model

The basic mechanism of the owner/possessor model has been explained above (section 2) in the context of restitution for interference. This model distinguishes between *bona fide* possessor for value, *bona fide* gratuitous possessor, *mala fide* possessor (extending to a possessor against whom an action is pending), and tortious possessor.

In this area, we find several rules which do make a difference to the unjustified enrichment approach towards recovery of unauthorized expenditure.[59]

As regards recovery for unauthorized expenditure, the *bona fide* possessor for value can claim reimbursement for necessary expenditure on the property under § 994 BGB, excluding normal maintenance costs. If it turns out that A has used a car without having title or any other right to use the car, A cannot claim from the owner the cost for having the car serviced, because these are normal maintenance costs. However, A can recover the cost of a new engine which A had to fit.[60] The possessor can recover for any other expense only to the extent that this expense has caused an increase in the value of the property which persists at the time when the owner regains possession. This follows from § 996 BGB.

It is perhaps no coincidence that this corresponds with the outcome in *Greenwood v Bennett*,[61] where the *bona fide* possessor of a stolen car was allowed to recover the value which he had added to the car (which in this case seemed to be identical to the expenditure on labour and materials). On the other hand, if B possesses a flat in good decorative order but decides to repaint it pink at great cost, B will not be allowed to recover that cost from the owner.

A *bona fide* possessor who did not pay for obtaining possession (the gratuitous possessor or *unentgeltliche Besitzer*) is entitled to the same measure of recovering unauthorized expenditure as the *bona fide* possessor for value.

On the other hand, a *mala fide* possessor (extending to a previously *bona fide* possessor from the moment that this person has been sued in

[59] See Verse, *Improvements*; Verse (1998) Restitution L Rev 85.

[60] Palandt, *Bürgerliches Gesetzbuch*, 68th edn (2009), § 994 no. 7 (Bassenge).

[61] *Greenwood v Bennett* [1973] 1 QB 195 (CA).

court for return of the property) will find it more difficult to recover for unauthorized expenditure. As regards necessary expenditure, § 994 BGB refers to the *negotiorum gestio* model (below, section 3.2). This implies that necessary expenditure can be recovered in full only if making the expenditure conformed to the actual or the implied will of the owner, whereby the possessor must consult the owner for this purpose if possible. Otherwise, the owner is liable only under the unjustified enrichment model and can therefore rely on disenrichment (below, Chapter 6, section 5). If the expenditure was not necessary to start with, the possessor cannot recover at all, unless the owner consented to the expenditure (§§ 996, 1001 BGB). This is still more generous than English law. As the *mala fide* possessor is not mistaken, it will be difficult to find an unjust factor which could support a claim for restitution.[62]

The following case (case no. 2) which was decided by the *Bundesgerichtshof* illustrates how the restitutionary claims and conterclaims interrelate in the case of a possessor who is not *bona fide*.[63] The claimant was the owner of a site which had been bombed during the Second World War. The defendant had constructed a building on the adjacent property, cleared part of the claimant's property of debris, and had used this space for storing building material and keeping a site hut, all in spite of the claimant's express prohibition. The claimant sued the defendant for the value of this use. The defendant raised a counterclaim for the expense which it had incurred in clearing part of the claimant's land of debris. It was beyond doubt that the claimant was entitled to claim from the defendant the value of the use of the property under §§ 990, 987. As regards the counterclaim, the most important question was whether this was a necessary or useful expense. Is it necessary to clear a property which is covered by rubble and debris, or is this merely useful? The *Bundesgerichtshof*, without any ado, thought it was merely useful, the reason presumably being that a bombed site does not need any upkeep in order to remain what it is. As the defendant was not *bona fide*, recovery for useful expense was excluded and the counterclaim therefore disallowed. As a result, the defendant was

[62] Similar Maier, 'No Basis: A Comparative View', in: *Mapping the Law*, 343, 357–358.

[63] BGH 25.3.1963, BGHZ 39, 186; below, Chapter 10, section 2 (translation).

exposed to the claimant's restitution claim under the owner/possessor model without the defendant being able to counterclaim for its own expense in obtaining this enrichment.

2. *Negotiorum gestio*

German law has inherited from Roman law a model of mutual liability in situations where one person takes care of some matter for another person, centred around a contract called mandate (*Auftrag*). Essentially, the mandator (*Auftraggeber*, the person whose business is managed) can claim from the mandatee (*Beauftragter*, the person who manages the business) anything which the mandatee obtains in the course of managing the mandator's business (§ 667 BGB), while the mandatee can recover for any expenses reasonably incurred for the purpose of the mandate (§ 670 BGB). However, unless stipulated otherwise in the contract, the mandatee is not entitled to be paid for this service (§ 662 BGB).

As in Roman law, the German law provisions on *negotiorum gestio* (*Geschäftsführung ohne Auftrag*, above Chapter 1, section 4.2) are modelled on mandate.[64] Let us assume that A sees smoke rising from her neighbour's house, and she knows that her neighbour is away. When no one answers the bell, A breaks open the door and attempts to put out the fire. *Negotiorum gestio* allows A to claim her reasonable expenses (§§ 683, 670 BGB), for example if A ruins her clothes, or empties her own fire extinguisher during the rescue operation, even if the entire building burns down in spite of A's heroic efforts. If *negotiorum gestio* were part of unjustified enrichment, if would be very difficult for A to claim her expenses in the latter situation, because the neighbour is not enriched if A does not succeed. And if A succeeds, the neighbour's enrichment does not consist in A's ruined clothes, but in the fact that the house still stands. *Negotiorum gestio* can therefore provide an adequate solution in situations which cause great difficulty in English law.

English law has traditionally been concerned with discouraging the 'officious intermeddler' and thus has been reluctant to subscribe to the notion of *negotiorum gestio*. In his broad comparative study, Kortmann showed that the idea of giving a remedy to someone who

[64] For a comparative treatment, see Kortmann, *Altruism in Private Law*.

suffers loss through an act of altruism is not entirely alien to English law after all.[65] It should also be mentioned that German law places some requirements on *negotiorum gestio* which are designed to exclude purely officious intermeddlers. Section 678 BGB makes liable in damages any intervener who ought to have realized that he or she acts against the actual or presumed will of the person on behalf of whom the intervention takes place (called *Geschäftsherr* in German, 'master of business' in a literal translation; for want of a better word in English, we will call this person the principal), even if the intervener has not been negligent in any other respect.

There are, however, also situations in which the actual or presumed will of the principal is irrelevant. Section 679 BGB provides that this is the case if the intervener's act corresponds with a duty of the principal, provided the fulfilment of this duty is in the public interest. Section 679 expressly applies to statutory obligations to pay maintenance. Furthermore, in emergency situations, the intervener is liable only for wilful and grossly negligent conduct.

Therefore there are several reasons why in our example of the burning house, the neighbour would not be heard with the defence that the fire was welcomed, perhaps because the building was dilapidated and the value of the property would have increased if the building had been razed to the ground. Even if the actual will of the neighbour after the event was that the building should burn down, this was not necessarily the will to be presumed at the time of A's intervention. Furthermore, there is a public duty to prevent the spread of fires. Finally, it was certainly not grossly negligent of A to put out the fire.

The measure of restitution which is attached to *negotiorum gestio*—recovery of expenditure—works well in most cases. It will, however, not always do justice to services provided by professionals in the course of *negotiorum gestio*. The surgeon who gives first aid to the unconscious victim of a traffic accident can, under §§ 683, 670 BGB, claim the costs for any dressing materials used, but not for a professional fee. However, the courts have meanwhile been convinced that the mandate model has to be modified in order to allow professionals and enterprises who are acting under justified *negotiorum gestio* also to claim their normal fee.

[65] Ibid.

This is illustrated by the above-mentioned case of the minor who managed to travel to New York on his ticket from Munich to Hamburg (above, Chapter 2, section 2.1, case no. 7).[66] In spite of the wording of §§ 683, 670 BGB, the *Bundesgerichtshof* allowed the flight operator to recover for the normal fare for the flight back from New York to Munich (and not just for expenses incurred) under *negotiorum gestio.* There was no contractual claim for payment for the return flight: German law has no equivalent to the necessaries rule,[67] and the minor's mother (as his statutory representative) could not be contacted while he was in New York. Furthermore, she subsequently refused to consent to the travel contract. A claim in unjustified enrichment would have been somewhat difficult to construct, as the flight operator when placing the minor on the return flight was fully aware that there was no contract, giving rise to the defence under § 814 BGB (above, Chapter 4, section 1). The solution was found in *negotiorum gestio.* As US immigration law imposed on the minor a legal obligation to return immediately, the flight operator was justified to assume that returning the minor was in the interest of his mother.

Finally, *negotiorum gestio* fails to escape one of the difficulties which an unjustified enrichment approach towards these cases presents, namely whether what the claimant did was a benefit for the defendant or for the claimant. The same question arises under the mandate model in deciding whether the claimant conducted the defendant's business or his or her own.

Case no. 3 provides another example.[68] The fire brigade of a local authority extinguished a forest fire which had been caused by sparks coming from a train engine. That is precisely what a fire brigade is for, therefore they were certainly conducting their own business. The *Bundesgerichtshof* nonetheless allowed the local authority to recover under *negotiorum gestio* from the *Bundesbahn* (Federal Rail). The court argued that the defendant was strictly liable for damage, and that it was therefore in the defendant's interest that liability should be limited by extinguishing the fire, regardless of the claimant's own duty to act. This can be contrasted with *Macclesfield Corptn v Gt Central*

[66] BGH 7.1.1971, NJW 1971, 609, 612; below, Chapter 10, section 7 (translation).

[67] Below, Chapter 9, section 2.2.C.

[68] BGH 20.6.1963, BGHZ 40, 28; below, Chapter 10, section 3 (translation).

Railway,[69] which concerned the costs for a bridge which the Macclesfield local authority had build over tracks owned by the defendant, who should in fact have built the bridge. The action under legal compulsion failed because the claimant could not show that they were under a duty to build the bridge. It is interesting to note that if Macclesfield had been under such an obligation (thus coming within reach of recovery under English law), this would have made their recovery under German law of *negotiorum gestio* more difficult, because the claimant would have had to show that it had acted in the defendant's interest in spite of acting under a duty of its own.

3. *Verwendungskondiktion*

If someone incurs expenditure on someone else's property, this is usually a case of performance, or covered by the owner/possessor model, or a case of *negotiorum gestio*. There is nevertheless a small residue of cases which are not covered by any of these institutions. This is where the *Verwendungskondiktion* (literally: *condictio* for expenditure) comes into play.

Actual cases in which a *Verwendungskondiktion* has been allowed are thin on the ground. In one case, the claimant had leased land from his aunt and had paid the legal costs for a will in which the aunt bequeathed this land to the claimant.[70] In anticipation of the inheritance, the claimant erected a building on the property. The aunt subsequently changed her mind, will, and heir alike, and died. The *Bundesgerichtshof* allowed the nephew to recover from the heir for the value of the building. This is a case of *Verwendungskondiktion*. The nephew did not perform towards anyone by building the house, so that there is no *Leistungskondiktion*. The owner/possesor model did not operate for various reasons, the most obvious being that the nephew was entitled to possession when the building was erected. Similarly, the nephew was conducting his own and no one else's business, so that *negotiorum gestio* was out of question. Unfortunately, however, the *Bundesgerichtshof* allowed the action not under *Verwendungskondiktion*, but under *condictio causa data causa non secuta*. This has received harsh and

[69] *Macclesfield Corptn v Gt Central Railway* [1911] 2 KB 528 (CA).
[70] BGH 29.11.1965, BGHZ 44, 321.

justified criticism, because there was not even a hint of performance in the case.[71]

This criticism may have reached the *Bundesgerichtshof* by the time it decided the only case in which it has expressly awarded a *Verwendungskondiktion.*[72] The claimants in that case were parents who had transferred the property in a mansion to the defendant, their son, keeping a lifelong proprietary right for the exclusive use of the swimming pool and stables, and communal use of the garden and some rooms in the basement. The son also agreed to pay a contribution to the parents' pension amounting to DM 1,200 (approx. €600) per month. The son and the parents subsequently fell out. There were several instances where the son tried to prevent the parents from using the pool, stables, and some basement rooms. Injunctions were issued and the parents eventually declared withdrawal from donation for gross ingratitude under § 530 para. 1 BGB. As the capitalized value of the pension amounted to less than 20 per cent of the net value of the land (discounting a mortgage and ignoring the value of the buildings), the court held that this 'mixed donation' (*gemischte Schenkung*) was predominantly a donation and applied donation rules. The court furthermore held that the withdrawal was justified in view of the aforementioned and a number of other occurrences. Under § 531 para. 2 BGB, the donor can then claim back the gift under the rules of unjustified enrichment. Amongst the various legal and physical changes which the son had made to the property, one is of particular interest in the present context, namely improvements he had made to the house. His counterclaim was successful to this extent, and granted by the *Bundesgerichtshof* under the *Verwendungskondiktion* to the degree that the value of the property continued to be improved at the time when the claimants declared withdrawal. This case demonstrates that there is a residual need for the *Verwendungskondiktion.* The owner/possessor model does not apply because the parents were not the owners

[71] Josef Drexl, in: Wolfgang Fikentscher, *Schuldrecht*, 8th edn (1992), no. 1107. This criticism has not prevented the *Bundesgerichtshof* from applying the *condictio causa data causa non secuta* to a case in which the claimant had bought and developed a commercial property and claimed for the value of the development when the seller terminated the contract on the ground of the claimant's failure to pay the agreed price: BGH 22.06.2001, NJW 2001, 3118; the solution should rather have been found under the rules on termination of contract, see above, Chapter 3, section 3.5.

[72] BGH 19.1.1999, BGHZ 140, 275.

when the improvements were made. Performance-based unjustified enrichment does not operate because the son did not intentionally shift wealth, and had no particular obligation in mind. *Negotiorum gestio* offers no help because the son was conducting his own business by making the improvements.

Both cases can be compared with *Hussey v Palmer*.[73] Here the claimant was an elderly widow, who was invited to live with her daughter and son-in-law, the defendant. The claimant paid £607 to have the home extended with a bedroom for her own use. When differences between the parties arose 15 months later, the claimant left and sued for the £607. Lord Denning MR held that there was probably no contract, but in any event a constructive trust for the £607. Therefore the action was allowed.

Hussey v Palmer must be contrasted with the recent case of *Yeoman's Row Management Limited and another v Cobbe*.[74] The parties agreed, subject to contract, on the sale of land owned by the defendant, on which the claimant (respondent) was to build residential units in accordance with a plan agreed between the parties. The defendant was to get an agreed share in the sales price of the units. The contract was to be signed as soon as the claimant had obtained the necessary planning permission. After permission had been granted, the defendant demanded a higher price which the claimant refused to pay. The contract was not signed. The claimant then sought to recover for the substantial expenditure he had incurred and the time spent in preparing the application and obtaining planning permission. The House of Lords rejected both proprietary estoppel and constructive trust, but held that the claimant could recover his costs and expenses as well as the value of his services in unjust enrichment. From a German perspective, this is obviously a case of expenditure on the defendant's property and outside the ambit of the owner/possessor model. However, the case concerned performance made on an anticipated contract which fell through, so that it would have been covered by performance-based unjustified enrichment in German law.

73 *Hussey v Palmer* [1972] 1 WLR 1286 (CA).
74 *Yeoman's Row Management Limited and another v Cobbe* [2008] UKHL 55.

Cases of *Verwendungskondiktion* can also raise very difficult problems of freedom of contract, which are discussed below (Chapter 6, section 4.3).

4. Performance of defendant's obligation

If one party pays a debt which another party owes to a third party, can the first party (the payer) recover from the second (the relieved debtor)?[75] English law has traditionally been reluctant to allow recovery, perhaps again for fear of officious intermeddlers, but also because the unjust factor approach allows little room for such claims. The payer will normally neither be mistaken nor expect a consideration which then fails. Compulsion offers the best chance for the payer, but only within its rather limited ambit, namely that the payer was forced to pay the third party. The same question would be more open if English law were to switch to the absence of basis approach proposed by Birks.[76]

German law has taken a more relaxed approach towards such payers. Section 267 BGB generally allows anyone to perform any obligation towards the creditor and makes an exception only for a performance which is owed in person. Consent of the debtor is not required. The creditor may refuse acceptance if the debtor disagrees, but not otherwise. As regards a right of the payer to recover from the debtor, this is largely regulated outside unjustified enrichment in German law.

Before we take a closer look at the mechanisms for recovery, it should be clarified that a party who has performed what the debtor owed to the creditor will normally be unable to recover from the creditor, because this is performance which is supported by a valid cause. The English case of *Aiken v Short* may serve as an illustration.[77]

[75] For a comparative analysis, see Daniel Friedmann and Nili Cohen, 'Payment of Another's Debt', in: *International Encyclopedia of Comparative Law*, Vol. 10 Ch. 10 (1991); Hector MacQueen, 'Payment of Another's Debt', in: *Unjustified Enrichment: Key Issues in Comparative Perspective*, 458ff; Charles Mitchell, 'Claims in Unjustified Enrichment to Recover Money Paid Pursuant to a Common Liability', (2001) 5 ELR 186 (pp. 193–197 on German law).

[76] Birks, *Unjust Enrichment*, 158–159 (covering some situations); Maier, 'No Basis: A Comparative Analysis', in: *Mapping the Law*, 359–361.

[77] *Aiken v Short* (1856) 1 H&N 210.

In this case, the claimant bank paid to Carter what Short owed to Carter in the mistaken belief of having a good security for the claim. Under both German and English law, the bank cannot recover from Carter. Under the unjust factor approach in English law, the explanation is complicated, in particular since any causative mistake is in principle sufficient to call for reversal of an enrichment. Unless *Aiken v Short* is overruled, a defence of 'good consideration' must be accepted, which would essentially be another way of saying that mistake is not sufficient if the enrichment is supported by a legal basis.[78] The German approach towards this case is straightforward. The bank's payment was supported by a valid legal ground, and that is the end of any claim by the bank against Carter.

1. *Cessio legis*

It has been mentioned above that most cases of what English law calls subrogation and treats as part of unjust enrichment are not enrichment cases in German law.[79] Whenever a *cessio legis*—an assignment by law—operates, the debtor is not relieved from any liability. Rather than being discharged, the debtor's obligation towards the creditor is transferred wholly or in part to the payer, who takes the place which was previously held by the creditor. This applies, for instance, to joint and several debtors, guarantors who pay instead of the principal debtor, insurers who compensate a tort victim, and persons who save the security which they have provided for a claim by paying a creditor who has a privileged security.

2. Contractual claim for recovery

In many cases, the person who performs instead of the debtor will do so under a contractual arrangement with that party, such as an insurance or banking contract, or an agency agreement. In these cases, the rules on mandate, or other contractual rules, are likely to allow the payer to recover from the debtor. For mandate, this is regulated by § 670 BGB, which generally allows for recovery of reasonable expenditure.

[78] See Virgo, 158, 175.
[79] See above, Chapter 1, section 4.6.

3. *Negotiorum gestio*

There are also cases in which the solution must be found in *negotiorum gestio*, for example if the claimant learns that the defendant, a relative or friend who is away for some time, unconsciously bounced a cheque or forgot to pay the household insurance premiums, and then steps in for the defendant. There is one decision in which the *Bundesgerichtshof* has even stated that someone who is paying the debt of another party will usually do so in carrying out that other party's business. [80] Therefore if the other requirements of *negotiorum gestio* are met—in particular if this performance corresponds with the actual or presumed intention of the debtor—the payer will usually be allowed to recover from the debtor under *negotiorum gestio* rules.

4. *Rückgriffskondiktion*

Psychology tells us that people who suffer from compulsive cleaning disorder—a disorder which may be more common in Germany than it is in England—will have one dirty corner in their otherwise sparkling, spotless, and germ-free house. If German law can properly be criticized for being overly concerned with conceptual consistency, the *Rückgriffskondiktion* or restitution by way of recourse can be held out as an example of the dirty corner where some unfinished business is hidden away and seems to defy the general concept. Perhaps the *Rückgriffskondiktion* is best described as a rag-bag of potential, rare cases which genuinely fall outside the *Leistungskondiktion*, and of other cases which are placed within enrichment in another way in order to avoid the defence of § 814 BGB, or in order to find a different defendant.

There are in particular three situations left to be covered by the *Rückgriffskondiktion* as the third of the generally accepted categories of 'enrichment in another way' under § 812 para. 1 sent. 1 BGB.

In the first situation, the claimant mistakenly believed he or she was obliged to perform towards a third party an obligation which was actually owed by the defendant. It has been mentioned above

[80] BGH 20.06.1968, Betriebs-Berater 1969, 194, confirmed in BGH 22.10.1975, Juristen-Zeitung 1976, 24–25.

(Chapter 2, section 1) that the *Leistungskondiktion* does not cover the case where the main shareholder pays her company's fiscal debt in the mistaken belief that she is jointly and severally liable for the debt. She cannot recover from the tax authorities because the fiscal debt provides the valid legal ground, and not from the company under the *Leistungskondiktion*, since she intentionally and purposefully performed what she thought was her own obligation towards the tax authorities, not towards the company. This is the hour of the *Rückgriffskondiktion*. Most would agree that she can recover under this *condictio* from the company.

This leads to the second and more problematic situation where the *Rückgriffskondiktion* serves to create a second defendant. In one such case (case no. 9), an accident insurance company mistakenly paid the medical bill for an 11-year-old girl and then succeeded in suing the father in recovery under the *Rückgriffskondiktion*.[81] In this case nothing would have prevented the insurance company from suing the actual recipient of the unjustified performance, namely the girl, under the regular *Leistungskondiktion*. For this reason, the Appeal Court had disallowed the action, but the *Bundesgerichtshof* granted restitution on equitable considerations, thus effectively allowing the insurance to leapfrog to the father. In a similar case, the *Bundesgerichtshof* ruled that a claimant could waive the right to claim restitution from the recipient and instead sue a defendant who had actually owed the debt which the claimant had mistakenly paid.[82] This would ultimately give the claimant a choice between two defendants, a situation which the *Leistungskondiktion* has been designed to prevent. We will return to this issue shortly.

The third situation concerns cases where the claimant paid the defendant's debt towards a third party in full knowledge that there was no obligation to do so. Precisely because of this full knowledge, § 814 BGB would defeat any action under the general performance-based enrichment clause, so that courts allow recovery under enrichment in another way.[83] One problem with this approach is that the defence of § 814 BGB should apply to all cases in which the claimant

[81] BGH 15.5.1986, NJW 1986, 2700; below, Chapter 10, section 9 (translation).
[82] BGH 14.7.1964, NJW 1964, 1898.
[83] BGH 22.10.1975, WM 1975, 1235.

has performed for the purpose of fulfilling an obligation. The wording of § 814 BGB makes no mention of the claimant's views as to whether it was the claimant or a third party who owed performance, and thus covers the payment of another party's debt.

The *Rückgriffskondiktion* is thus used to escape certain limitations of performance-based restitution in situations in which the enrichment clearly occurred by performance. It is untidy, to say the least, to tuck this into non-performance-based restitution as a third alternative next to infringement (*Eingriff*) and expenditure (*Verwendung*). The *Rückgriffskondiktion* should instead be removed from the realm of 'enrichment in another way', and be reformulated as exceptions to the general rules on performance.

The first situation, in which the claimant mistakenly believed he or she was obliged to perform towards a third party an obligation which actually was owed by the defendant, could be treated as an exception to the rule that the notion of performance as an intentional shift of wealth from one party to another with a particular obligation in mind, identifies not only the right claimant but also the right defendant. We have seen that the main purposes of basing unjustified enrichment on performance are to protect parties against insolvency risks they have not assumed, against losing defences, and against being subjected to defences which parties have acquired from relationships with third parties.[84] None of these purposes is served if in our example the shareholder cannot recover from the company.

The second situation could be treated in the same way, as an exception to the rule that leapfrogging is not allowed. Such an exception can be made when none of the above-mentioned dangers can materialize. It is noteworthy that the policy considerations on which the *Bundesgerichtshof* relied for allowing direct recourse against the father of the 11-year-old girl (case no. 9)[85] are indeed largely identical with those three performance-related policy considerations.[86]

[84] Canaris, 'Bereicherungsausgleich'; Larenz and Canaris, 204ff; above, Chapter 3, section 2.

[85] BGH 15.5.1986, NJW 1986, 2700; below, Chapter 10, section 9 (translation).

[86] Above, Chapter 3, section 2.

The third situation—avoiding the 'no mistake' defence of § 814 BGB—is not helped by moving this from performance-based restitution to 'enrichment in another way' restitution, because the wording of this provision applies also to the latter. If there are good reasons for making this exception, they would be equally as good if this were understood to form part of performance-based restitution.

In summary, the German law of unjustified enrichment has no need for this dirty corner, the *Rückgriffskondiktion*. Time has come for a spring clean.

6

The Measure of Restitutionary Liability

The measure of liability in unjustified enrichment is governed by §§ 818–820 BGB. The wording of these provisions makes no distinction between different types of unjustified enrichment claims. It is indeed the prevailing belief that §§ 818ff BGB contain a unitary system of consequences of liability which covers all of unjustified enrichment, including both performance and non-performance-based restitution, even if strong criticism of this view has been mounted by a number of authors.[1] The focal point for this discussion is gain-based restitution, about which more will be said below.

To a certain extent, this mirrors the previous discussion on whether performance and non-performance-based restitution flow from the same or from two different concepts of unjustified enrichment, where the opposite view (two different concepts) has gained the upper hand—again, following the wording of the BGB, which in § 812 BGB distinguishes between enrichment by performance and enrichment in another way. From a common law perspective, it is also worth noting that there is no 'proprietary divide' in the measure of restitutionary liability in German law. The measure of recovery under §§ 818–820 BGB does not depend on whether any proprietary right is involved.[2] It is only by way of concurrent liability that in situations of unauthorized possession the owner/possessor model will prevail and provide some (mostly marginally) different solutions.[3]

[1] See Schäfer for a historical analysis of this discussion.

[2] It should be noted that it may be easier to obtain gain-based damages under the *Eingriffskondiktion*, which, however, is not limited to infringements of proprietary rights. See below, section 3, and above, Chapter 5, section 2.

[3] See above, Chapter 5, section 2.1 for the owner/possessor model, and below, Chapter 7, section 5 for rules on concurrent liability.

Sections 818–820 are characterized by a three-step approach. The first 'measure' of enrichment is not truly a measure, but the actual object of enrichment, rather than its value. Put into two words, what must be returned is the 'object received', indicating a clear preference for restitution of that object in kind (below, section 1). This object is not normally replaced by other objects, at least not to the degree allowed by the English law of tracing (below, section 2). The gain which the defendant has made through the enrichment is normally relevant only if this can be considered to be a benefit associated with the enrichment, rather than as a result of the skill or luck of the defendant (below, section 3). If the initial object of enrichment cannot be returned, it is replaced by step 2, namely 'value received', and the recipient must pay that value (below, section 3). Step 3 turns this into 'value remaining' in the majority of situations, taking account of the disenrichment which has occurred since the time of receipt (below, section 5). This measure of liability is increased for defendants who are *mala fide* or for other reasons less worthy of protection. They cannot rely on disenrichment, and therefore remain at step 2, 'value received'. They are also exposed to some additional liability (below, section 6).

It has been mentioned above that §§ 818ff BGB offer a set of remedies which is borrowed by other areas of the law,[4] just as unjustified enrichment borrows from its main rival, the owner/possessor model, for situations in which the defendant seems less worthy of protection.[5]

1. Restitution in kind

Just as specific performance is the primary remedy in the German law of contract, restitution in kind (*Naturalrestitution)* is the primary remedy in the German law of restitution under § 818 paras 1 and 2 BGB, and also in the law of damages (which applies to contract and tort law) under § 249 BGB.[6] However, restitution in kind as a measure of damages differs from restitution in kind as a measure

[4] Above, Chapter 1, section 3.2.
[5] Below, section 6.2.
[6] See also Reuter and Martinek, 516.

of restitution. The former is concerned with making good loss, the latter with reversing an unjustified enrichment. If A fraudulently obtains from B, and then publishes without B's consent, a picture which gives the false impression of B being caught in a compromising situation, restitution in kind under tort law (§§ 823, 249 BGB) would include a public declaration that the impression is indeed false, while restitution in kind under unjustified enrichment (§ 818 BGB) would require A to return the picture to B.

Section 818 para. 2 BGB makes it clear that restitution other than in kind can be required or may be given only if the defendant is unable to provide restitution in kind. In our example, the picture itself can be given back in kind, but not any benefit which is associated with having published the compromising picture. The precise extent to which the restitution claim primarily focuses on the object (*Gegenstand*) or on the value (*Wert*) of the enrichment is still under debate; the wording of § 818 para. 2 suggests the former.[7] From an English perspective, however, the German position seems very much object- rather than value-oriented. It has been mentioned above that, contrary to popular belief, even an object without any commercial value must be given up under § 812 BGB as long as restitution in kind is possible, such as an IOU which has been proved to be inaccurate.[8]

In cases of restitution based on performance, it can generally be said that anything which will give the performance back to the claimant is considered restitution in kind. If performance consisted in payment of a sum of money, repayment will also be considered restitution in kind, just as a claim for payment of the purchase price in a sales contract is considered a claim for (specific) performance of the contract.

Restitution in kind will thus often cover situations which appear to have little connection with making something good by its nature rather than by financial recompense. If, for instance, the unjustified enrichment consists in the defendant having acquired a claim against the claimant without a legal ground, §§ 812, 818 BGB will require the defendant to release this claim to the claimant, by which the situation prior to the unjustified enrichment will be restored. This entitlement

[7] For an account of this discussion see Reuter and Martinek, 516–523.

[8] Above, Chapter 2, section 2.1.

to restitution can also be used as a defence under § 821 BGB, should the defendant decide to sue under the original claim.

2. Tracing and substitution

With its focus on the object rather than the value of the enrichment, German law could perhaps be expected to provide for extensive rules whereby the initial object of an unjustified enrichment can be replaced by another object, which would serve to keep the focus away from the financial aspect. That, however, is not the position under German law. The fallback position is that to the extent that the defendant is unable to provide restitution in kind, this is replaced by restitution of value. Some exceptions are allowed by virtue of property law rules on mixing and mingling (see 1 below), and by rules on substitution (see 2 below).

1. Tracing and related proprietary techniques

Tracing in German law is disappointingly narrow from an English perspective, and from a purely proprietary viewpoint it is possible to say that it barely exists. If tracing consists in giving the previous owner of object A title to object B on the ground that object B has replaced object A, there is very little indeed which is comparable with German law. Such tracing exists if chattels are inseparably combined into a new object, or become inseparably mixed or intermingled, as provided for by §§ 947 and 948 BGB. In these cases, the owners of the combined or mixed objects become joint owners of the new object. However, as case no. 5 (the young bulls case discussed above) illustrates, if chattels (the bulls) are processed into new products (meat and sausages), the owner of the processed object loses property and must rely on unjustified enrichment by virtue of §§ 950, 951 BGB.[9] This is, of course, the *specificatio* of Roman law, which has also had some influence on English law.

[9] BGH 11.1.1971, BGHZ 55, 176, below, Chapter 10, section 5 (translation), discussed above, Chapter 3, section 2.

Tracing into anything other than physical objects is virtually impossible. If A steals €1,000 in banknotes from B, opens a new bank account and deposits the €1,000 in that account, B has no property in this sum. B cannot trace her banknotes into this account. The bank account will be perceived as a mere claim which A has against the bank.

No assistance is to be expected from trusts in providing proprietary remedies. Trusts in the English sense do not exist.[10] Fiduciary relationships over someone else's corporeal property are accepted but will always require that possession in the property has passed from the settlor to the trustee. Constructive trusts do not exist at all. There are a few functional equivalents to what English law would call equitable liens, in the sense that in some situations liens will arise by virtue of the law without being negotiated between the parties. For example, landlords have statutory liens under § 559 BGB in chattels which tenants have brought into a dwelling. These liens will secure any outstanding rent.[11] However, courts cannot attribute a lien to a party on grounds of equity. Liens must be provided by statute.

There is a remarkable chiasmus as regards equitable considerations in the German and English laws of obligations and of property. The German law of obligations, as interpreted by the courts, appears to be drenched in equity and good faith, and, if push comes to shove, barely any statutory provision seems to be safe from being overridden on the ground of good faith. English law has traditionally frozen equity in a separate category of case law with fixed and limited institutions (such as trusts) or remedies (such as an account of profits). Outside equity, English law will often rather apply the maxim of 'hard cases make bad law' than water down the law of obligations.

We can observe the reverse phenomenon in property law. German law suddenly becomes rigid. There is a fixed and definite list of property rights, and with very few exceptions it will prevent the smallest

[10] Many of the situations for which a trust is required or particularly useful under English law are covered by German contract law, which has never had a doctrine of privity of contract, and which allows for gratuitous contracts such as donation. More on gratuitous contract and their relevance for unjustified enrichment below, Chapter 9, section 2.3.

[11] See RG 1.12.1922, RGZ 105, 408 for an interesting unjustified enrichment case which centred around this lien.

drop of equity from oiling the wheels. Legal certainty in the interest of the public will usually prevail over other considerations. On the other hand, English law becomes incredibly flexible in property law. Proprietary rights are extended by tracing to a range of potential additional defendants.[12] Resulting trusts, equitable liens, and even constructive trusts are created and granted in order to achieve the desired outcome in a given case.[13] To the continental lawyer, nothing seems more flexible in English law than that of trusts. However, as the recent case of *Yeoman's Row Management Limited and another v Cobbe* shows, English law currently tries to reduce some of this flexibility in favour of clarity.[14]

Be that as it may, restitutionary remedies *in personam* must cover many of these situations in German law. One consequence of this orientation on personal claims is that German law makes it extremely difficult to sue in restitution anyone other than the person who was initially enriched. In principle, there are only two exceptions: third parties can be sued if they have obtained the enrichment gratuitously from the enriched party under § 816 para. 1 sent. 2, or under § 822.[15] It should be remembered, though, that the concept of performance can serve to find defendants other than those who were most directly enriched.[16] Another exception will occasionally be provided by the following rules on substitution.

2. Substitution

Substitution is a technique by which, for the purpose of restitution under contract law[17] or unjustified enrichment law (but not as a matter of property law!), the initial object of enrichment is replaced or

[12] See e.g. Lionel Smith, *The Law of Tracing* (1997).

[13] See e.g. Robert Chambers, *Resulting Trusts* (1997).

[14] *Yeoman's Row Management Limited and another v Cobbe* [2008] UKHL 55, rejecting both proprietary estoppel and a constructive trust, the latter in contrast with *Hussey v Palmer* [1972] 1 WLR 1286 (CA).

[15] For § 816 para. 1 sent. 2 BGB, see above, Chapter 5, section 2.4, for § 822 BGB, below, section 5.3.

[16] Above, Chapter 2, section 2.2.

[17] See above, Chapter 3, section 3.2.C.

supplemented by another object. Within unjustified enrichment, substitution occurs under § 818 para. 1 BGB. The replacement is commonly referred to as *Surrogat*. If the initial object of enrichment is destroyed, has been damaged, or withheld from the defendant, anything that the defendant has obtained on the basis of such destruction, damage, or withholding can be claimed by the defendant. Dawson once thought that substitution was 'a loophole through which tracing could be introduced',[18] but if that possibility existed it has failed to materialize. It is only within a limited set of circumstances that substitution can arrive at results which are similar to tracing under English law.

Substitution under § 818 para. 1 BGB does not occur if a *bona fide* defendant has freely given up the initial enrichment, for example goods in which the defendant had acquired title, to a third party against payment. Such payment does not substitute for the goods.[19]

On the other hand, substitution generally operates for claims which the defendant has acquired against a third party for compensation, restitution, or surrender. The claimant can require the defendant to assign any such claims under §§ 812, 818 BGB, so that eventually the claimant will be in a position to sue a third party. Thus, leapfrog claims along a line of several shifts of wealth are possible if A shifts wealth onto B without a legal ground, and B shifts the same wealth onto C and also without a legal ground. In this case, B is enriched by a restitutionary claim against C, which A in turn can require B to give up. The end result is that A can sue C. Of course, C remains free to rely against A on any defences C could have invoked against B. Nevertheless, some cases of a successful so-called double *condictio* or *Doppelkondiktion* can be found.

In one such case, A (the claimant) was a bank who agreed to give a loan to B (the defendant).[20] The money was to be paid directly to C,

[18] Dawson, 149, referring to substitution under § 281 (now § 285) BGB.

[19] Confirmed in spite of some academic criticism by BGH 11.10.1979, BGHZ 75, 203, where, however, the defendant was *mala fide*. Section 816 BGB applies if the defendant did not have title in the goods (see above, Chapter 5, section 2.4), § 819 to *mala fide* defendants, and § 819 para. 4 to defendants against whom a claim is pending (below, section 6.1); such defendants are required to give up the payment which they have received in exchange.

[20] BGH 15.3.1990, ZIP 1990, 915.

who—with the full knowledge of A, but probably not of B—intended to use the money to operate a brothel on a ship in the Mediterranean. C became insolvent, and A sued B for return of the money. A could not succeed in contract, because the loan contract was void on the ground of illegality.[21] However, A could sue B in restitution for performance (because B was, probably, *bona fide*, the *in pari turpitudine* rule in § 817 sent. 2 BGB did not directly apply).[22] B's enrichment was reduced to her restitutionary claim against C therefore A could require B to relinquish the claim.

Equally, substitution occurs under § 818 para. 1 BGB if the unjustified enrichment consists in a right which has been realized or transformed. If the initial object of enrichment consists in a lottery ticket, the ticket will be substituted by any prize which the ticket attracts. However, substitution does not occur if the enriched party exchanges the enrichment for another object under a contract between the enriched party and a third party, unless this is covered by § 816 BGB. Therefore, if A receives a payment without legal ground and buys a lottery ticket with that money, any prize which the ticket gains is no substitute for the original enrichment, and therefore need not be given up.[23]

We will now look at the consequences which this would have on some English cases. In *Banque Belge pour l'Etranger v Hambrouck*,[24] the defendant obtained credit on his bank account by forging cheques at the expense of the claimant bank. He withdrew money from the account and gave it to the second defendant, his mistress, who placed the money in her own account with a different bank. The claimant bank was allowed to trace into that account. No tracing would have occurred under German law, but what about substitution? The money which Hambrouck withdrew from his account was a substitute for the credit which he had obtained against his bank. German law would consider him the owner of the banknotes. By giving the notes to his

[21] Section 134 BGB in conjunction with § 180a StGB. Section 180a StGB has since been reformed and makes running a brothel a criminal offence only if prostitutes are kept in situations of personal or economic dependency.

[22] For this defence, see above, Chapter 4, section 3.

[23] Staudinger-Lorenz § 818 no. 17; this follows from RG 24.3.1915, RGZ 86, 343, 347 and RG 16.2.1921, RGZ 101, 389, 391, although these cases did not concern lottery tickets.

[24] *Banque Belge pour l'Etranger v Hambrouck* [1921] 1 KB 321 (CA).

mistress, he transferred title, but not at the expense of the bank in the sense of § 816 BGB, since he was the owner. (Similarly, no claim would arise against the mistress under § 822 BGB, because Hambrouck was not *bona fide*.[25]) Did Hambrouck receive anything in exchange? It is possible to consider a claim in unjustified enrichment. Such a claim could arise under § 812 BGB if there was no underlying valid contract of donation between Hambrouck and his mistress. Even if such a contract were to be void on the ground of immorality under § 138 BGB (possible at the time, but at present rather doubtful), this would still leave the problem of Hambrouck's own wrongdoing as a defence under § 817 BGB. Therefore, the claimant would already have found it difficult to sue the mistress, let alone her bank. And *Lipkin Gorman v Karpnale Ltd* would have been a non-starter.[26] The case concerned a certain Cass, a partner in the claimants' firm of solicitors, who had lost large sums which he had drawn from the claimants' account by gambling at the defendants' casino. First, under German law there could not have been substitution into gambling gains or losses because Cass had gambled out of his own motion. Secondly, Cass had no claim in unjustified enrichment against the defendants. While the gambling agreement would not have been enforceable under German law, it would, once completed, provide a legal ground for the casino to retain the money under § 762 para. 1 sent. 2 BGB.[27] Therefore Cass had no claim against the defendants which could have substituted for Lipkin Gorman's claims against Cass. Finally, § 816 BGB would not have operated because the casino did not acquire the money gratuitously.[28] *Lipkin Gorman* thus illustrates how German law keeps unjustified enrichment within failed relationships, in particular in order to attribute insolvency risks to the party which assumed them. It can be argued that Lipkin Gorman were in a much better position both to assess the risk of entrusting

25 See below, section 5.3.

26 *Lipkin Gorman v Karpnale Ltd* [1991] 2 AC 548 (HL).

27 See above, Chapter 2, section 6.2.D.

28 BGH 25.4.1967, BGHZ 47, 393, departing from BGH 12.7.1962, BGHZ 37, 363, where an action similar to the one in *Lipkin Gorman* had been allowed under § 816 BGB. See generally, Carsten Zülch, 'Bona Fide Purchase, Property and Restitution: Lipkin Gorman v Karpnale in German Law', in: *The Limits of Restitutionary Claims*, 106–140. For § 816, see above, Chapter 5, section 2.4.

Cass with their client's account and of Cass becoming insolvent than the casino could ever have been.

3. Secondary benefits and gain-based recovery

We have already seen above that gain-based recovery, which has attracted much discussion in English law,[29] is not understood to be the standard measure of liability in the German law of unjustified enrichment, which instead focuses on the initial object by which the defendant has been enriched. There are nevertheless some inroads which German law has made into measuring the enrichment which a party has to surrender by the gain which that party has made. The most important ones are the increased liability of *mala fide* defendants (below, section 6.2), the inclusion of secondary benefits which the defendant has derived from the enrichment, and the provision of § 816 para. 1 sent. 1 BGB (above, Chapter 5, section 2.4).

Within its area of application,[30] § 816 para. 1 sent. 1 BGB generally includes gains which the defendant has made by disposing of the object of the enrichment. If the defendant receives possession (but not ownership) of goods under a contract which does not materialize, and sells them on at a good profit to an unsuspecting third party, the owner of the goods can claim the purchase price which the defendant has received. If the third party has not yet paid, the claimant may instead require the defendant to assign this claim for the purchase price.

For other unjustified enrichment claims, § 818 para. 1 extends the scope of what is owed to benefits which the defendant has gained from using the enrichment. We have seen above in the context of terminated contracts that German law uses for this purpose the concept of *Nutzungen*, defined in § 100 BGB as 'the fruits of a physical object or a right as well as the advantages which is offered by the use of the physical object or the right'. If D has obtained an unjustified title to E's house,[31] and rents the house to a tenant or lives in the house

[29] See in particular Edelman, *Gain-based Damages*.

[30] See above, Chapter 5, section 2.4.

[31] If D gains possession of the house without acquiring ownership, the owner/possessor model will prevail. See above, Chapter 5, section 2.1.

herself, the rent will be classed as fruits, and her having lived there will count as an advantage. Reasonable expenses can be deducted from these secondary benefits. This would also cover the so-called 'Kentucky cave case',[32] in which the defendant admitted the fee-paying public to an onyx cave which was accessible from the defendant's property, but of which approximately one-third belonged to land owned by the claimant's estate.

Benefits also include interest, provided it was actually gained on the amount which the defendant received at the claimant's expense. If the defendant is a business, a presumption will operate in favour of the claimant that the defendant has gained interest at a rate which is typical under the given circumstances.[33] Likewise, if the defendant has used a monetary enrichment for paying off debts, the interest which the defendant has thus saved is considered a benefit which the defendant must give up to the claimant.[34]

Taken together, this implies that any gain made by use of the initial enrichment will normally have to be given up—with the exception of a gain made by selling the initial enrichment outside the scope of § 816 para. 1 sent. 1. This may serve as a basic rule for the basic measure of recovery, but needs to be qualified in a number of situations.

First, when looking at German court practice, the above appears to reflect forensic reality mainly in subtractive enrichment, in particular within performance-based restitution. For some situations, this has been the subject of some dispute. For example, if the object of enrichment consists of an entire business (as would be the case if the contract for the sale of the business is invalid), must the defendant return not only the business itself, but also an account of the profits? Earlier cases tended to reject this, arguing that profits depended on the defendant's personal ability and achievement.[35] Over the years, however, the *Bundesgerichtshof* has changed its mind, and will now regularly require

[32] *Edwards v Lee's Administrator* 96 SW 2d 1028 (Kentucky CA 1936), used as an example e.g. by Birks, *Unjust Enrichment*, 84.

[33] BGH 4.6.1975, BGHZ 64, 322.

[34] BGH 6.3.1998, BGHZ 138, 160.

[35] E.g. BGH 25.9.1952, BGHZ 7, 208, 218.

the recipient to hand over the entire business together with the profits which were made.[36]

Outside subtractive enrichment, the situation may be different, in particular for intellectual property rights.[37] It has been mentioned above that courts will usually allow the claimant to recover for an appropriate licence fee (representing the value of the initial enrichment), and not generally for any profit which the defendant has made by using the claimant's intellectual property right.[38] Such a restriction may be problematic in light of a concept of benefits which includes those derived from a right. It has, however, also been mentioned that the courts have traditionally allowed for an account of profits if the infringement was intentional—not normally using unjustified enrichment for this purpose, but claims in unjustified *negotiorum gestio*.[39] Defendants may also be required to disgorge profits made through violations of intellectual property under several statutory provisions. Section 97 *Urheberrechtsgesetz* (UrhG, Copyright Act) allows courts to 'consider' the profits made when assessing 'compensation' for negligent and intentional violations of copyright. The same is true for designs and § 42 *Geschmacksmustergesetz* (Designs Acts), patents under § 139 *Patentgesetz* (PatG, Patent Act), and trademarks under § 14 *Markengesetz* (MarkenG, Trademarks Act).

The wider academic debate on gain-based enrichment as a general measure of recovery (i.e. including gains made by selling the initial enrichment) is ongoing.[40] Proponents of a general gain-based recovery point to § 816 para. 1 sent. 1 and would prefer to see this generalized for consistency. Opponents point to the different regime for *mala fide* defendants and wish to keep full gain-based recovery for situations of increased liability, § 816 para. 1 sent. 1, and intentional infringements.

[36] BGH 5.7.2006, NJW 2006, 2847.

[37] It should be borne in mind that many situations in which the defendant has used chattels or real property belonging to the claimant will be covered by the owner/possessor model, see above, Chapter 5, section 2.1.

[38] Above, Chapter 5, section 2.2.A.

[39] Above, Chapter 5, section 2.3.

[40] See e.g. Lieb in *Münchener Kommentar*, § 818 nos 18–24.

4. Restitution in money and methods of valuation

If the defendant is not in a position to provide restitution in kind, the value of the enrichment will be used as the measure of recovery under § 818 para. 2 BGB. This concerns services, construction of buildings, transport, the use of facilities, and many other situations.

1. Objective methods of valuation

Section 818 para. 2 BGB speaks of *Wert* (value), without indicating the standard by which this value is to be ascertained. The courts have for long held that the valuation standard is objective,[41] i.e. does not depend on the subjective appreciation by the parties.[42]

But there is already disagreement about whether enrichment is to be measured by the market value of the service, construction, transport, use, etc. which has been provided, or by the increase which the defendant's assets have achieved by the enrichment. The *Bundesgerichtshof* has for some time been oscillating between both approaches. On the one hand, the normal fee will indicate the value of a service for the purpose of measuring the enrichment.[43] But the same court has also repeatedly held that unjustified enrichment claims must generally not reverse enrichment beyond the actual increase in the defendant's assets, with the proper measure being the balance between increases and decreases in the value of the defendant's assets which are associated with the enrichment.[44] These two ways of measuring enrichment will usually coincide if the defendant has actually saved expense by the claimant's performance or other expenditure, but that will frequently not be the case.

41 RG 3.5.1935, RGZ 147, 396, 398; BGH 27.2.1952, BGHZ 5, 197.

42 The opposite view which favours subjective valuation was pioneered by Hans-Georg Koppensteiner, 'Probleme des bereicherungsrechtlichen Wertersatzes (II)', Neue Juristische Wochenschrift 1971, 1769ff and remains controversial in the literature, see Lieb in *Münchener Kommentar* § 818 no. 44 (who advocates an objective approach).

43 BGH 1.2.1962, BGHZ 36, 321, confirmed in BGH 25.6.1962, BGHZ 37, 258.

44 BGH 19.1.1951, BGHZ 1, 75; BGH 7.1.1971, NJW 1971; below, Chapter 10, section 7 (translation).

The two approaches came to loggerheads in the aforementioned underage flyer case (case no. 7).[45] In that instance, the minor's assets were certainly not increased by flying to New York and back instead of leaving the plane at his scheduled destination in Hamburg. Yet the *Bundesgerichtshof* allowed full recovery of the usual cost for both legs of the journey.

2. Subjective methods of valuation

This case can at the same time serve as an opener to the question of subjective methods of valuation. Subjective valuation is used here as a generic term for techniques which replace a market-based approach to measuring enrichment by a subjective approach from the perspective of the defendant. This can also imply that the enrichment is worth less, and perhaps even worth more than an objective increase or decrease in the assets of the defendant. In English legal terminology, the former is connected with the term subjective devaluation,[46] while the latter can become relevant under whatever may be left of the doctrine of free acceptance.[47]

Let us add three more examples to the case of the underage flyer (case no. 7). What if the minor had been on a flight to Hamburg and the plane had been hijacked and flown to New York? What if the minor had fallen asleep and thus failed to leave the plane at Hamburg? What if the minor had mistakenly been put on the wrong plane to start with, i.e. a plane to New York rather than to Hamburg? In all these cases the minor would have obtained a flight to New York without a legal ground. In all these cases, the minor would not have saved any expenses. Therefore the *Bundesgerichtshof*'s more restrictive approach to valuation would save the minor from restitutionary claims by the airline. But the same result could also be obtained by a subjective method of valuation. In our examples, the minor did not want to go to New York, and for this reason the trip was worthless if not a nuisance. Subjective devaluation could easily defeat the claim.

[45] BGH 7.1.1971, NJW 1971, 609; below, Chapter 10, section 7 (translation); discussed above, Chapter 2, section 2.1 and Chapter 5, section 3.2.

[46] See e.g. Birks, *Unjust Enrichment*, 54.

[47] Goff and Jones, 1–019 to 1–022; Tettenborn 16–17; critical Burrows 402–407.

At the same time, subjective valuation could give an answer why the minor was correctly held liable in the real case: because by sneaking back on board, the minor had made clear that this was an enrichment which he wanted, even if he did not intend to pay for it. The English doctrine of free acceptance, which demonstrates that there are subjective methods of establishing not only of defeating an enrichment, might thus come to the aid of those German legal scholars who favour a subjective approach for measuring enrichment.[48]

Subjective valuation as a tool for defeating an unjustified enrichment claim tends to surface in particular in the context of unauthorized expenditure on someone else's property. If the expenditure has led to an increase in the market value of the property, any objective approach will find it very difficult to defeat a claim in restitution for the increased value. This would effectively force the results of contracts onto the owner and thus undermine the owner's free choice whether to enter into the contracts.

3. Imposed enrichments

In the same way, unjustified enrichment could seriously disturb the equilibrium which the law of contract attempts to establish between the parties by denying the existence of a contractual obligation. In other words, unjustified enrichment would no longer remedy unwanted results created by other areas of law, and instead end up creating results which other areas of the law aim to prevent. In German law, these matters are discussed under the heading 'imposed enrichment' (*aufgedrängte Bereicherung*).

In one leading case,[49] the claimant took a lease of the defendant's agricultural property and erected a massive building without permission from the defendant, who then terminated the lease. The claimant requested that the defendant should pay for the value of the building. The *Bundesgerichtshof* disallowed the claim, arguing that the building was imposed on the defendant against his will, and that

[48] Hans-Georg Koppensteiner, 'Probleme des bereicherungsrechtlichen Wertersatzes (II)', Neue Juristische Wochenschrift 1971, 1769; see also Lieb in *Münchener Kommentar* § 818 no. 44.

[49] BGH 21.12.1956, BGHZ 23, 61, below, Chapter 10, section 1 (translation).

the building could be put to commercial use only by incurring considerable additional expense. Rather than paying for the value of the enrichment, the defendant was entitled to remove the building or, if this was unreasonable because of the costs involved, to require the claimant to remove the building. It is noteworthy that, had the same case been decided under present English law, it would have been difficult for the claimant to find even an unjust factor, since his improvement of the land was not based on mistake, nor freely accepted by the defendant, and even failure of consideration would be problematic.

Similar problems can also arise with performance-based unjustified enrichment. A contractor deceives a house-owner into having double glazing installed by pretending that double glazing has recently become a statutory requirement. The law of contract tells us that the house-owner can rescind the contract on the ground of deceit (*arglistige Täuschung*, § 123 BGB) even after the contractor has installed the double glazing. If unjustified enrichment forces the house-owner to pay the contractor a *quantum meruit*, the contract rules on deceit are deprived of their effect. Again, subjective valuation can help: if the owner did not initially want double glazing to be installed, this should equally defeat an unjustified enrichment claim.

5. Disenrichment (change of position)

Section 818 para. 3 BGB provides that restitution is not owed 'to the extent that the recipient is no longer enriched'. What German law calls *Wegfall der Bereicherung* (literally: lapse of enrichment) corresponds with the English notion of change of position.[50] Birks suggested a change of terminology, namely to speak of 'disenrichment' rather than change of position.[51] We will use this term because it better reflects the German approach.

[50] For a detailed comparison, see James Gordley, 'Restitution without enrichment? Change of position and *Wegfall der Bereicherung*', in: Johnston and Zimmermann, 227ff.

[51] Birks, *Unjust Enrichment*, 208; see Gareth Jones, 'Some Thoughts on Change of Position', in: *Mapping the Law*, 65ff. For a comparative analysis, see James Gordley, 'Restitution without enrichment? Change of position and *Wegfall der Bereicherung*', in: *Unjustified Enrichment: Key Issues in Comparative Perspective*, 227ff.

In German law, disenrichment is so wide a defence that many have doubted whether it is a defence at all or rather a rule, i.e. whether remaining value is the main rather than the third measure of enrichment in German law.[52] As a consequence, what is said here would have been very surprising to an English lawyer until 1990. However, *Lipkin Gorman v Karpnale Ltd*[53] has bridged much of the former gap.

First and foremost, disenrichment—regardless of whether it is a rule or a defence—is a way of measuring liability (see 1 below). Secondly, the wisdom of allowing a party to rely on disenrichment can be called into question in situations of failed contracts (see 2 below). Thirdly, disenrichment can create a new defendant in some situations (see 3 below).

1. Disenrichment as measure of liability

If the enrichment which the defendant initially received has since been diminished or has disappeared altogether, disenrichment as a measure of liability will limit unjustified enrichment claims to the increase of assets which still remain in the hands of the defendant. In a way, this mirrors and complements gain-based enrichment, which also postpones measuring enrichment beyond the time of initial receipt.

Defendants generally need not show that they have reasonably relied on the enrichment being justified. This is similar to what Burrows calls the wide concept of change of position, the approach taken by English law after *Lipkin Gorman*.[54] *Mala fide* defendants and those against whom a claim under unjustified enrichment is pending are not allowed to rely on disenrichment (below, section 6).

Broadly speaking, most cases fall into one of the following four categories.

1. The enrichment consists in a physical object, and the defendant can show that the object is lost, destroyed, or given away. To the extent that there is no substitution (above, section 2.2), there is disenrichment. *Grosso modo*, the same will apply to choses in action or other rights.

[52] See e.g. Schlechtriem, *Schuldrecht BT*, nos 778–780.
[53] *Lipkin Gorman v Karpnale Ltd* [1991] 2 AC 548 (HL).
[54] Burrows, 512–517.

2. The enrichment consists of a one-off payment. In order to be allowed to rely on disenrichment, the defendant must show that:

(a) the defendant has spent the money, and
(b) the defendant would not have spent money in the same way had it not been for the enrichment.

Furthermore, there must be no substitution or other increase in the defendant's assets which is causally linked with the money being spent.

Blowing the enrichment on a luxury cruise or gambling are textbook examples. However, in one case the *Oberlandesgericht* Hamm disallowed the gambling defence on what were essentially causation arguments.[55] The defendant had tried to defeat an argument that he was *mala fide* by claiming that he had been expecting an outstanding payment from a third party, which he actually received a few weeks after allegedly having lost the claimant's money by gambling. The court held that by not allowing the defendant to rely on disenrichment, the defendant was merely put in the position which would have existed had he not mistaken the source of the payment, in which case he would have wasted his own money.[56]

3. The enrichment consists in continuous overpayment of wages, pensions, maintenance, or similar regular payments. If the defendant can show that he or she has not built up specific savings or other permanent assets as a result of the overpayment, there is a rebuttable presumption—in particular for defendants who are on a low to medium income—that the enrichment has been spent on an improved lifestyle. In one such case (case no. 14), the defendant was a divorcee who had received overpayments of maintenance from her former husband while an action for reducing the maintenance payments was pending.[57] She relied on § 818 para. 2. BGB. The claimant argued that the defendant had used the maintenance payments for paying off debts, and that this amounted to a remaining enrichment. This was in principle accepted, but the defendant was in a position to show that she

[55] OLG Hamm 6.11.1989, NJW-RR 1991, 155.

[56] For a critical view, see Peter. Schlechtriem, 'Rechtsprechungsbericht zum Bereicherungsrecht—Teil 3', Juristen-Zeitung 1993, 185, 189.

[57] BGH 17.6.1992, BGHZ 118, 383; below, Chapter 10, section 14 (translation).

had also continued to pay off the same debts on a lower income. As a consequence, the husband's claim was disallowed.

4. The defendant has incurred expenses for the upkeep or improvement of the enrichment object. To the extent that these cannot be deducted from secondary benefits, they may be deducted under disenrichment.[58]

Both German and English law primarily understand disenrichment or change of position as reflecting a diminution of what the defendant has initially received. This makes it somewhat problematic for considering under disenrichment any decrease in the assets of the defendant which occurred before the defendant received the initial enrichment. There are, however, cases in which a causal link between enrichment and disenrichment can be established even where the enrichment does not precede the disenrichment. This is perhaps best illustrated by *Dextra Bank Trust v Bank of Jamaica*.[59] In this case, the claimant made a payment on the mistaken assumption that this was the payout of a secured loan. The defendant thought it was buying US dollars in exchange for the equivalent in Jamaican dollars, which it had paid out in anticipation to individuals understood to be nominated on behalf of the claimant. One of the questions to be decided was whether the defendant could rely on its payout to the nominated individuals as change of position even though they made the payout before having received the claimant's payment. The Privy Council held that it could. A much more complicated German case can be read in the same way, namely that a party may deduct under § 812 para. 3 assets which it disposed of in reliance on a subsequent enrichment.[60]

2. Disenrichment and counter-restitution

If two parties have performed under a void contract, can one party rely on disenrichment, with the effect that one party must shift back its wealth while the other need not? In German law this is perceived

[58] BGH 11.1.1980, NJW 1980, 1790.

[59] *Dextra Bank Trust v Bank of Jamaica* [2001] UKPC 50.

[60] BGH 21.3.1996, BGHZ 132, 198, 210. But see also BGH 5.11.2002, BGHZ 152, 307, below, Chapter 10, section 16 (translation); discussed above, Chapter 3, section 2. In that case, the defendant believed it was receiving repayment of a loan; its previous payout of what it believed to be a loan could not have been deducted under change of position.

as a specific problem of disenrichment. In English law this was traditionally covered by impossibility of counter-restitution as a bar for rescinding a contract, but this view may be gradually giving way to viewing this also as an issue of change of position.[61]

The first implication of this difference in approach is that impossibility of counter-restitution is no bar to recovery in German law. If counter-restitution is indeed impossible, the question is whether this can amount to disenrichment, or whether performance is replaced by its value under § 818 para. 2. We have seen above that the same question can arise for contracts which have been terminated (rather than being void or voidable), and that § 346 BGB indeed allows for a number of situations in which one party can claim back its own performance without having to provide counter-restitution of the other party's performance. The fallback rule in this area of contract law, however, is not to allow a party to rely on such a lapse of enrichment.[62]

However, as § 818 para. 3 BGB provides no express exception for performances made in exchange for another performance, parties should in principle be allowed to rely on disenrichment if their case falls under unjustified enrichment (rather than contract) rules. If two parties have performed under a void contract, each party can claim back performance, and each party can individually rely on disenrichment if the object of the performance has disappeared, etc. This is the view of the so-called *Zweikondiktionenlehre*, i.e. doctrine of two *condictiones*.[63]

The opposite view is taken by the so-called *Saldotheorie*, or doctrine of the balance.[64] This doctrine is based on the assumption that the contract between the parties, even if it is void, nevertheless provides a tie between performance and counter-performance. This tie prevents a claimant from obtaining restitution for performance while at the same time relying on disenrichment for the defendant's counterclaim. In this situation, the claimant is entitled only to claim the balance between the value of his or her performance and the defendant's

[61] Burrows, 540–541, pointing out that counter-restitution operates irrespective of bad faith of the defendant.

[62] See above, Chapter 3, section 3.2.B.

[63] See e.g. Schlechtriem, *Schuldrecht BT*, no. 795.

[64] For a detailed description of the *Saldotheorie*, see Krebs, *Restitution at the Crossroads*, 101–104.

performance (hence the name of the theory). If, therefore, the claimant has entered into a void agreement under which the claimant was to pay €1,000 for an object which is worth €800, and this object is destroyed while in the claimant's possession, the claimant can claim €1,000 – €800 = €200 from the defendant. From a comparative viewpoint, it is worth noting that Krebs has pointed out that the gradual abolition of the 'total failure of consideration' requirement in English law would require English law to develop rules similar to the German *Saldotheorie*,[65] whereas Burrows, not long after *Lipkin Gorman* and quite independently of the German experience, proposed a variant of the English rule on counter-restitution which was somewhat similar to the *Saldotheorie*.[66] *Goss v Chilcott* can also be read as indicating that change of position is not normally available as a defence in a contractual situation if a claim is based on failure of counter-performance.[67]

In German law, the dispute between the two doctrines remains unresolved, and has created a minefield for practitioners and law students alike. In fact, a leading decision by the German Federal Constitutional Court on judicial review of university examinations was triggered by what examiners had initially marked as an erroneous application of the *Saldotheorie*.[68] It seems that there are few purists who wish to apply their doctrine to each and every case. The *Bundesgerichtshof* will generally apply the *Saldotheorie*,[69] but resort to the *Zweikondiktionenlehre* if the contract in question has been rescinded on the ground of deceit, or is void on the grounds of usury or lack of contractual capacity.[70]

This makes perfect sense if A is deceived into buying a car with serious safety defects, and these defects cause an accident in which the car

[65] Krebs, 121–123; similar Mindy Chen-Wishart, 'In Defence of Unjust Factors: a study of rescission for duress, fraud and exploitation' (2000) Oxford U Comparative L Forum 2 at <http://ouclf.iuscomp.org>, text following note 76.

[66] Andrew Burrows, *The Law of Restitution*, 1st edn (1993), 135–136.

[67] *Goss v Chilcott* [1996] AC 788 (PC); this view has been taken by Robert Stevens, in: Andrew Burrows et al., 'The New Birksian Approach to Unjust Enrichment' (2004) Rest L Rev, 260, 271.

[68] BVerfG 17.4.1991, BVerfGE 84, 34.

[69] For a recent case, see BGH 6.8.2008, Neue Zeitschrift für Miet- und Wohnungsrecht 2008, 886.

[70] See e.g. BGH 16.11.2007, Neue Zeitschrift für Verwaltungsrecht 2008, 591 (deceit); BGH 23.6.2006, NJW 2006, 3054 (usury); BGH 17.1.2003, NJW 2003, 3271 (incapacity).

is written off. In this instance, A can rely on disenrichment and still claim back the purchase price.

However, sometimes the results are less convincing. In case no. 6, the claimant bought a used car from the defendant on the fraudulent misrepresentation that the car had never been in an accident. Three weeks later, the claimant negligently wrote off the car in an accident unrelated to the defects. The *Bundesgerichtshof* allowed the claimant to rely on disenrichment as regards the car, and yet to recover for the full purchase price. The court argued that without the fraudulent representation, the claimant would not have bought that particular car and therefore would not have written it off. The court stated that this was not too remote (*adäquat*) because there was always the possibility of an accident.[71] With great respect, the remoteness argument is fundamentally flawed. The German doctrine of remoteness will specifically prevent this damage from being attributed to the wrongdoing. It is generally recognized that a certain consequence is too remote if the tortfeasor's act did nothing to increase the risk of that consequence occurring.[72] And the risk of writing off that particular car was exactly the same as that of writing off any other car. Cases such as *Carslogie Steamship Co v Royal Norwegian Government* indicate that English law might agree.[73]

The same question remains in dispute in academic writing. Some authors propose fault-based approaches to disenrichment in this situation. Others attach greater importance to the ground why the contract is void.[74]

It should also be borne in mind that the new contractual rules on restitution after termination of contract (above, Chapter 3, section 3.2.B) allow for five exceptions where a party may claim restitution without providing counter-restitution. This could put pressure on the courts to reduce the application of the *Saldotheorie* in order to avoid the situation where rules which make a contract void in order to protect the weaker party will leave that party exposed to the *Saldotheorie* where the same party, if the contract had been valid,

[71] BGH 14.10.1971, BGHZ 57, 137, 141–142; below, Chapter 10, section 6 (translation).

[72] See e.g. BGH 21.2.1961, Versicherungsrecht 1961, 465.

[73] *Carslogie Steamship Co v Royal Norwegian Government* [1952] AC 292 (HL).

[74] For a full discussion, see Staudinger-Lorenz § 818 nos 41–46, including comparisons with French, Swiss, English, and Canadian law.

could have escaped the consequences of the *Saldotheorie* by terminating the contract.

3. Disenrichment and third parties

Section 822 BGB caters for the situation where the *bona fide* enriched party has gratuitously passed on the enrichment to a third party. The initially enriched party can rely on disenrichment, as the initial enrichment has lapsed and no substitution has occurred. In this situation, the claimant can sue directly the third party, which is treated as if it had received the enrichment from the claimant.

However, this comes nowhere near to the English technique of tracing and would not have been of any help in cases such as *Banque Belge pour l'Etranger v Hambrouck* [1921] 1 KB 321 (CA) or *Lipkin Gorman v Karpnale Ltd* [1991] 2 AC 548 (HL). In both of these cases, the parties who were originally enriched were *mala fide* and for this reason could not rely on disenrichment.

There is a German film (*Lina Braake*, 1975) which is based on § 822 BGB, and which has the following plot. An old lady of little means is driven out of her flat by a greedy bank. On the advice of a retired lawyer, she later gains credibility with the bank in the guise of a wealthy businesswoman, and deceives the bank into giving her a large loan. She gives the money to a *bona fide* Italian migrant family whom she has befriended, and who use the money for buying a family home in Sardinia, where the old lady merrily spends her old age as everybody's darling.

The plot is watertight. The bank cannot recover from the lady because she is penniless, and not from the family under § 822 BGB because the lady cannot rely on disenrichment. The script benignly forgets the criminal prosecution to which the lady has exposed herself, and so both family and lady live happily ever after. The *Bundesgerichtshof* confirmed this outcome in 1998: the fact that the (first) *mala fide* recipient is insolvent is not sufficient for making the (second) *bona fide* gratuitous recipient liable under § 822; only if the first recipient can rely on change of position will the second recipient become liable under § 822.[75]

[75] BGH 3.12.1998, NJW 1999, 1026. The court relied on the drafting history of § 822 to show that the legislator intended to exclude a general liability of gratuitous second recipients.

6. Increased liability

The rules on disenrichment aim to protect innocent recipients. Similar to the rules on recovery of benefits, they intend to cream off an enrichment, but without making the recipient lose wealth as a consequence of the initial enrichment. Such protection is not always required, in particular if the recipient is not *bona fide*.

1. Matters pending before a court

According to § 818 para. 4 BGB, once a claim for restitution is pending at court, the recipient will be liable under the general provisions. This is a reference to §§ 291 and 292 BGB. Interest is due on the litigated amount according to § 291, while § 292 refers to the owner/possesor model as regards liability for an object which must be given up. As outlined above, this will (a) make the recipient liable for any use gained, plus (b) any use which the recipient negligently failed to gain, and it will (c) be very difficult for the recipient to recover for any unauthorized expenditure. More importantly, (d) the recipient can no longer rely on disenrichment. Finally, (e) the recipient may be liable to gain-based recovery: if the initial enrichment cannot be returned because the recipient has sold it to a third party, the claimant may recover the purchase price even if this exceeds the value. Such recovery becomes possible because the reference in § 818 para. 4 to the 'general provisions' includes § 285 on substitution (above, Chapter 1, section 4.5).

It should be noted, though, that the pending claim must be the claim for unjustified enrichment. It is not sufficient that a different claim or other action is pending on the same set of facts. In the abovementioned maintenance case (case no. 14), the defendant could rely on disenrichment even though an action was already pending for decreasing the monthly maintenance payments.[76] This was not an action for return of the overpayment.

[76] BGH 17.6.1992, BGHZ 118, 383; below, Chapter 10, section 14 (translation).

2. *Mala fide* defendant

By virtue of § 819 BGB, the same stricter rules apply once the defendant knows of the lack of legal ground for the enrichment, or if the defendant acted unlawfully or immorally by accepting the claimant's performance.

In a case decided by the *Bundesgerichtshof* in 1979, parties had negotiated the sale of a lorry to the claimant whereby the defendant company was to accept a used lorry in partial payment.[77] The deal fell through. The defendant nevertheless sold the used lorry to a third party. The court held that the claimant was entitled to the purchase price which the defendant had obtained. Since the defendant was aware that the deal had fallen through when it sold the old lorry, it was held to be aware of the lack of legal ground for its enrichment.

It is worth noting, though, that knowledge of all the facts is not the same as knowledge of lack of legal ground. This was affirmed in the above-mentioned maintenance case (case no. 14).[78] This means that both mistake of fact and mistake of law protect a disenriched defendant.

3. Defendant aware of uncertainty

Finally, § 820 BGB regulates the increased liability of defendants who are exposed to *condictiones causa data causa non secuta* and *ob causam finitam*, respectively. Recipients who knew that it was uncertain whether the performance could achieve the desired result (*causa data causa non secuta*), or who knew that the legal ground for which performance was made might later lapse (*causa finita*) are treated as if an action had been pending at the time when they received the performance. This is varied in para. 2 for interest (which, incidentally, is the only express provision on interest in §§ 812–822 BGB): which is due only from the time when the recipient learned that the desired result would not be achieved or that the legal ground had lapsed. Other benefits need to be surrendered only to the extent that they remained in the hands of the defendant at that same time.

77 BGH 11.10.1979, BGHZ 75, 203.

78 BGH 17.6.1992, BGHZ 118, 383; below, Chapter 10, section 14 (translation).

Section 820 BGB was tested in a recent judgment (case no. 17) in which the *Bundesgerichtshof* returned to its unfortunate previous practice of resolving property disputes between divorcees or other estranged partners by using the *condictio causa data causa non secuta*.[79] As it is common knowledge that many relationships turn sour, is not every partnership uncertain, and even more so if the partners have not committed to live together until parted by death? If the answer is yes, this would mean that there is increased liability from the beginning, and no party can rely on having been disenriched. The *Bundesgerichtshof* held that, although partners were aware that their relationship could come to an end, they would normally see this as a remote possibility, and that was not good enough for an uncertainty in the sense of § 820 BGB. The result is correct as a matter of policy, but the argument is another excellent example of 'backward reasoning'.

[79] BGH 9.7.2008, NJW 2008, 3277, below, Chapter 10, section 17 (translation); discussed above, Chapter 3, section 1.1.

7

Concurrent Liability

We have seen in many instances above that certain claims take precedence over others, therefore it may prove helpful to have an overview of issues of concurrent liability.

1. Concurrent liability within unjustified enrichment

Under the principle of subsidiarity (above, Chapter 3, section 2), performance-based unjustified enrichment claims take precedence over unjustified enrichment claims that are not based on performance. This is generally true for relationships which involve only two parties. Occasionally, exceptions will be made as regards restitution between three or more parties. While the performance concept generally serves to find the right claimant and the right defendant in these situations, some modifications are occasionally permitted by the courts. It has been mentioned above (Chapter 3, section 2) that banks can sometimes sue recipients if they have mistakenly paid to them more than their clients had instructed. Equally, cases involving performance will occasionally be re-labelled under enrichment in another way in order to allow a claimant to sue a person other than the one to whom he or she has performed. This is in particular true for the *Rückgriffskondiktion* (above, Chapter 5, section 4.4).

However, § 816 BGB as a specific instance of non-performance-based unjustified enrichment defies the principle of subsidiarity. When this provision applies, we will nearly always have performance between the unauthorized person and the third party, and yet the entitled person is allowed to recover directly from the third party, if the third party obtained the benefit gratuitously.

2. Unjustified enrichment and contract law

In theory, no concurrent liability rule applies between unjustified enrichment and contract in German law. Nothing will prevent a claimant from suing the same defendant both under §§ 812ff BGB and in contract. However, in nearly all cases a claim will lie in either contract or unjustified enrichment, but not in both. This is due to the fact that in German law, unlike in the present English law, contract and restitution run in tandem: a claimant can generally claim back anything which the claimant gave to the defendant, provided the defendant has no legal ground to keep the enrichment. Usually, the law of contract will decide whether the defendant is entitled to keep the enrichment. If there is a valid contract under which the claimant owed performance to the defendant, no claim lies in unjustified enrichment. On the other hand, if there is no valid contract, no claim will lie in contract law.

Another difference to English law is that the BGB regulates the consequences of termination of contract within the law of contract. Under German law, termination will not destroy a contract, but create contractual obligations on each party to return to the other what he or she has received under the contract (above, Chapter 3, section 3). Again, because the contract provides the legal ground for the defendant's or the claimant's enrichment, there is no room for unjustified enrichment in these cases. Admittedly, though, the difference between this and a rule on concurrent liability is mainly a matter of terminology. In English law, this would be covered by unjust enrichment for failure of consideration.

That said, there is one true situation of conflict between the laws of contract and unjustified enrichment. This is the *condictio causa data causa non secuta*, by which a claimant can claim back an enrichment which he or she gave to the defendant if the purpose of the enrichment can no longer be fulfilled. We have seen above (Chapter 3, section 1.1) that courts will occasionally ignore existing contracts and the legal ground which they provide for this enrichment and allow a claim under § 812 para. 1 sent. 2, 2nd alternative. This is a rare case of unjustified enrichment prevailing over the law of contract, and a sloppiness which German law could well do without.

3. Unjustified enrichment and *negotiorum gestio*

In case of a justified intervention, *negotiorum gestio* will provide a legal ground for enrichments that the intervener has conferred on the person whose business the intervener was conducting. Similarly, the intervener can claim his or her expenses in return. As a rule, therefore, nothing will be left to unjustified enrichment in cases of justified *negotiorum gestio*. If the intervention was not justified, particularly in cases of wilful interference with another's rights, disgorgement of profits under § 687 para. 2 BGB (above, Chapter 5, section 2.3) concurs with liability for unjustified enrichment.

4. Unjustified enrichment and tort law

As with the rules on contract and *negotiorum gestio*, the law of tort can provide a legal ground for a performance which has been made, such as paying damages to an injured party. Apart from this, claims in unjustified enrichment and in tort are concurrent, and there is no necessity 'to waive the tort' in German law. The only possible exception is where an unauthorized person makes an ineffective disposition which the entitled person decides to ratify in order to make a claim under § 816 BGB (above, Chapter 5, section 2.4).

5. Unjustified enrichment and property law

It has also been mentioned that, within its sphere of application, the owner/possessor model takes precedence over unjustified enrichment, so that there is a clear rule on concurrent liability in this area.[1] However, the owner/possessor model does not cover the situation where the possessor consumes or sells the property. In such cases, courts have allowed previous owners to sue former possessors under §§ 812 and 816 BGB. The decision in the young bulls case (case no. 5) contains

[1] Above, Chapter 5, sections 3.1 and 2.1.

a full discussion of concurrent liability between the owner/possessor model and §§ 812ff BGB (under 3), to which the reader is referred.[2]

Otherwise, there is no conflict between proprietary remedies and those in unjustified enrichment. In particular, unjustified enrichment claims are always claims *in personam*, not *in rem* (above, Chapter 1, section 1).

If performance has been made under a void contract by delivering goods, and the title has not passed, a proprietary claim for the return of the goods lies under § 985 BGB, whereas a claim for the return of possession in the goods (*condictio possessionis*) can lie under § 812 BGB. If title has passed—and title can pass in spite of the contract being void under German (and occasionally also under English) law—the former owner can claim surrender of both possession and ownership under § 812 BGB. There is some debate whether the courts are correct to insist that the owner/possessor model should always have the last word as regards secondary benefits.[3]

It should be noted, however, that the subsidiarity of §§ 812ff BGB to owner/possessor claims will not generally lead to a situation where restitution is disallowed. Rather, it will establish different consequences of liability for some marginal cases.

[2] BGH 11.1.1971, BGHZ 55, 176, below, Chapter 10, section 5 (translation).

[3] Staudinger-Lorenz, Vorbem zu §§ 812ff, nos 40–44.

PART II
THE WIDER COMPARATIVE PERSPECTIVE

8

Classification and Consequences

1. Scope, taxonomy, and approach

Comparative lawyers are familiar with a phenomenon which makes their work both more interesting and more difficult. Different legal systems subscribe to different perceptions of particular areas of law. These areas may be construed more narrowly or more widely. The German law of contract includes gratuitous agreements, the English law does not. They may push borderline issues into one or other area of law. For example, German law tends to push borderline issues between tort and contract into contract law, English law pushes them into tort law. The approach may be based on different principles, such as *faute* for the French law of torts, or breach of duty for the English law of negligence, or as wrongful and culpable violation of a right under § 823 BGB. They may operate different taxonomies, such as negligence as the flagship of English tort law, which is surrounded by some 70 torts and 'torticles',[1] or the three pillars of violation of rights, breach of statute, and intentional infliction of harm under German tort law.

The law of unjust(ified) enrichment reveals similar differences in scope, taxonomy, and approach.

1. Scope

We have seen above that the German law of unjustified enrichment and the English law of unjust enrichment show an overlap which is substantial, but far from complete.[2] As §§ 812ff BGB exclude claims

[1] Bernard Rudden, 'Torticles' 6/7 Tulane Civil L Forum 105, 109f (1991–1992).

[2] Above, Chapter 1, sections 4–5.

between owners and possessors, in *negotiorum gestio*, and between parties to a terminated contract, and as legal assignment replaces the English law of subrogation, the German law of unjustified enrichment is substantially smaller in scope than would be what many still call the law of restitution in English law.

What makes the comparison of scopes difficult is the fact that there is no agreement as to how wide or narrow is the English law of unjust enrichment. Is there an overarching principle of unjust enrichment which covers all restitution cases?[3] Should 'restitution for wrongs' form a separate category?[4] Or are there even three separate principles (those against unjust enrichment, against profiting from wrongdoing, and for vindication of property rights)?[5] The courts have not resolved this dispute. While *Lipkin Gorman* could be read as establishing a broad principle against unjust enrichment, the recent case of *Yeoman's Row Management* almost gives the impression that unjust enrichment, claims for a *quantum meruit*, and failure of consideration represent three different areas of law.[6] And in *Foskett v McKeown*, Lords Browne-Wilkinson and Steyn disagreed whether tracing forms part of unjust enrichment.[7]

Interestingly, while German unjustified enrichment law excludes a number of areas which are within the English law of unjust enrichment on any of the above three understandings, 'restitution for wrongs' is firmly within unjustified enrichment in Germany.

2. Taxonomy

In spite or perhaps even because of the tireless work of Peter Birks, the English law of unjust enrichment is still not sufficiently settled for a predominantly accepted taxonomy to have emerged. There appears to be broad agreement that restitution for wrongs, if at all part of

[3] Burrows, 5ff.

[4] Birks, *Unjust Enrichment*, 13.

[5] Virgo, 6ff.

[6] *Lipkin Gorman v Karpnale Ltd* [1991] 2 AC 548 (HL); *Yeoman's Row Management Limited and another v Cobbe* [2008] UKHL 55, para. 3 (per Lord Scott).

[7] *Foskett v McKeown* [2001] 1 AC 102 (HL). Lord Browne-Wilkinson states: 'We are not dealing with a claim in unjust enrichment'. Lord Steyn discusses unjust enrichment issues within tracing, whereas Lord Hope discusses tracing and unjust enrichment next to each other.

unjust enrichment, at least forms a separate category. The distinction between subtractive and non-subtractive enrichment appears now also well established, and the further distinction between participatory and non-participatory enrichment has gained ground.[8] These distinctions offer powerful analytical tools, but do not by themselves provide a full classification within unjust enrichment claims. We have seen above that German courts and—with some modifications and disagreements—German academics largely subscribe to the taxonomy proposed by Wilburg and von Caemmerer which distinguishes between performance and non-performance-based unjustified enrichment, whereas the latter is subdivided into interference (*Eingriff*), expenditure (*Verwendung*), and recourse (*Rückgriff*).[9]

Comparative scholars also tend to keep 'restitution for wrongs' and expenditure on (or improvements of) the defendant's property as separate categories, but also to distinguish further within subtractive enrichment and/or performance-based unjust(ified) enrichment. The extensive comparative study by Schlechtriem groups performance of a non-existing debt together with failure of purpose and treats both recovery after termination of contract and return of gifts separately.[10] Visser's contribution to the *Oxford Handbook of Comparative Law* distinguishes similarly between reversal of an unowed payment and winding-up of failed contracts, but adds conferral of a benefit in a public law context as a separate category, and also subrogation.[11] The recently published Draft Common Frame of Reference distinguishes between transfer of assets on the one hand, and services or work rendered on the other.[12] And some scholars doubt whether unjust(ified) enrichment should be an area of law in its own right, and whether in particular contract and tort law are not better suited to provide their own restitutionary remedies.[13]

[8] See above, Chapter 2, section 1.

[9] Above, Chapter 2, section 1 and Chapter 5, section 1. See also Schäfer, 718, who believes that any taxonomy of unjust(ified) enrichment will at some level have to distinguish between these four categories.

[10] Schlechtriem, *Restitution und Bereicherungsausgleich*.

[11] Visser, 969ff.

[12] Article VII.-4:101 DCFR.

[13] Wendehorst, 113–131; similar Hedley, 1, 25ff (emphasizing strong analogies between contract and restitution); Steve Hedley, 'Unjust Enrichment as the Basis of Restitution—An Overworked Concept' (1985) 5 Legal Studies 56; this similarity is noted by Wendehorst, 122.

This great variance or even uncertainty of how unjust(ified) enrichment claims should be typified reveals another underlying uncertainty, namely concerning the best general approach.

3. Approach

Two famous English cases and two equally famous people may help us to explore the different fundamental approaches towards unjust(ified) enrichment.

A. Kelly v Solari *and the man on the Clapham omnibus*

In *Kelly v Solari*, an insurance company paid out a premium to a widow and afterwards realized that the policy held by the deceased husband had lapsed.[14] What kind of conversation is likely to develop if the proverbial man on the Clapham omnibus is asked for his views as to whether the insurance company should be allowed to claim back the premium?[15]

(1) 'Yeah, they should get the money back.' Q: 'Why?' A: 'Well, they didn't owe her anything, the policy had lapsed, hadn't it.' Q: 'Doesn't it matter that they paid her anyway?' A: 'Well, no, they made a mistake.'

(2) 'Yeah, they should get the money back.' Q: 'Why?' 'Well, they made a mistake.' Q: 'We make mistakes all the time, can we always get our money back?' A: 'No, mate, but you say the policy had lapsed, they didn't owe the money, did they.'

(3) 'Dunno, really. Hard to say. Depends.' Q: 'On what?' A: 'Well everything, like is she a poor old lady, whose fault is it, is it fair for the insurance company to get the money back?'

(4) 'No.' Q: 'Why not?' A: 'They should look after their money better.'

[14] *Kelly v Solari* (1841) 9 M&W 54.

[15] The 'man on the Clapham omnibus' has featured regularly in English judgments ever since Collins MR in *McQuire v Western Morning News Company Ltd* [1903] 2 KB 100 (CA) ascribed to Lord Bowen.

The first three answers represent the three basic approaches towards unjust(ified) enrichment. Answer 4 could imply that there should be no such thing as a law of unjust(ified) enrichment, and it finds little support in the law. Answer 3 represents an approach based on equitable or policy considerations, and can be found in some legal systems.[16] Answer 2 represents the unjust factor approach. The question whether the money was owed arises in the form of a defence—of good consideration. And answer 1 represents unjustified enrichment, whereby an enrichment must be returned unless supported by a legal ground. Mistake, that is, lack of it, figures as a defence.

Readers are invited to ask this question to a representative sample of men and women on the Clapham or any other bus—preferably without using leading words such as 'mistake' or 'owe', I would be very interested to learn of the outcome. My personal experience is that answer 1 is most common, followed by answer 3. I have to date not heard answer 2 from anyone who is not trained in the English law of unjust enrichment. My own limited empirical experience is therefore completely at odds with a view commonly held in English academic writing, namely that the unjust factor approach is 'more readily recognisable by the layperson as based upon the reasons given in every day discourse for meriting restitution',[17] and that '[n]o passenger on the Clapham omnibus ever demanded restitution for want of legally sufficient basis'.[18]

It is submitted that the probable reason why 'mistake' is not the first thing to come to mind for most laypeople when asked for their views on *Kelly v Solari* is the fact that many of them have learned, and most actually the hard way, that making mistakes can be costly, and that if you do make one you do not generally expect to get your money back. It would be wise not to be mistaken about how solvent, reliable, or trustworthy other people are. For all that laypeople may have learned about the law, the lesson is unlikely to have been 'all your mistakes will be forgiven and remedied, the law will treat you as if you had not made that mistake'. How could they know that any simple causative

[16] Schlechtriem, *Restitution und Bereicherungsausgleich*, Vol. I 1, no. 119, with descriptions of Swedish, Danish, Norwegian, and Finnish law at nos 78–106.

[17] Robert Stevens, in: Andrew Burrows et al, 'The New Birksian Approach to Unjust Enrichment' (2004) Rest L Rev 260, 273.

[18] Birks, *Unjust Enrichment*, 115.

mistake is enough for them to get their money (or whatever else they gave away) back if, and only if, they move into an area of law which they have not heard of, and which most lawyers find very difficult to explain to non-lawyers?

On the other hand, the notion of owing or not owing something, which lies behind the 'absence of basis' approach, is not at all difficult for laypeople to grasp.[19] Most people will presumably harbour a strong belief that they should be able to get their money back if they have paid too much.

The third approach, which is based on equitable or policy considerations, is equally understandable to a layperson. This seems to turn a legal into a moral or policy question. People may disagree about the results in individual cases, but they are at least familiar with solving moral dilemmas.

Whichever views will most commonly be held on the Clapham bus about *Kelly v Solari* will not determine which of the above three approaches is to be preferred for English, German, or any other law. If a complicated area of law can be structured in such a way that it is comprehensible for laypeople, all the better, but if that is not the case, then so be it. We will therefore move on to the legal sphere for a further evaluation of those three approaches.

B. Moses v Macferlan *and Lord Mansfield*

In *Moses v Macferlan*, Lord Mansfield summed up his view of the English law of unjust enrichment (for the action for money had and received) in a mere two sentences:[20]

> It lies only for money which, ex aequo et bono, the defendant ought to refund: it does not lie for money paid by the plaintiff, which is claimed of him as payable in point of honor and honesty, although it could not have been recovered from him by any course of law; as in payment of a debt barred by the Statute of limitations, or contracted during his infancy, or to the extent of principal and legal interest upon an usurious contract, or, for money fairly lost at play: because in all these cases, the defendant may retain it with a safe conscience, though by positive law he was barred from recovering. But it lies for money

[19] Similar Sheehan (2008) Oxford U Comparative L Forum 1, text adjacent to note 94: 'The layman would hardly understand that he could get money back because there was no legal basis; he would, though, understand getting money back because he didn't owe it'.

[20] *Moses v Macferlan* (1760) 2 Burr 1005.

paid by mistake; or upon a consideration which happens to fail; or for money got through imposition, (express, or implied;) or extortion, or oppression; or an undue advantage taken of the plaintiff's situation, contrary to laws made for the protection of persons under those circumstances.

The first sentence contains a negative list of situations in which the defendant had no enforceable claim to the enrichment he had received from the claimant but was still allowed to keep the benefit. This negative list includes *inter alia* debts which were time-barred, and gambling and betting debts.

The second sentence contains a positive list of situations in which an unjust enrichment action will lie. The situations include, in modern terminology, mistake, failure of consideration, fraud, duress, and undue influence.

Both sentences and both lists are concerned with the return of benefits for which the defendant could not have sued the claimant successfully. The first sentence, which includes the negative list, makes two references to the fact that Lord Mansfield is talking about a benefit which was not due. The second sentence does not repeat that requirement.

This raises the question of how to find out whether a case not clearly covered by one of the lists will fall within the first list or the second. According to Lord Mansfield, those cases will make the positive list where 'the defendant, upon the circumstances of the case, is obliged by the ties of natural justice and equity to refund the money' or, as is stated at the outset, ought to refund *ex aequo et bono*.

In modern language, the rule in *Moses v Macferlan* can therefore be summed up as follows: the law of unjust enrichment (or at least that part of it which has developed from the action for money had and received) is concerned with the surrender of benefits which the defendant received, but could not have claimed, from the claimant. It is established that in some of these situations the claimant is entitled to restitution of the benefit, but not in others. In their decision whether such a claim is allowed, courts will be guided by equity and natural justice.

At the core, Lord Mansfield's dictum in *Moses v Macferlan* is therefore an elaborate version of what has been indicated above as answer 3, a law of unjust enrichment which is guided by equitable and policy considerations. It is important to understand that this is fundamentally different from both the present English law of unjust enrichment (an elaborate version of answer 2 above), and the present German law of unjustified enrichment (an elaborate version of answer 1 above).

2. A tale of unexpected similarities

It is against this backdrop that it will be shown that the tale of unjust enrichment under present English law and unjustified enrichment under present German law is one of unexpected similarities. In fact, much of what unites English and German law marks a departure from *Moses v Macferlan*.[21]

1. Introduction of a general rule

Both English and German law have chosen to combine one general rule with a list rather than using the two-list approach as formulated in *Moses v Macferlan*. The departure by English law from the two-list approach was a gradual one. In 1802, Sir William Evans based his treatment of the action for money had and received on *Moses v Macferlan*. He also made it clear at the outset that this action concerned payments which were not due.[22] He then reversed the sequence in *Moses v Macferlan* by beginning with the positive list, which received a fuller treatment than the subsequent negative list, where Evans concentrated in particular on settlements and the effects of judicial proceedings.[23] Most modern English textbooks have dropped the negative list. For what is now called either subtractive enrichment,[24] or benefits which the defendant has acquired from or by the act of the plaintiff,[25] the general rule is that there is no recovery unless the claim

[21] *See* David Ibbetson, *A Historical Introduction to the Law of Obligations* (2000), 263ff for a historic account of the English law of unjust enrichment and an outlook for its future.

[22] Evans, 9.

[23] Evans, 81ff. One more general item on the negative list is mentioned though, namely money 'paid in pursuance of a moral obligation', at 86.

[24] Following Birks, *Introduction*, 99.

[25] Goff and Jones, section 1.

falls within one of the established items on the positive list.[26] Some elements on the negative list survive as a defence to a claim which falls in a positive-list category.[27] English courts, while having gradually come to terms with recognizing unjust enrichment as a general principle, have at least until recently held consistently that restitution based on that principle is limited to particular unjust factors,[28] or, in previous parlance, 'particular situations'.[29]

So whenever an enrichment has occurred which falls within the categories embraced by Lord Mansfield's two lists, the general rule is that there will be no recovery unless the case can be placed on the positive list. The negative list has been dissolved into a negative general rule, and what remains is a positive list of what is now called unjust factors.

The German law of unjustified enrichment has also dissolved one of the two lists into a general rule and kept the other list. It just happened that those who drafted the *Bürgerliches Gesetzbuch* dissolved the positive rather than the negative list. In all situations covered by Lord Mansfield's lists—namely a shift of wealth from one party to another which was not supported by a legal ground—the general rule is that the recipient must give up the enrichment. Thus, an enrichment is unjustified (*ungerechtfertigt*) rather than unjust (*ungerecht*), unless there is a specific legal reason why it should be kept. Naturally, in itself this general rule is the exact opposite of the English general rule that the enrichment need not be given up.

[26] Goff and Jones, 1–052; Burrows, 41–44; Virgo, 119–130; Mitchell, in: *English Private Law*, 18.40–18.45. Tettenborn distinguishes between 'unjust factors' (13–17) and 'factors justifying retention' (20–32), but treats the latter as factors defeating a prima facie case for restitution (20).

[27] Goff and Jones, 1–061ff; Burrows, 51; Mitchell, in: *English Private Law*, 18.260–18.308 ('unjust-related defences').

[28] In *Woolwich Equitable Building Society v Inland Revenue Commissioners* [1993] AC 70 (HL), Lord Goff gives a convenient list of those unjust factors which allow recovery of money paid. The door was left open for future development in *Deutsche Morgan Grenfell Group Plc v Inland Revenue Commissioners* [2006] UKHL 49 by Lord Hoffmann at 21: 'at any rate for the moment, . . . unlike civilian systems, English law has no general principle that to retain money paid without any legal basis (such as debt, gift, compromise, etc) is unjust enrichment'. See Häcker (2007) LQR 177.

[29] *Orakpo v Manson Investments Ltd* [1978] AC 95 (HL), at 104, per Lord Diplock.

2. Rejection of the principles of equity and natural justice

Dissolving one of the lists into a general rule has enabled both English and German law to discard what is perhaps the most important rule in *Moses v Macferlan*, namely that it should be considerations of equity and natural justice (or good faith, as German courts would be inclined to say) which should ultimately decide whether a claim for restitution lies. Keeping one negative and one positive list calls for such a guiding principle, which helps to decide on which of the two lists a given case should be. On the other hand, once it is known that a case falls within a general rule, all that is needed is to find whether one of the recognized exceptions applies.

To say that equitable considerations have no place in the law of unjust(ified) enrichment, as currently practised in England and Germany, would be an overstatement. English law makes some use of constructive trusts for this purpose, even if it may not go quite as far as the dictum by Cardozo according to which 'a constructive trust is the formula through which the conscience of equity finds expression'.[30] As we have seen above, German courts have also occasionally stated quite openly in difficult cases that their solution is guided by considerations of good faith.[31] On the other hand, it is largely accepted at present in both English and German law that the law of unjust(ified) enrichment is a system of legal rules rather than a compilation of general considerations as to what is just and fair. So while it can be said that equitable considerations have played a historical part in formulating those rules,[32] it nevertheless appears that neither English nor German law have followed the main proposition made by Lord Mansfield in *Moses v Macferlan*.[33] This marks a clear contrast with Scandinavian laws of unjust enrichment, which Schlechtriem in his elaborate comparative study has described as desisting from formulating rules which

[30] *Beatty v Guggenheim Exploration Co* 225 NY 380, 386 (1919); *see* Birks, *Introduction*, 64.

[31] BGH 31.5.1990, BGHZ 111, 308, at 312, below Chapter 10, section 12 (translation); BGH 15.5.1986, NJW 1986, 2700, below, Chapter 10, section 9 (translation).

[32] See e.g. Lionel Smith, 'Property, Subsidiarity, and Unjust Enrichment' (2000) Oxford U Comparative L Forum 6 at <http://ouclf.iuscomp.org>, text adjacent to notes 88ff.

[33] See e.g. Birks, *Introduction*, 19.

make claims dependent on the fulfillment or certain requirements in favour of compiling various factors of assessment into a flexible system, from which courts can choose in an individual case on a balancing approach.[34]

3. Elaboration and expansion of lists

Both English and German law have invested considerable efforts in the formulation and refinement of the list they have retained. And both English and German law were under some pressure to hedge the main danger which general rules tend to have: they usually catch more than was initially intended. This danger has been frequently noted for the civil law approach of a positive general clause,[35] but exists equally for negative general rules. There are two main ways of reducing this danger, namely by restricting the general rule, and by elaborating the exceptions. We will begin with the latter and German law, which put most limitations of the general principle in place when the BGB was enacted.

We have seen above how by stating quite generally that benefits acquired at the expense of another person need to be returned unless this shift of wealth is supported by a legal ground, German law has removed nearly all questions addressed in Lord Mansfield's positive list from the ambit of the law of unjustified enrichment and left those issues to be decided by other areas of law, including in particular contract, tort, family, and inheritance law.[36] For it is those other areas of law which provide a defendant with the legal ground, which is generally understood to be a claim or other right which entitles the defendant to keep the benefit. This, however, requires all those rules to be written with the possibility of unjustified enrichment in mind. For example, a rule which prevents a contract from becoming enforceable

[34] Schlechtriem, *Restitution und Bereicherungsausgleich*, Vol. I 1, no. 119, with descriptions of Swedish, Danish, Norwegian, and Finnish law, at nos 78–106. See also M Schulz, Unjust Enrichment—Sweden, <http://www.juridicum.su.se/user/masc/unjustenrichment.htm> (last accessed 21 December 2008).

[35] Dawson, 8 noted this as the main danger of the civil law approach and a general principle of unjust enrichment.

[36] Above, Chapter 3, section 6. From a comparative viewpoint, see also Daniel Friedmann, 'The Creation of Entitlements through the Law of Restitution', in: *Structure and Justification in Private Law*, 185: these other areas of law are the 'source of entitlement' for restitution.

will not necessarily be best served by allowing restitution after the unenforceable contract has been mutually performed.

Lord Mansfield's negative list is thus mostly relocated. We have seen above that § 222 para. 2 BGB generally prevents restitution if someone has performed on a claim which was barred by prescription.[37] Section 762 para. 1 sent. 2 on gaming and betting turns these into so-called 'natural obligations' which cannot be enforced, but where no restitution is allowed once debts have been paid, covering Lord Mansfield's 'money fairly lost at play'.[38] Forms provisions cover a considerable number of essential negative list items. We have seen that a lack of form may be healed in some cases by performance, and that the very purpose of those provisions which heal this lack of form is to prevent claims in unjustified enrichment.[39]

The wide range of gratuitous contracts which are available under German law—including donation, gratuitous lending, gratuitous loan, the gratuitous provision of services, and of works—will also prevent many situations from appearing on Lord Mansfield's negative list, unless the gratuitous contract can be set aside as a matter of contract law.[40]

Finally, one general consideration on Lord Mansfield's negative list was turned into a general defence against a claim for the return of an enrichment obtained by performance. Even if there was no legal ground to support this shift of wealth, it may be retained under § 814 BGB if the enrichment is supported by a moral duty or considerations of decency.[41]

While in Germany most negative reasons were drafted and elaborated on at the same time the general rule was introduced, the gradual introduction of the English negative general rule was not initially accompanied by a similarly thorough elaboration of the positive grounds for unjust enrichments. As Dawson noted in 1951:

> But the English law of restitution as a whole gives a remarkable example of the effects of freezing doctrine—still more of freezing minds—in an area still incompletely explored at the time the freeze set in.[42]

[37] Chapter 2, section 6.2.C.
[38] Chapter 2, section 6.2.D.
[39] Chapter 2, section 6.2.B.
[40] But see above, Chapter 3, section 1.1 for the *condictio causa data causa non secuta*.
[41] Chapter 4, section 2.
[42] Dawson, 21.

At present, the situation is almost reversed. While there has been comparatively little movement in the German law of unjustified enrichment over the past few years, English law has undergone dramatic developments. Preceded and assisted by academic writing,[43] English courts have unfrozen the law of restitution and have, in less than a decade, achieved a rapid development which in other areas of law might have taken a century.[44] Some major expansion did take place within the grounds of recovery for unjust enrichment. In the present context, it is only necessary to mention some of those which occurred on Lord Mansfield's positive list. Over the last twenty years, English courts have been increasingly generous in setting aside (and providing restitutionary relief for) guarantees or mortgages provided by individuals to secure loans taken out by their relatives or other persons with whom they have a relationship of trust and confidence.[45] The previous requirement that restitution for failure of consideration is granted only if the failure was total has been gradually eroded.[46] And, most significantly, the decision by the House of Lords in *Kleinwort Benson v Lincoln City Council* has closed what was perhaps the biggest single gap in the English law of unjust enrichment, namely the rule that only mistakes of fact, as opposed to mistakes of law, entitled to recovery of a benefit which the defendant had received at the claimant's expense.[47] Ironically, the closure of this gap will leave English law with no other

[43] Many have contributed to this debate. Three milestones will be mentioned: the American Law Institute's *Restatement of the Law of Restitution, Quasi Contracts and Constructive Trusts* (1937) by Austin W Scott and Warren A Seavey; Robert Goff and Gareth Jones, *The Law of Restitution* 1st edn (1966); Birks, *Introduction*.

[44] The most rapid phase of development was between 1991 and 1999: *Lipkin Gorman v Karpnale Ltd* [1991] 2 AC 548 (HL); *Woolwich Equitable Building Society v Inland Revenue Commissioners* [1993] AC 70 (HL); *Barclays Bank plc v O'Brien* [1994] 1 AC 180 (HL); *Westdeutsche Landesbank Girozentrale v Islington London Borough Council* [1996] AC 669 (HL); *Kleinwort Benson Ltd v Lincoln City Council* [1999] 2 AC 349 (HL). However, cases such as *Royal Bank of Scotland v Etridge* [2001] UKHL 44, *Deutsche Morgan Grenfell Group plc v Her Majesty's Commissioners of Inland Revenue* [2006] UKHL 49 and *Yeoman's Row Management Ltd and another v Cobbe* [2008] UKHL 55 show that the phase of development continues.

[45] *Bank of Credit and Commerce International SA v Aboody* [1990] 1 QB 923 (CA); *Cheese v Thomas* [1994] 1 WLR 129 (CA); *Barclays Bank plc v O'Brien* [1994] 1 AC 180 (HL).

[46] *Rover International Ltd v Cannon Film Sales Ltd* [1989] 1 WLR 912 (CA); *Westdeutsche Landesbank Girozentrale v Islington London Borough Council* [1996] AC 669 (HL); *Goss v Chilcott* [1996] AC 788 (PC).

[47] *Kleinwort Benson Ltd v Lincoln City Council* [1999] 2 AC 349 (HL).

option but to draw up once again a negative list, namely in the form of reasons for keeping an enrichment which trump a mistake of law. This is because every item on Lord Mansfield's negative list can be reshaped into a mistake of law. A claimant may, for example, mistakenly have believed that the limitation period was longer than it actually was.[48]

4. Restrictions of the general rule

In spite of these efforts by both English and German law to limit the scope of their general rule by expanding the scope of the exceptions, pressure remained on both to further reduce its impact. This was achieved to some degree by way of taxonomy, and to some degree by a policy-based approach. German law has concentrated more on the former, and English law more on the latter.

One reduction of the scope of the German general clause, which generally requires enrichments to be given up, was achieved by giving a wider meaning to the 'legal ground' which entitles the recipient to keep the enrichment. It does not need much of an extension to cover those two items on the negative list which were the chief concern of Sir William Evans in 1802.[49] The first are settlements, which are contracts in their own right under § 779 BGB, and therefore cause no further problem because they are capable of modifying the legal relationship between the parties. The second are judgments and enforceable administrative decisions, which, once they have become final, provide for a legal ground even if they are wrong as a matter of substantive law. And in one further expansion, 'legal ground' in the context of the recognition of a debt does not refer to the validity of the recognition agreement itself, but to the existence of the debt which was recognized.[50]

However, the most significant reduction of the German general clause was achieved by way of taxonomy, namely by the Wilburg and von Caemmerer divide between performance and non-performance-based

[48] It is worth noting from a comparative perspective that the *Restatement of the Law of Restitution, Quasi Contracts and Constructive Trusts* (1937) by Austin W Scott and Warren A Seavey already contained a similar negative list for liability mistakes in § 61.

[49] Evans, 86–102.

[50] Above, Chapter 2, section 6.2.E.

unjustified enrichment.[51] We have seen above that in order for performance-based unjustified enrichment to operate, it is not sufficient that the defendant's gain was at the expense of the claimant and unsupported by a legal ground. In addition, the defendant must have received the benefit as the result of a performance by the claimant, which is understood as a conscious shift of assets to the defendant with a particular obligation in mind. And while it is the claimant's view which determines whether a shift of wealth was an act of performance, it is the recipient's view which determines whether this was performance by the claimant, or by another party. Effectively, this serves to keep restitutionary claims within the legal relationships from which they arise, and prevents leapfrogging in search of a solvent defendant. Furthermore, performance-based restitution takes precedence over non-performance-based restitution, which, as we have seen, includes what English law would classify as restitution for wrongs, most of ignorance, and some of mistaken improvements.[52] Whatever its disadvantages may be, the performance/non-performance taxonomy has been rather effective in preventing the German general rule from catching more than it initially bargained for.

In part, English law has also resorted to taxonomy in order to limit the effects of its general rule, namely by placing some enrichment claims in the area of trust, in particular constructive trusts. Such trusts have occasionally been employed for claims which were based on the defendant's enrichment even where there appeared to be no sign of an unjust factor.[53]

Mainly, however, English law has resorted to policy considerations in order to curb its general rule of non-recovery. Some of these would be clear-cut restitution cases under the German legal system. An example is the policy-based rule in *Woolwich Equitable Building Society v Inland Revenue Commissioners* which allows taxpayers quite

[51] Above, Chapter 2, section 1.

[52] Above, Chapter 5.

[53] A case in point is *Hussey v Palmer* [1972] 1 WLR 1286 (CA), discussed above, Chapter 5, section 3.3. The claimant was an elderly widow who was invited to live with her daughter and son-in-law, the defendant. The claimant paid £607 to have the home extended by one bedroom for her use. She left the home fifteen months later, after having fallen out with her son-in law. Her claim for £607 could hardly have succeeded under failure of consideration at the time, but was allowed with the help of a constructive trust (at 1289–1290, per Lord Denning).

generally to recover taxes they were wrongly charged by tax authorities, regardless of whether their payment was affected by a mistake, compulsion, etc.[54] In effect, English law has thus not only limited, but reversed the general rule of non-recovery for an entire area of law. English law can therefore be said to operate a small positive general clause which functions in the same way as performance-based restitution in German law.

There is another, although somewhat disputed, ground of restitution in English law which is based on policy considerations, namely illegality.[55] One case where recovery was allowed on the ground of illegality is *Kiriri Cotton v Dewani*, which concerned an illegal premium which a tenant had been charged for obtaining the premises.[56] This is a rather complicated area of law, because in both German and English law, illegality can appear not only as a reason for, but also as a defence against a restitutionary claim.[57] It is nevertheless important to mention illegality in this context because both English and German courts will frequently make their decision dependent on whether the policy which prohibits a certain transaction will ultimately be best served by allowing, or disallowing, restitution. These considerations also accounted for the decision in *Tribe v Tribe*, where a father transferred his assets to his son when the father's creditors were closing in, but was allowed to recover his assets from his then uncooperative son after the father had been able to pay off the creditors.[58] Perhaps this is the area where, in spirit if not in letter, the two lists plus general guiding principle approach of Lord Mansfield is to a certain degree applied by both English and German courts. There are known situations where

[54] *Woolwich Equitable Building Society v Inland Revenue Commissioners* [1993] AC 70 (HL).

[55] This ground of restitution is recognized i.e. by Burrows, Ch. 12; critical e.g. William Swadling, 'The Role of Illegality in the English Law of Unjust Enrichment' (2000) Oxford U Comparative L Forum 5 at <http://ouclf.iuscomp.org>. Goff and Jones, 24–001 see a limited role for illegality as a ground of restitution.

[56] *Kiriri Cotton v Dewani* [1960] AC 192 (HL). Other explanations for this award would have been difficult to find, as at the time mistake of law was not a ground of restitution. But see now *Kleinwort Benson Ltd v Lincoln City Council* [1999] 2 AC 349 (HL).

[57] For German law, see above, Chapter 4, section 3. English law recognizes both the defence of *nemo auditur turpitudinem suam allegans* (no one will be heard pleading his own wrongdoing) and of *in pari delicto potior est conditio defendentis* (where parties have wronged equally, the position of the defendant is better), see *Holman v Johnson* (1775) 1 Cowp 341, and *Tinsley v Milligan* [1994] AC 340 (HL), at 354.

[58] *Tribe v Tribe* [1995] 3 WLR 913 (CA).

a party cannot recover what was transferred under an illegal contract. There are others where recovery is allowed. And policy considerations will ultimately decide which of those lists a case should join.[59]

It should be noted that in Germany, England, and apparently quite generally throughout Europe, it is increasingly recognized that the policy reasons which make a certain contract void are sometimes better served by allowing recovery, and sometimes by disallowing it, and that such policy considerations therefore have an important role in defining whether and to what measure restitution should be allowed.[60] Interestingly, the English swaps litigation cases have shown that the same questions can surface in claims based on failure of consideration rather than on illegality.[61]

5. Partial oblivion

The previous sections (1)–(4) have been largely of a positive nature in setting out how German and English law, by going in different yet at the same time similar ways, have both managed to build a modern law of unjust(ified) enrichment which can currently be said to often reach similar results in similar cases. There are, however also a few less positive ways in which English and German law, by going their different ways, have both left behind something which appeared obvious at the time of *Moses v Macferlan*. This section will deal with partial oblivion, and the next with rationalizations of the general rule.

This partial oblivion relates to the features of the Roman *condictio indebiti*, which has influenced both *Moses v Macferlan* and the German law of unjust enrichment. German law relies heavily on the

[59] While this tendency can be observed in both English and German law, it is more apparent in German law; see above, Chapter 4, section 3.4.

[60] Schlechtriem, *Restitution und Bereicherungsausgleich*, Vol. I 3 no. 695 notes a general trend in Europe to define both the effect and the scope of the illegality defence with a view towards the purpose of the prohibitory norm which has been violated. Art. VII.-6:103 DCFR on illegality provides that 'the enriched person is not liable to reverse the enrichment to the extent that the reversal would contravene the policy underlying the principle or rule'.

[61] The speech by Lord Justice Waller in *Guinness Mahon & Co Ltd v Council of the Royal Borough of Kensington & Chelsea* [1999] QB 215 (CA) discusses in detail the question whether the purpose of the statutory prohibition of local authorities entering into swaps transactions requires that councils may keep the profit from closed transactions decision is based on failure of consideration rather than on illegality. (The question is answered in the negative.)

condictio indebiti, which served as a model for the German general clause. In English law, mistake as a ground for unjust enrichment also owes much to the *condictio indebiti*.[62]

This most general amongst the Roman law *condictiones* allows recovery of a benefit which the defendant has received from the claimant, providing two additional conditions are met. The first is that this benefit was not due to the defendant. And the second is that the claimant was labouring under an error when providing the benefit.[63] Both German and English law have chosen to concentrate heavily on one of the requirements, and to move the other to backwaters where it will occasionally be overlooked. Once again, though, German and English law differ in their choice. The entire German law of unjustified enrichment builds on the notion of the legal ground. German law has thus concentrated on the *indebitum* aspect of this *condictio*, while mistake receives only the most fleeting mention in the statute, judgments, and academic writing. English law focuses heavily on the second requirement, i.e. the mistake, whereas the question whether the benefit was due received little attention in textbooks and judgments alike until Birks proposed that English law should shift to an absence of basis approach.[64]

One notable exception in the recent case law is the speech of Lord Hope (unsurprisingly, a Scottish judge) in *Kleinwort Benson*, where he made the following comparative obiter dictum:[65]

> The approach of the common law is to look for an unjust factor, something which makes it unjust to allow the payee to retain the benefit: Birks, An Introduction to the Law of Restitution, 2nd ed. (1989), pp. 140 et seq. It is the mistake by the payer which, as in the case of failure of consideration and

[62] This is perhaps most evident in Evans, 6–22, whose writing on the action for money had and received in general, and on mistake in particular, is heavily based on the *condictio indebiti*. See also e.g. Birks, *Introduction*, 153.

[63] See Zimmermann, *The Law of Obligations*, 848–851.

[64] Birks, *Unjust Enrichment*, Ch. 5, adopting the conclusions of a detailed analysis of the use of a legal ground analysis (or its failure) in English cases of mistake by Sonja Meier, *Irrtum und Zweckverfehlung* (1999). See also Sonja Meier and Reinhard Zimmermann, 'Judicial Development of the Law, Error Iuris, and the Law of Unjustified Enrichment—A View from Germany' (1999) 115 LQR 556–565. The authors believe that a distinction between mistakes which do and which not do give rise to an action in unjust enrichment is not possible without a legal ground based analysis (at 563) and conclude that *Kleinwort Benson* has reintroduced the *condictio indebiti* through the back door (at 565).

[65] *Kleinwort Benson Ltd v Lincoln City Council* [1999] 2 AC 349, 409 (HL).

compulsion, renders the enrichment of the payee unjust. The common law accepts that the payee is enriched where the sum was not due to be paid to him, but it requires the payer to show that this was unjust. Whereas in civilian systems proof of knowledge that there was no legal obligation to pay is a defence which may be invoked by the payee, under the common law it is for the payer to show that he paid under a mistake. My impression is that the common law tends to place more emphasis on the need for proof of a mistake. But the underlying principle in both systems is that of unjust enrichment. The purpose of the principle is to provide a remedy for recovery of the enrichment where no legal ground exists to justify its retention.

What Lord Hope calls a different emphasis has led to some undesirable side effects in both German and English law.

We have seen above how German law has turned the mistake requirement into a defence, namely that there is no claim in restitution for performance if the claimant had positive knowledge that he or she did not owe the benefit to the enriched party.[66] Mere doubts do not suffice, but a reservation—unless made as standard procedure[67]—will prevent the defence of § 814 sent. 1 BGB.[68] Perhaps more significantly, if most German judgments and legal writing are considered, German law appears to have lost sight of the role which mistake plays in bringing about situations of unjustified enrichment. Together with the restrictions imposed by the performance/non-performance taxonomy, this implies that cases of mistaken performance are somewhat artificially dissected. Situations where the claimant performed an obligation which the defendant owed to a third party are considered to be outside the realm of performance-based restitution and are tucked away in the second alternative of § 812 subs 1 sent. 1 BGB, namely 'enrichment in another way', to which the 'no mistake' defence in § 814 BGB is held not to apply.[69] Thus, mistake is lost as a factor which in some cases might, for example, separate the deserving from the less deserving cases where one party pays another party's debt.

English law, on the other hand, has to some degree neglected the requirement which gave the *condictio indebiti* its name, i.e. that the

[66] Chapter 4, section 1.

[67] OLG Koblenz 20.9.1983, NJW 1984, 135. This concerned insurance companies which had added standard reservation clauses to their payout forms.

[68] BGH 17.2.1982, BGHZ 83, 278.

[69] See BGH 22.10.1975, Wertpapier-Mitteilungen 1975, 1235.

benefit was not due to the defendant, and which, as indicated above, Lord Mansfield mentioned twice when setting out his view on the action for money had and received in *Moses and Macferlan*. The 1856 case of *Aiken v Short* turned out to be a watershed.[70] Platt B denied a bank recovery for having paid off the first mortgagee in the mistaken belief that the bank had bought the property. He argued that the payment 'was actually due to her, and there can be no obligation to refund it'. This is an argument which any German court would be happy to entertain. In English law, however, the judgment is mostly remembered for Bramwell B denying the claim on the ground that 'the mistake must be as to a fact which, if true, would make the person paying liable to pay the money', which relegated the legal ground to a sub-category of mistake, i.e. the requirement of a liability mistake. This requirement in turn was given up in *Barclays Bank v Simms*, where a bank had overlooked an instruction by its client to stop a cheque to a recipient who had gone into receivership.[71] The question of whether the payment was due was considered as a defence against the establishment of an enrichment: the discharge of an existing obligation was held to be a consideration which would prevent an enrichment claim. But as the bank had no authority to discharge this debt, the defence was held not to apply. The question of whether the benefit was due to the defendant has thus been turned into the question whether the defendant lost something (a claim) by accepting the benefit. As in German law with mistake, moving the issue of whether a benefit was due to the defendant to the backwaters carries some risks which, although manageable in most cases, can cause confusion and uncertainty. Because it is not completely certain whether the consideration and ratification rationale employed for the discharge of an existing debt applies outside contract law, the following simple case can cause problems for English law:

A keeps a dog which one day comes home with a piece of cloth in his mouth which looks as if it had just been torn from a dress.

[70] *Aiken v Short* (1856) 1 H&N 210; see: Daniel Friedmann and Nili Cohen, 'Payment of Another's Debt', sec. 60–61, in: *International Encyclopaedia of Comparative Law*, Vol. X (P. Schlechtriem, chief ed.).

[71] *Barclays Bank Ltd v W J Simms Ltd* [1980] 1 QB 677. Goff J (as he then was), noted the difference between those views in his argument why Bramwell B's remark was obiter dictum.

The next day A receives a note from Mrs Smith who lives along the road, which confirms this suspicion and demands payment for the dress. A immediately sends, to the address indicated, a cheque for the amount with an apologetic note. When attempting to apologize in person to the nice Mrs Smith whom he has known for years, A finds out that the note came from, and that he has paid, another neighbour with the same name, whom he loathes and whom he would never have paid. A sues for return of the money. There is no doubt that A paid under a causative mistake and is thus, in principle, entitled to get his money back. Can the English law of unjust enrichment prevent this claim, as in my view it should? Or do we have to resort to set-off or other non-enrichment-based defences, which would place the burden of proof again on Mrs Smith?

6. Rationalization of the general rule

General rules not only tend to catch more than was intended by those who drafted them. They also have a dangerous tendency to justify themselves in situations where neither the expansion of exceptions, nor any hedging through taxonomy or by policy considerations will be sufficient to counteract this effect. Dawson warned of the dangers of what he called a general principle of unjust enrichment as he observed it to exist in France and in Germany:[72]

> Yet once the idea has been formulated as a generalization, it has the peculiar facility of inducing quite sober citizens to jump right off the dock. This temporary intoxication is seldom produced by other general ideas, such as 'equity,' 'good faith,' or 'justice,' for these ideals themselves suggest their own relativity and the complexity of the factors that must enter into judgment. The ideal of preventing enrichment through another's loss has a strong appeal to the sense of equal justice but it also has the delusive appearance of mathematical simplicity. It suggests not merely the need for a remedy but a measure of recovery. It constantly tends to become a 'rule,' to dictate solutions, to impose itself on the mind.

Dawson was proven to be right. Some ten years after he wrote those lines, German courts gave up what Dawson considered to be the best attempt of the German legal system to counteract and control this

[72] Dawson, 8.

danger, namely the limitation of unjust enrichment to cases of 'direct enrichment'.[73] Dawson at the time noted that it was 'ingenious', but also that it was 'fairly clear that we cannot use it'.[74] It turned out that even German law could no longer use it, and that it had to be replaced with a tighter reading of the general clause, namely the performance/non-performance taxonomy.

What Dawson did not note was that the general negative rule adopted by English law carries the same dangers. While it may not exactly 'induce quite sober citizens to jump right off the dock', it does tend to dictate solutions, impose itself on the mind, and serve to rationalize a deficiency in the law rather than resolving it.

The rationalization of the English general rule is called 'security of receipts'. This is not to say that there is no value in keeping receipts secure, just as it would be wrong to deny considerations of equity, of corrective justice, or of promoting legality in any role. But these considerations are not often in themselves sufficient to justify a general rule, regardless of whether it is a negative or a positive one. A continental observer would feel inclined to think that the consideration of security of receipts has been somewhat overstretched in English law. In the same way that it was previously used to rationalize rules which have since been discarded (such as the mistake of law rule), it is currently employed on the new frontiers of restitution.

A case in point is *Nurdin & Peacock v D B Ramsden & Co Ltd*,[75] which extended mistake of law based restitution. In a relatively complicated lease arrangement, the claimants were tenants who had discovered that they had for some time been overcharged by the defendants, their landlords, and had thus paid too much rent. While this was disputed by the defendants, the claimants made one more payment of rent at the higher rate, which later was indeed found to have included an overcharge. They then initiated proceedings against the defendants and made four more payments at the higher rate while the claim was pending. The claimants were motivated to pay first and discuss later by two factors. One was that underpayment could lead to forfeiture

[73] Above, Chapter 2, section 4.

[74] Dawson, 121.

[75] *Nurdin & Peacock v D B Ramsden & Co Ltd* [1999] 1 All ER 941.

and repossession of the property by the landlords. The other was their belief that they could recover the overpayment. Neuberger J (as he then was) ruled that nothing could be done about the first motive, because it did not fit into the established category of duress. But he expanded the new mistake of law rule in *Kleinwort Benson* and allowed recovery on the second motive. We will return to the merits of the case below. In the present context, it is worth noting that this judgment attracted instant criticism on the ground that this led to an intolerable inroad into the security of receipts.[76]

The claimants could always have recovered their initial overpayments for a mistake in fact. No security of receipts argument would have rushed to the aid of the then entirely unsuspecting defendants. But when defendants receive an additional overpayment in the knowledge that there is now a serious dispute between parties as to their entitlement, and together with a note which clearly states that the claimants would attempt to recover any overpayment, security of receipts becomes an issue. Security of receipts even remains an issue after the defendants have been sued for all overpayments and receive four more of them. And for all five overpayments, the other end of unjust enrichment, the defence of change of position, tells us that the defendants were not entitled to rely on keeping them.

Whenever grounds of restitution are expanded, security of receipts probably looks like a natural argument to a person trained in the common law.[77] To a continental observer, this presents itself as a rationalization of a general rule which has been overstretched. But it is also reassuring to see that English and German courts alike have, although frequently with some delay, often decided to resist the temptation which Dawson described.

[76] G Virgo, 'Recent Developments in Restitution of Mistaken Payments' [1999] 58 Camb L Journal 478, 480; maintained in Virgo, *Principles of the Law of Restitution*, 162: 'the judge undermined the bar on restitution of voluntary payments, a bar which is of crucial importance to maintain the security of receipts'.

[77] Virgo, 129, also relies on 'security of receipts' as an argument against an absence of basis approach: 'This principle of security of receipt is important in the development of the law of restitution. . . A move to an absence of basis approach could destabilize commercial transactions'.

3. Conclusions

We have seen throughout this tale of unexpected similarities that the English unjust factor approach and the German absence of legal ground approach are much closer to one another than at first meets the eye. They have both moved unjust(ified) enrichment largely out of the realm of equity and policy considerations into a rule-based and hence more predictable system. They have both adopted a general rule with a list of exceptions. They have struggled to limit the injustice and turmoil which their general rules are capable of creating by refining and expanding the exceptions to those rules. The approach they have each chosen has made them neglect some important aspects, and at times led them to rationalize rather than remedy deficiencies. And while they start from opposite ends, they employ very similar techniques for achieving what are often similar results. As Reynolds has put it:

> . . . legal systems come on to the stage from opposite doors, but then proceed to meet somewhere in the middle, with comparatively slight variations in marginal cases, resulting from the different starting points.[78]

If we stay with this metaphor, the next question will be whether a legal system can re-enter the stage through the opposite door.

[78] Francis Reynolds, *The Diversity of the Common Law: A Warning for Unification Projects* (2000), 24.

9

Lessons to Be Learned?

1. Introduction

This chapter will examine whether the comparison between German and English law of unjust(ified) enrichment can be used for developing the law in both legal systems. The fact that the emphasis will be more on how English law can use the German experience than the other way round does not reflect any superiority. We have seen above that the German law of unjustified enrichment is far from perfect, and that the two laws have much more in common than first meets the eye. There are two reasons for this book to focus more on German lessons for English law than on English lessons for German law.

The first reason concerns the audience. This book is primarily written for common law readers, who are frequently more interested in persuasive authority which could help in the development of the common law than in remedying deficiencies in foreign legal systems.

The second reason is the current debate which Peter Birks sparked by proposing that English law should give up the unjust factor approach, whereby a disenriched party may claim back the enrichment only if a specific unjust factor can be found, and adopt an absence of basis approach whereby a defendant must return an enrichment made at the expense of the claimant if this enrichment is not supported by a legal basis.[1] This proposition, which has initiated a wide debate,[2] makes it particularly interesting to look at the German law of unjustified

[1] Birks, *Unjust Enrichment*, Ch. 5.

[2] See e.g. Burrows et al (2004) Rest L Rev 260–298; Giglio (2003) 23 OJLS 455; Häcker, (2007) LQR 177; Sheehan (2008) Oxford U Comparative L Forum 1, and the contributions by Burrows, Dannemann, and Maier to *Mapping the Law*. For a similar discussion on South African law, see Scott, *Unjust Enrichment by Transfer in South African Law*.

enrichment, which has operated on an absence of basis approach for more than a century.

Comparative law can be a tricky business.[3] More than three decades of discussing 'legal transplants' have shown us that legal institutions have migrated across substantial distances in time, space, and culture,[4] but also that their success may largely depend on the legal environment in which they are embedded.[5] That is particularly true for unjust(ified) enrichment.

We will therefore first look at those other areas of law which can provide the legal basis for enrichments under an absence of basis approach, and in particular contract law.[6] Existing differences between English and German contract law imply that an absence of basis approach should not simply be transplanted into English surroundings without a careful examination as to the effects which these differences in contract law can have on unjust enrichment law (see section 2).

Having thus placed an absence of basis approach in context, we will look at the modificiations which would then become necessary or advisable within unjust enrichment law (section 3). This concerns some English case law which cannot be reconciled with an unjust enrichment approach. It includes issues of taxonomy, in particular whether switching to an absence of basis approach should also entail the adoption of the performance/non-performance divide eventually adopted by German law in the 1960s, or whether English law would do better without this divide and operate a general absence of basis approach more similar to the pre-1960 system in Germany.

Finally, we will look at what German law could learn from the comparison with English law (section 4).

[3] Robert Stevens, in: Andrew Burrows et al, 'The New Birksian Approach to Unjust Enrichment' (2004) Rest L Rev 260, 270, calls it even a 'dangerous business'.

[4] Alan Watson, *Legal Transplants: An Approach to Comparative Law*, 2nd edn (1993; 1st edn 1974).

[5] See Michele Graziadei, 'Comparative Law as the Study of Legal Transplants and Receptions', in: Mathias Reimann and Reinhard Zimmermann (eds), *The Oxford Handbook of Comparative Law* (2006), 441ff.

[6] See above, Chapter 2, section 6.

2. Bases for enrichment in English law

1. Property and intellectual property law

Regardless of whether 'restitution for wrongs' is to be understood as part of unjust enrichment in English law, a shift to an absence of basis approach is likely to have rather a limited influence on the interaction between unjust enrichment, tort, property, and intellectual property law. If 'wrong' is understood as unjust factor, infringements of property or intellectual property rights are regularly at the same time both a wrong and lack a legal basis. If there is a legal basis for interference with property or intellectual property rights, such interference will normally not amount to a wrong. The much-discussed question as to which wrongs are anti-enrichment wrongs (wrongs which require an award of restitution) is essentially the same for both unjust factor and the absence of basis approach.[7] Likewise, for breach of contract as a wrong, the question whether gain-based restitution should be allowed does not depend on whether recovery is based on an unjust factor or on an absence of basis approach.

2. Contract law

A valid contract provides a legal basis which allows a recipient to keep the enrichment. A void contract cannot provide such a basis. But what about terminated or terminable, voidable and unenforceable contracts?

Terminated contracts are easily dealt with. Once terminated, a contract can no longer provide a legal basis for an enrichment. This must not be confused with the question whether restitution after termination belongs to unjust(ified) enrichment, as in English law, or to contract law, as in German law.[8] German contractual rules on restitution after termination take precedence over general unjustified enrichment rules because they are more specific, not because § 812ff BGB could not handle restitution after termination.

[7] Above, Chapter 5, section 2.2.A.

[8] Above, Chapter 3, section 3

Terminable and voidable contracts are a little more difficult. Under German law, they continue to provide a legal basis for keeping an enrichment for as long as the right to terminate or to avoid a contract is not exercised. Birks, however, believed that terminable and avoidable contracts cannot provide a legal basis.[9] An absence of basis approach can operate on either one of these views, although arguable more easily on the German position. One of the consequences of the view taken by Birks is that if A sells B a painting for £10,000, B makes a down-payment of £5,000, and A fails to deliver, then B can sue A simultaneously for specific performance (on the contract, because it has not been terminated) and return of his deposit (under unjust enrichment, because the contract could be terminated). This is not exactly German law's idea of contract and unjustified enrichment running in tandem.

The most interesting questions arise from contracts which are not enforceable. Birks agreed that these require a different treatment.[10] We have seen above that Lord Mansfield in *Moses v Macferlan* presented not only the well-known positive list of what are now understood to be unjust factors, but also a negative list composed of unenforceable claims.[11] We are told that a claim in unjust enrichment

> does not lie for money paid by the plaintiff, which is claimed of him as payable in point of honor and honesty, although it could not have been recovered from him by any course of law; as in payment of a debt barred by the Statute of limitations, or contracted during his infancy, or to the extent of principal and legal interest upon an usurious contract, or, for money fairly lost at play: because in all these cases, the defendant may retain it with a safe conscience, though by positive law he was barred from recovering.[12]

For many years the negative list was neglected in English law because in most of these situations no unjust factor could be detected. This changed, however, when in *Kleinwort Benson Ltd v Lincoln City Council* the House of Lords abolished the rule that mistake of law could not justify a claim for restitution.[13] Now, every item on Lord Mansfield's

[9] Birks, *Unjust Enrichment*, 125–126.
[10] Birks, *Unjust Enrichment*, 126.
[11] Chapter 8, section 1.3.B.
[12] *Moses v Macferlan* (1760) 2 Burr 1005 (KB).
[13] *Kleinwort Benson Ltd v Lincoln City Council* [1999] 2 AC 349 (HL).

negative list can be described in terms of mistake.[14] For example, the payer may have mistakenly believed that a claim was not time-barred. Regardless of whether an unjust factor approach or an absence of basis approach is followed, the time has come to take a fresh look at reasons which could justify the retention of such enrichments.

Meier and Krebs have illuminated this issue from an Anglo-German perspective.[15] Sheehan has taken a closer look at Lord Mansfield's negative list, providing powerful arguments that English law still recognizes natural obligations which, although unenforceable, can explain why no claim will lie in unjust enrichment if they have been performed.[16]

Birks agreed that, under an absence of basis approach, English law could no longer afford to ignore the issue of natural obligations.[17] Where no legally enforceable claim exists, natural obligations give a legal facet to moral obligations. In Birks' view, they operated in the form of a defence against a claim which would otherwise lie in unjust enrichment.

Classifying natural obligations, or reclassifying Lord Mansfield's negative list, under defences makes sense for an unjust factor approach. The claimant has paid a debt which was time-barred under the mistaken assumption that it was not; the existence of the debt as a natural obligation provides a defence. It is submitted, however, that on an absence of basis approach, the majority of Lord Mansfield's negative list, and most natural obligations, should feature not as a defence, but rather as justification for the enrichment. The enrichment is not unjust, but can be explained by an obligation which, although not enforceable, allows the defendant to keep the enrichment once the claimant has performed.

Limitation rules provide an important example for such unenforceable obligations. Limitation extends beyond contractual claims, but in the present context is best discussed with other unenforceable claims, most of which arise from contracts or other agreements.

14 See Dannemann, 79 Texas L Rev 1844–1845 (2001).

15 Meier, 301–353; Krebs, Ch. 14.

16 Sheehan (2004) LMCLQ 172ff, distinguishing between three types of natural obligations, of which only the first serves as a defence against a claim in unjust enrichment. See also Krebs, 267ff.

17 Birks, *Unjust Enrichment*, 258.

A consideration of the function of limitation rules will help to explain why they do not destroy a legal basis for keeping an enrichment.[18]

The rules on limitation of claims are directed against the enforcement of obligations after a certain time has passed. They seek to protect the debtor, who after the period has lapsed may rely on keeping the assets. They offer finality.[19] However, limitation rules do not seek to prevent the voluntary execution of such obligations. They offer no explanation for why the recipient should not keep the benefit.

This marks a clear distinction between limitation rules and rules which aim to make a contract void, such as rules in illegality. These are directed not only against the enforcement of, for example, agreements to launder money or to conceal assets from creditors, but equally against the execution of such agreements. Such void obligations cannot form a basis on which the recipient may keep the enrichment.[20]

What does the above imply for Lord Mansfield's negative list, or Sheehan's list of natural obligations? We will now take a closer look at the most important examples: (1) limitation of claims, (2) requirements of form, and (3) contracts beyond the capacity of minors. Gambling agreements would have been included in this list until s 335 of the Gambling Act 2005 made all lawful gambling agreements enforceable, so that they now provide the same basis for an enrichment as, say, a contract for the sale of goods.

A. Limitation of claims

Limitation features on the lists of both Lord Mansfield and Sheehan.[21] Time-barred claims, while not enforceable, nevertheless provide a basis for an enrichment once they have been honoured. We have seen above that limitation rules aim to protect defendants, but do not strike at the payment of time-barred debts. Section 214 para. 2 BGB contains an express provision to this effect.[22]

[18] For a comparative analysis based on German, English, Dutch, and Greek limitation rules, see Gerhard Dannemann, Fotios Karatzenis, and Geoffrey Thomas, 'Reform des Verjährungsrechts aus rechtsvergleichender Sicht', Rabels Zeitschrift für ausländisches und internationales Privatrecht (1991), 697ff.

[19] *Chitty on Contracts*, 28–001.

[20] Recovery may nevertheless be refused because illegality may be available as a defence. See Birks, *Unjust Enrichment*, 247, and above, Chapter 4, section 3.

[21] Sheehan (2004) LMCLQ 188, who, however, views time-barred claims as 'anomalous natural obligations when seen against other examples'.

[22] Above, Chapter 2, section 6.2.C.

B. Requirements of form

It is interesting to note that Lord Mansfield's negative list does not mention requirements of form, even though the Statute of Frauds preceded *Moses v Macferlan* by 87 years. On the other hand, Sheehan counts contracts which are void for lack of formality amongst natural obligations.[23]

Section 4 of the Statute of Frauds provides that certain agreements are not actionable unless they are evidenced in writing; in its present version, the section applies to guarantees.[24] Although unenforceable, an oral guarantee can nevertheless provide a basis for the guarantor's payment. No one has suggested that a guarantor who has paid should be able to recover on the ground that the guarantee agreement was not evidenced in writing; strong authority suggests that no such claim should lie.[25] The same is true for contracts which are caught by s 2(1) Law of Property (Miscellaneous Provisions) Act 1989. This Act has gone beyond the 'evidenced in writing' requirement established by its predecessors[26] and provides in s 2(1):

> A contract for the sale or other disposition of an interest in land can only be made in writing and only by incorporating all the terms which the parties have expressly agreed in one document or, where contracts are exchanged, in each.

In *Tootal Clothing v Guinea Properties*, the Court of Appeal limited the effects of this section to contracts prior to their performance.[27] Scott LJ stated:

> However, section 2 is of relevance only to executory contracts. It has no relevance to contracts which have been completed. If parties choose to complete an oral land contract or a land contract that does not in some respect or other comply with section 2, they are at liberty to do so. Once they have done so,

[23] Sheehan (2004) LMCLQ 188. See also Krebs, 263ff.

[24] See *Actionstrength Ltd v International Glass Engineering Ltd* [2003] UKHL 17, [2003] 2 AC 541, where the House of Lords refused to override the requirement of writing in equity on the ground that the recipients had relied on an oral guarantee.

[25] *Thomas v Brown* (1876) 1 QBD 714. The High Court (Quain J) rejected an action for recovery of a deposit under a contract for the sale of land which was void under s 4 of the Statute of Frauds because it did not disclose the vendor.

[26] Section 40 of the Law of Property Act 1925; s 4 of the Statute of Frauds.

[27] *Tootal Clothing v Guinea Properties* (1992) 64 P&CR 452 (CA); see also Goff and Jones, 21–001; Sheehan (2004) LMCLQ 189.

it becomes irrelevant that the contract they have completed may not have been in accordance with section 2.

It is unlikely that Scott LJ intended this dictum to dovetail with an absence of basis approach, but if he had, he could hardly have formulated it better. The form requirement lapses once the oral contract has been completed, and the contract stands as a basis which defeats a claim in unjust enrichment.

There are, however, some statutory requirements of form which provide for a different solution. The case of *Wilson v First County Trust Ltd* involved as defendant a pawnbroker who had lent the claimant borrower a sum of money for six months on the security of her car.[28] The agreement did not state the total amount of credit as required by s 61(1) Consumer Credit Act, with the consequence that, under ss 65(1) and 127(3), the agreement could not be enforced against the debtor. Therefore the borrower was allowed to keep the money and did not have to pay interest. Furthermore, the pawnbroker had no defence against the borrower's claim for recovery of her car.

This makes it clear that s 127(3) of the Consumer Credit Act is not limited to executory contracts and that it is unlikely that an agreement which falls short of the requirements of ss 65(1) and 127(3) can provide any basis for the mutual enrichments exchanged under such a contract. This is best understood as a baseless enrichment, and the result—which provides a windfall to the borrower, and appears somewhat harsh on the lender—as a policy-motivated defence which is given to the borrower only, not for the individual borrower's benefit but in order to provide a strong incentive for lenders to observe the requirement of form. Lord Nicholls put the point in this way:[29]

> But when legislation renders the entire agreement inoperative, to use a neutral word, for failure to comply with prescribed formalities the legislation itself is the primary source of guidance on what are the legal consequences. Here the intention of Parliament is clear.

Other statutory requirements of form must be examined in the same way to discover whether they too aim to make executed contracts void.[30] The wording of the provisions in question may often offer no more

[28] *Wilson v First County Trust Ltd* [2003] UKHL 40, [2004] 1 AC 816.

[29] Ibid, at para 49.

[30] Similar Krebs, 263, also arguing from an Anglo-German perspective; see also Meier, 301ff.

than limited guidance. For example, s 18 of the Gambling Act 1845 (now repealed by s 334 of the Gambling Act 2005) made gambling agreements 'null and void', yet at the same time prohibited the recovery of any deposit made for that purpose. *Lipkin Gorman* confirmed that parties could not recover what they had paid under a null and void agreement of that type.[31] Similarly, although s 1 of the Infants Relief Act 1874 made certain contracts entered into by minors 'absolutely void', this did not mean that infants could recover what they had performed.[32] On the other hand, even where a statute provides that lack of form will render a contract 'unenforceable', the recipient of performance under such a contract may be liable in unjust enrichment, as the Australian case of *Pavey and Matthews v Paul* shows.[33]

We have seen above for form provisions what is generally true for invalidating provisions in German law, namely that they are usually written with unjustified enrichment in mind.[34] The general rule is that lack of form will not only render a contract unenforceable, but also void. A contract which lacks the required form does not provide a legal basis which would allow a recipient to retain a benefit received under such a contract. However, there are several statutory provisions which, for particular situations, provide that a lack of form is healed when the contract is executed. This makes such a contract valid, and the recipient may therefore retain such benefits.

It is doubtful, however, whether any similar, or even opposing, general rule can be extracted from English law. For an absence of basis approach in English law, this implies that only careful statutory interpretation will reveal whether a contract which lacks a required form can provide a basis which entitles the recipient to keep the enrichment.

[31] *Lipkin Gorman v Karpnale Ltd* [1991] 2 AC 548, 577.

[32] *Pearce v Brain* [1929] 2 KB 310, see below, Chapter 4, section 2.2.C. This category of 'absolutely void' contracts was abolished by s 1 of the Minors' Contracts Act 1987. See *Chitty on Contracts*, 8–005.

[33] *Pavey and Matthews Proprietary Ltd v Paul* (1987) 162 CLR 221 (HCA). A builder was entitled to a *quantum meruit* (not the contractual rate) for work provided under a building contract which was 'unenforceable' for lack of written form required by s 45 of the Builders Licensing Act 1971 (NSW). Birks, *Unjust Enrichment*, 127 appeared to take a different view as he treated Mrs Paul's refusal to pay as repudiation. But can one-sided performance suffice for making the contract enforceable vis-à-vis the other party?

[34] Chapter 2, section 6.2.B.

C. Contracts beyond the capacity of minors

Under English law, minors are capable of entering into contracts, in particular those which provide a minor with 'necessaries'. Additionally, contracts involving the acquisition of a permanent interest in property are binding on a minor unless they are repudiated. Furthermore, on attaining full age, a person may ratify contracts which had previously not been binding for lack of capacity.[35] All three types of valid contract are of no further interest in the present context. But what about contracts which go beyond necessaries and which are either repudiated or not ratified?

Such contracts appear on Lord Mansfield's negative list, whereas Sheehan argues that they will often be unable to produce a natural obligation, because this would frequently undermine the protective purpose of provisions on capacity.[36]

These different views indicate that it can be difficult to reconcile existing rules on the personal incapacity of minors with general rules of unjust enrichment law, regardless of whether an unjust factor approach or an absence of basis approach is followed. At the risk of considerable oversimplification, the following general patterns can be observed:

(1) Minors are not liable to return any performance made under an agreement which is unenforceable against them for lack of capacity,[37] even if there has been failure of consideration or a mistake as to the minor's age. This common law rule is modified by a statutory provision which allows courts to order restitution of property acquired by a minor on a discretionary basis.[38]

(2) On the other hand, a minor can in principle recover what he or she performed under an agreement which is not subsequently ratified, or after it has been repudiated. It appears, however, that this is possible only where failure of consideration has been total, which will frequently not be the case. The main authorities for this view date from the 1920s, namely *Steinberg v Scala*

[35] See *Chitty on Contracts*, 8–002 to 8–044.

[36] Sheehan (2004) LMCLQ 191.

[37] *Chitty on Contracts*, 8–049.

[38] Under s 3 of the Minors' Contracts Act 1987 it is at the discretion of the courts whether the minor should return to the other party any property acquired under this type of invalid agreement, but s 3(2) also states that '[n]othing in this section shall be taken to prejudice any other remedy available to the [other party]'.

(Leeds) Ltd, for contracts which were repudiated,[39] and *Pearce v Brain* for contracts which were not ratified.[40]

Some writers have criticized this view. Burrows has argued forcefully that greater prominence should be given to the protective policy of rules on contractual capacity of minors, so that the requirement of total failure must be reconsidered.[41] Sheehan believes that recovery would now be possible in the case of a minor's mistaken belief that the contract was enforceable (mistake of law).[42] Meier, who points out that there are other situations in which minors will more easily obtain restitution, is critical of the general inconsistency.[43] Be that as it may, both of the above restrictions—which, incidentally, are unknown to German law[44]—are not easily squared with the modern understanding of failure of consideration as an unjust factor, where the 'total' requirement has otherwise been substantially eroded.[45] Nor could they be reconciled with an absence of basis approach. Whereas the first restriction can be formulated as a policy-based defence aimed at the protection of minors, it is difficult to find any explanation for the second.

3. Non-contractual agreements

'Non-contractual agreements' are agreements which are not considered to be contracts in English law. They include agreements which

[39] *Steinberg v Scala (Leeds) Ltd* [1923] 2 Ch 452 (CA). A minor who had bought shares in a company was not allowed to have her name removed from the register, and to receive her money back, on the ground that there had not been a total failure of consideration. Whittaker sees this as part of a general rule whereby restitution is not allowed for performance made prior to repudiation: *Chitty on Contracts*, 8–040.

[40] *Pearce v Brain* [1929] 2 KB 310. A minor had exchanged a motorcycle and sidecar worth £30 for a car worth £15; the rear axle of the car broke after the minor had driven some 70 miles. Recovery was disallowed because failure of consideration had not been total.

[41] Burrows, 415.

[42] Sheehan (2004) LMCLQ 191.

[43] Meier, 323f. She points out that minors can generally claim back what they have performed, as long as the other party has not performed, even if the other party is willing to do so: *Corpe v Overton* (1833) 10 Bing 252, last cited and distinguished in *Steinberg v Scala (Leeds) Ltd* [1923] 2 Ch 452, 460f.

[44] For an account of German rules on the contractual capacity of minors from an unjust enrichment perspective, see Krebs, 180ff.

[45] See Burrows, 333ff.

either do not require consideration (such as express trusts) or which are not enforceable for lack of consideration (in particular gifts, some agency agreements, and some situations of bailment).

Readers may think that this category of non-contractual agreements under English law exists only in the imagination of the present author. They may have a point.[46] We will see below, however, that if English law adopts an absence of basis approach, this would create strong incentives for recognizing that there is such a thing as an English law of non-contractual agreements.

There are many situations in which one party has knowingly enriched the other in order to execute an agreement which is not a contract under English law, notably because one of the parties has not provided any consideration. No unjust factor has hitherto called for the restitution of such a benefit when everything goes according to plan, and this result is usually correct. An absence of basis approach, though, may struggle to find the right basis which allows recipients to keep their enrichments.

A. *Gifts and trusts*

Birks was well aware that English law, with its comparatively narrow understanding of contract, must venture further and include in particular gifts and trusts, both of which he considered to provide a legal basis which justified enrichment.[47] However, the German experience shows that there are many other agreements under which one party is to receive something for nothing, and that these should also be 'unjust enrichment-proof', i.e. considered as providing a legal basis.

B. *Gratuitous use*

A person may give money, chattels, or real property to another person not for keeping, but for using:

- A asks Z: 'Can you lend me £100 until the end of the month?'
- B, who needs to pick up a friend at the airport, is offered the use of her neighbour Y's car.

[46] But see Ben McFarlane, 'The Enforcement of Non-Contractual Agreements to Dispose of Interests in Land' (2005) 16 Kings College Law Journal 174ff.

[47] Birks, *Unjust Enrichment*, 148ff. It is an altogether different matter that gifts can be more easily revoked on the ground of mistake than contracts.

- C is allowed to use the flat of his acquaintance X while X is away on holiday.

A, B, and C duly return what has been given to them. Can Z, Y, and X claim in unjust enrichment for the value of this use? There can be no doubt that A, B, and C have been enriched by being allowed to use Z's, Y's, or X's money, car, or flat at their expense. Z, Y, and X could try to find some unjust factor, but this would be an uphill struggle if the circumstances indicate that the use was intended to be gratuitous.

How could an absence of basis approach defeat such claims? Such a basis can be provided by agreements between the parties involved. German law recognizes several agreements which fit this bill, all of which are considered to be contracts.

We saw above that gratuitous use of money is covered in German law by §§ 488–498 BGB on contracts of loan.[48] Parties are free to stipulate that no interest should be paid. Therefore a contract for a gratuitous loan explains why, under German law, Z cannot sue A in unjust enrichment for interest on the amount lent to A.

In English law, it is uncertain whether this can be a contract before the loan is paid over, because the promise of a loan is not supported by any consideration, except perhaps the promise to pay the money back. In *Chitty on Contracts* Guest notes that 'there appears to be no authority on this question'.[49] Birks took the view that the loan was paid over voluntarily, but with the purpose of imposing a contractual obligation of repayment on the recipient.[50] Once we have a valid contract of loan, this provides the basis on which A is entitled to the free use of Z's money. Gratuitous loans are therefore unproblematic for an absence of basis approach.

We saw above that §§ 598–606 BGB on *Leihe* cover gratuitous lending of chattels or real property.[51] The agreement by which Y allows B to use his car is such a contract of *Leihe*, and provides a basis for B's enrichment. The closest English equivalent, i.e. gratuitous bailment in the form of a *commodatum*,[52] is not a contract, but situated

[48] Chapter 2, section 6.2.A.

[49] *Chitty on Contracts*, 38–223 note 1103.

[50] Birks, *Unjust Enrichment*, 144f.

[51] Chapter 2, section 6.2.A.

[52] *Coggs v Barnard* (1703) 2 Ld Raym 909, 916, per Holt CJ; *Chitty on Contracts*, para 33–041. This is not to be confused with deposit, an agreement for gratuitous

somewhere between contract, tort, and property law—an agreement made in connection with the transfer of possession of a chattel under which the bailee is allowed to use the chattel without charge.

Can bailment be the basis for this shift of value which would prevent Y from subsequently charging B for the use of his car? This is largely uncharted territory. The preferable view is to see the bailment agreement as a basis for this enrichment, with the result that there is from the outset nothing unjust about the enrichment. This view is most consistent with the main characteristic of the absence of basis approach, which simply leaves it to other areas of law (such as contract, tort, or property) to discover whether a shift of wealth is justified. Bailment explains this enrichment equally as well as a car rental contract would, because both agreements allow B to use Y's car.

Whereas the German *Leihe* covers both chattels and real property, bailment is limited to the former. It offers no help for explaining why X should not be allowed to sue C for the value of the use of his flat. The classification of this type of agreement under English law is not straightforward—perhaps a gratuitous licence,[53] which could explain C's entitlement to possession not only for the purpose of property law, but also in terms of enrichment.

C. *Gratuitous services*

An absence of basis approach would also force English law to look more closely at agreements whereby one person is to provide gratuitous services to another.

- D, who lives in London, has been offered a job in Carlisle and asks W, her cousin who lives locally, to find and rent for her a two-bedroom flat.
- E asks his friend V: 'I wonder whether you could look after my children this evening. I have to go to a parents' meeting.'
- F, who is painting her house, is pleased when her neighbour U offers to help and spends hours doing the fiddly jobs.

safekeeping (*Coggs v Barnard* at 913), to which the closest German equivalent is *Verwahrung*, §§ 688–700 BGB.

[53] See *Ramnarace v Lutchman* [2001] UKPC 25, [2001] 1 WLR 1651, 1656; *Manchester Airport plc v Dutton* [2000] 1 QB 133 (CA).

D, E, and F are enriched by services or work provided by W, V, and U. Under German law, both contracts for services (§§ 611–630 BGB) and contracts for works (§§ 631–651 BGB) can be entered into as gratuitous agreements.[54] There is also a contract entitled *Auftrag* or mandate (from the Roman *mandatum*) whereby one party agrees to carry out someone else's business gratuitously (§§ 662–674 BGB).[55] All three contacts provide a legal basis for the enrichment which occurs when these contracts are performed.

Can English law provide similar bases? Gifts are not an option if the traditional view is taken that these are limited to gratuitous transfer of property.[56] It is interesting to note that unjust enrichment lawyers have broadened the notion of gifts. Goff and Jones include gratuitous services,[57] Birks even included what he called a 'grudging gift', knowing transfers of benefits which the donor cannot help but make, for example if I heat my room in the knowledge that the fuel I pay will also make the room of my upstairs neighbour warmer.[58]

If it was appropriate to warn above of dangerous knock-on effects which a legal transplant from another system (such as an absence of basis approach) can have on its surroundings (such as the English law of gifts), this could have served as an example. Such a notion of gift is so wide that its main function has become that of explaining aspects of a different area of law (unjust enrichment), but not to explain and regulate legal aspects of gifts.[59] It is safe to predict that no promise of such a gift would ever be made under deed. Rules on revocation of gifts will either render this 'grudging gift' of rising heat meaningless,[60] or will not fit into this wide notion. It could have puzzling implications for rules on taxation of gifts, on limiting or registration of gifts made to holders of public office, or on confiscation of gifts made from

54 See above, Chapter 2, section 6.2.A.

55 Above, ibid. Remuneration would make this a *Geschäftsbesorgungsvertrag* under §§ 675–676 BGB.

56 *Halsbury's Laws of England*, 4th edn reissue, vol. 20, 16.

57 Goff and Jones, 1–062.

58 Birks, *Unjust Enrichment*, 158–159; see also below, section 3.2.A.

59 There is a paucity of academic writing on the English law of gifts. Richard Hyland, *Gifts A Study in Comparative Law* (Oxford University Press, forthcoming 2009).

60 Gifts can be made revocable, see e.g. *Earl Grey v Attorney-General* [1900–1903] All ER 268 (HL); *Tikiri Banda Dullewet v Padma Rukmani Dullewe* [1969] 2 AC 313. Any grudging gift-giver could simply revoke and thus destroy the gift as a legal basis.

the proceeds of crime. It is for good reason that we think in terms of sales contracts (as the remunerated equivalent in contract law to the traditional notion of gifts) rather than in terms of the 'provision of a benefit in exchange for money, including grudging provision'. As Birks has stated elsewhere, 'That which is stretched and distorted soon becomes difficult to understand and impossible to apply'.[61] Therefore a solution other than the boundless inflation of gifts needs to be found for English law. It is argued here that the best way forward is to build on all existing non-contractual agreements in English law, and to expand their number where necessary.

Much of what German law covers with *Auftrag* can be understood in English law as an agency agreement, which can also be made outside contract law.[62] Again, this appears to have been little explored in terms of unjust enrichment, but it is suggested that the agreement provides the basis which entitles the principal to retain the benefit of the agent's work without having to pay for the value of the service in unjust enrichment. For this reason, in our example, W should not be allowed to claim in unjust enrichment a fee for having acted as D's agent.

English law will find it more difficult to cover the gratuitous provision of other services, or of works. For a rather limited range of cases, one particular form of bailment, i.e. mandate (also derived from the Roman *mandatum*), can assist, as mandate is characterized by the undertaking of the bailee to perform a gratuitous act, normally some service to be performed in relation to the bailed chattel.[63] However, mandate can provide no explanation if possession in the chattel does not pass, or in the large majority of cases where the gratuitous service is not related to any chattel, as in our example of V babysitting for E.

It may become necessary to resort to a general notion of agreements outside contract law, going beyond those which are presently recognized in English law, such as gifts, express trusts, bailment, and certain

[61] Peter Birks, 'The Law of Restitution at the End of an Epoch' (1999) 28 U West Aust LR 13, 28.

[62] *Chitty on Contracts*, 31–020.

[63] *Coggs v Bernard* (1703) 2 Ld Raym 909, 918, per Holt CJ, drawing on Bracton; *Chitty on Contracts* (note 49) para 33–040. The case concerned the gratuitous storage of a consignment of brandy; the defendant was held liable for his negligence. It is noteworthy that Holt CJ, at 920, found consideration in the bailor having entrusted his goods to the bailee.

forms of agency.[64] Gifts are unenforceable due to the lack of consideration but, once executed, they provide a legal basis for an enrichment. We have seen that there are many other agreements which are also unenforceable for lack of consideration, but which can equally well explain a shift of wealth. An absence of basis approach towards unjust enrichment is best served by treating all such agreements alike, regardless of whether they fall within recognized categories of non-contractual agreements.

3. Adjustments within unjust enrichment

In looking at the adjustments which a switch to an absence of basis approach would necessitate or at least make advisable for English law, particular attention must be paid to those areas of unjust(ified) enrichment where the English unjust factor approach and German law do not overlap. Most of these situations can be found in subtractive enrichment.

1. Wider scope of unjust factors

We have seen that there are situations where an unjust factor can be identified, but where the recipient can point to a legal ground which supports the enrichment. We have looked above at the example of A sending a cheque to Mrs Smith to pay for the damage which his dog caused to her dress, not realizing that she was not the nice Mrs Smith whom he had known for years, but another neighbour he loathed.[65] A cannot recover under § 812 BGB because the payment is supported by a legal ground in the form of Mrs Smith's tort claim against A as the dog owner, and most would agree that this is the correct result. But A can recover under English law, because A paid under a causative mistake, and because it is at least uncertain whether discharge of an

[64] It should be noted that Gerard McMeel, 'On the redundancy of the concept of bailment', in: Alastair Hudson (ed), *New Perspectives on Property Law, Obligations and Restitution* (2004) 247, has argued that 'bailment has no autonomous legal content' and should be dissolved into 'concepts of consent, wrongdoing, unjust enrichment or property'.

[65] Above, Chapter 8, section 2.5.

obligation can defeat enrichment outside contract law. The difficulties which this simple case can create for an unjust factor approach makes an absence of basis approach seem quite simple.

2. Wider scope of absence of basis

Potentially more numerous and more difficult are situations in which an enrichment has been made without legal ground, but where no unjust factor would call for restitution. Precisely how numerous these are depends on whether an absence of basis approach is supplemented by the performance/non-performance divide.

A. 'Rising heat'—non-performance enrichments

This is perhaps best illustrated by the 'rising heat' example used by Birks, which we encountered above in the context of non-contractual agreements.[66] When I heat my room, I cannot help that some of that heat will end up in the room of my neighbour upstairs. My heat loss is a disenrichment, the neighbour's heat gains an enrichment. Birks finds a legal basis for this enrichment in a 'grudging gift' which I make to my neighbour.

This case is unproblematic for an unjust factor approach, because no unjust factor can be found which would allow me to recover from my neighbour. There is no mistake (but see next paragraph), no compulsion, no failure of consideration. The same case is equally unproblematic for German law. This is not a case of performance, nor of infringement, nor of owner/possessor claims, nor of *negotiorum gestio* (as heating my room is my own business). It is possible to think about constructing this as expenditure under the *Verwendungskondiktion*, but that would be a very long shot and certainly stretch the notion of *Verwendung*.[67]

This case is, however, highly problematic for an absence of basis approach which does not rely on a performance/non-performance divide.

[66] Birks, *Unjust Enrichment*, 158–159; above, Chapter 9, section 2.3.C.

[67] It is interesting to note that von Caemmerer, 351, uses another heating example to illustrate the *Verwendungskondiktion*, namely if a caretaker mistakenly uses his own fuel to heat a building, rather than the landlords' fuel. Recovery is unproblematic: mistake is available as unjust factor, the *Verwendungskondiktion* will lie, and there can be no question of a 'grudging gift'.

The explanation of 'grudging gift' is not only questionable in its very broad approach to what a gift can be,[68] it is also not workable. Not everyone is as familiar with the laws of physics as was Birks. What about those people who would be surprised to hear that they had been heating their neighbours' flats for years? Extending 'grudging gifts' further to 'unconscious gifts' would take us back to conceptual monstrosities such as 'pseudo-quasi-contract'[69] which unjust enrichment has overcome. As 'gift' is not an option, this means that people can sue their neighbours for the value of the heat which has risen as long as they did not know that their neighbour was benefiting. They can incidentally do the same under an unjust factor approach if they can also show that they would have turned down their heat had they only known that their neighbour was benefiting, because in this case the neighbour's heat gain was based on a causative mistake.

For those who knew that the heat was rising, the law of gifts offers another way to a claim. Gifts can be made revocable.[70] Therefore before I turn on my heat in the autumn, I drop a note in my neighbour's letterbox which states that I give my neighbour this heat as revocable gift. In spring, I revoke my gift and claim the value as unjust enrichment. And if we were really to accept that there is such a thing as grudging gifts—gifts which a party does not want to make but feels powerless not to make—these should probably even carry the presumption of being revocable.

Could we instead attempt to solve this problem by giving a wider notion to legal basis, perhaps in line with the Canadian 'juristic reason'?[71] Rather than relying on other areas of law such as property or contract law for a legal basis,[72] unjust enrichment could then create its own basis for keeping an enrichment. That, however, is very likely to take us back to an approach to unjust enrichment which is based on

68 Above, section 2.3.C.

69 Percy Winfield, *The Province of the Law of Tort* (1931), 148: 'The phrase is barbarous, but we can think of no other'.

70 *Earl Grey v Attorney-General* [1900–1903] All ER 268 (HL); *Tikiri Banda Dullewet v Padma Rukmani Dullewe* [1969] 2 AC 313.

71 *Pettkus v Becker* [1980] 2 SCR 824. See generally Lionel Smith, 'Demystifying Juristic Reason' (2007) 45 Can Bus Law J 281ff.

72 Both property and contract law can be used to address the issue of heating costs, usually by distributing costs for operating a central heating system between co-owners or co-tenants. Those solutions are, however, outside unjust enrichment.

equity and policy considerations, a solution which has been rejected by both English and German law.

Situations which are comparable to that of the rising heat can be found outside subtractive enrichment. Birks gave the following additional example of a 'grudging gift': 'Similarly, if you have a flat which overlooks the Oval you will be able to watch test matches without paying.'[73] Should everyone who can see a sports ground, outdoor stage or cinema screen be made to pay for the performances they can watch from their living room? Certainly not. But it is hard to find any legal basis for such an enrichment. The German performance/non-performance divide will again make such a search unnecessary and agree with the unjust factor approach that no claim will lie in unjust(ified) enrichment.

B. *Enrichment between three or more parties*

In situations involving three or more parties, the unjust factor will frequently help to find the right claimant as the person who was mistaken, whose expected consideration failed, who was compelled to act, etc. The unjust factor approach is frequently less helpful in finding the right defendant. We have seen that in cases such as *Barclays Bank v Simms*, this approach permits a choice of potential defendants which German law would normally exclude.[74] However, we have also seen that an absence of basis approach per se gives a wide choice between potential claimants and potential defendants. We have used above the example of a tenant who has instructed a glazier under a contract (which is void for mistake) to install a window, and where the work is carried out by the glazier's apprentice.[75] Possible claimants are the apprentice (the labour being the disenrichment) and the glazier, possible defendants are the tenant and the landlord. Mistake as an unjust factor would narrow down the choice of claimant to the glazier, but leave us with two potential defendants (tenant and landlord).

An absence of basis approach will reveal that no legal basis can be found for the enrichment for any of the four potential claims

[73] Birks, *Unjust Enrichment*, 158.

[74] Above, Chapter 3, section 2; *Barclays Bank Ltd v W J Simms Son & Cooke (Southern) Ltd* [1980] 1 QB 677 (QBD).

[75] Chapter 2, sections 2.2 and 3.2

apprentice–tenant, apprentice–landlord, glazier–tenant, and glazier–landlord.

It is only the performance-based taxonomy for unjustified enrichment which tells us that it is the glazier who must sue the tenant, as it is the glazier who, by sending the apprentice, was attempting to discharge an obligation towards the tenant (and not towards the landlord).

If English law is to switch to an absence of basis approach, this would give it a choice between widening or narrowing the number of potential unjust enrichment claims in situations involving three or more parties. The wide choice between claimants and defendants which a mere absence of basis approach makes possible runs contrary to both English law instincts and comparative experience.[76] French law opened up precisely such a wide choice in the famous *Boudier* case, where an unpaid seller of fertilizer to a lessee of agricultural property was allowed to sue the owner of the fertilized property after the lessee had terminated the lease. French law has since had to hedge *Boudier* liability to such a degree that many think the case would be decided differently today.[77]

The German experience offers two such choices for narrowing the number of potential claimants and defendants.

The first is the requirement of a 'direct shift' which the courts applied for the first sixty years after the BGB entered into force. It is of no use in the glazier example, as it would point to the apprentice as claimant and the landlord as defendant. As we have seen above, 'direct shift' has in general proved to be untenable in German court practice.[78] The second is the performance/non-performance divide. This has functioned rather well in carving out what could be the largest possible area of unjustified enrichment law in which the inquiry whether the enrichment is unjustified can be left completely to other areas of law. It has also achieved reasonably good results in

[76] For a comparative analysis of unjust(ified) enrichment between three or more parties, see Schlechtriem, *Restitution und Bereicherungsausgleich*, Vol. II, Ch. 7. French law opened up unjust enrichment to this effect in the *Boudier* case: Cass. req. 15.6.1892, S. 1893.1.281, but was eventually forced to give up, see Schlechtriem Vol. I 1 no. 6; 2 no. 197 note 742.

[77] For a comparative discussion, see Zweigert and Kötz, 586; Schlechtriem, *Restitution und Bereicherungsausgleich*, Vol. II 7 nos 18ff.

[78] Chapter 2, section 1.

defining the right claimant and the right defendant,[79] even though we have seen that it is not always easy to maintain a sense of direction in the sea of case law which German courts have produced.[80]

C. *Execution of ill-founded disputed claims*

It is submitted that a shift towards an absence of basis approach may help to close what is the only remaining substantial gap within the unjust factor approach, a gap which generally produces highly unsatisfactory results, and exceptionally produces satisfactory results, but at the expense of consistency and clarity. A string of English cases are variations of the following standard situation:[81]

G makes a *bona fide* request for payment from T. T disputes the claim, but pays under protest in order to avert grave consequences threatened by G. Later, it transpires that G's demand was not justified.

The basic rule in English law is that T cannot recover. The reason for this is simple to say and difficult to explain: compulsion is not an autonomous unjust factor, but borrowed from contract law. This may have been done more by accident than by design: most other unjust factors are autonomous.

Mistake as a doctrine of contract law is very narrow. It is only under the most exceptional circumstances that a mistake will make a contract void.[82] Within unjust enrichment, mistake follows autonomous rules. These are diametrically opposed to the contract rule: any mistake which has caused the claimant to transfer assets to the defendant will

[79] Above, Chapter 2, sections 2–3.

[80] Chapter 3, section 2.

[81] *CTN Cash and Carry Ltd v Gallaher Ltd* [1994] 4 All ER 714 (CA): in order to avert the threatened withdrawal of a voluntary credit facility, the claimants had paid for goods which were destroyed before the risk had passed. *Maskell v Horner* [1915] 3 KB 106 (CA): the claimant was forced to pay unjustified market tolls by defendant seizing his goods or threatening to do so. *Twyford v Manchester Corporation* [1946] Ch 236: the unsuccessful claimant had paid under protest a fee unlawfully charged for the permission to 're-cut, re-paint or re-guild' inscriptions on gravestones in their cemetery. Similarly, *Still v Equitable Life Assurance Society Of United States* 54 SW 2d 947 (SCt Tenn 1932): the insured claimant was not allowed to recover the premiums which he had paid under protest in order to avert the lapse of his policy, after the insurer had wrongly, but in good faith, refused a contractually stipulated waiver of premiums on the ground of the insured's total disability. See the following text for two further examples.

[82] See *Great Peace Shipping v Tsavliris Salvage* [2002] EWCA Civ 1407.

allow the claimant to claim back those assets in unjust enrichment. This dramatically wider scope of mistake in unjust enrichment makes sense. If A mistakenly overpays a bill for £423 by paying £432 there is no reason to inquire whether an additional payment of £9 would have fundamentally altered the nature of the contract. Although it would obviously not have done so, A can claim back the £9 on the ground of his causative mistake.

The same is true for failure of consideration. Its contract law equivalents—in particular frustration and termination—are much more narrow. Again, there is no reason to inquire in unjust enrichment whether the failure of consideration is 'going to the root' of the relationship between claimant and defendant.

Compulsion is different. Except for 'legal compulsion' it is not an autonomous unjust factor, but merely a shorthand for the contractual doctrines of duress and undue influence. If B pays under threat, B can recover if the compulsion was so strong that it would have amounted to duress, and not otherwise. Any other 'causative compulsion' is not good enough, even if no hint of a contract can be found which could have explained his payment. If the same rationale were applied to mistake, A could not claim his overpayment of £9 in the previous example.

This difference in treatment may be accidental rather than intentional. No English judge appears ever to have contemplated whether compulsion in unjust enrichment must be as narrow as duress in contract law.[83] Neither does it appear that academics have wasted much thought on how it can be right that A can recover if A pays what he does not owe due to a stupid mistake, but B cannot recover if B makes the same unwarranted payment under pressure to his economic livelihood.

Why English judges and academics have not contemplated making compulsion an autonomous unjust factor is even more puzzling when considering that many find the results which this narrow construction of compulsion as unjust factor achieves to be very unattractive. *CTN Cash & Carry v Gallaher* shows that English judges will shake their heads in disbelief that reputable companies such as Gallaher should

[83] Recovery was indeed allowed in *Maskell v Horner* [1915] 3 KB 106 because the compulsion would have been strong enough to set aside a contract on the ground of duress to goods. There was, of course, no such contract in that case.

refuse to pay back what they were not owed, and regret that they cannot order them to do so.[84]

Therefore what English judges have done is to limit this damage for some situations by sending a knight in shining armour to the rescue of the claimant. Such a knight appeared in the guise of an ingenious and circular mistake of law in *Nurdin & Peacock v D B Ramsden*.[85] Under the threat of forfeiture of lease and repossession, the claimants had overpaid their rent. Neuberger J (as he then was) allowed them to recover on the ground that they had mistakenly believed that they were entitled to do so—with the effect that they had not been mistaken at all. Shining knights may save the day, but they come at a price.

More interesting in the present context is *Woolwich v Inland Revenue*.[86] The claimants had paid an *ultra vires* tax demand under protest, in order not to be branded as tax evaders and ultimately exposed to the sanctions of HM Revenue & Customs. The House of Lords allowed recovery by introducing the absence of basis approach into a particular area of the English law of unjust enrichment, namely demands made by public authorities.

Woolwich shows what would happen in other cases of execution of ill-founded disputed claims if an absence of basis approach were to be adopted for the entire English law of unjust enrichment. In all the above situations, T could claim back what was paid under protest, because no basis could be found on which G would be allowed to retain the enrichment.[87] *CTN Cash & Carry* would therefore need to be overruled, and *Nurdin & Peacock v D B Ramsden* would find a much more satisfactory explanation.

For the same reason, English law would need to take a fresh look at what Goff and Jones have called 'assumption of risk' and 'submission to an honest claim'.[88] In the present landscape of unjust factors, these are normally viewed as two separate issues located partly within

[84] *CTN Cash and Carry Ltd v Gallaher Ltd* [1994] 4 All ER 714, 719 (Steyn LJ) and 720 (Sir Donald Nicholls V-C).

[85] *Nurdin & Peacock v D B Ramsden & Co Ltd* [1999] 1 All ER 941.

[86] *Woolwich Equitable Building Society v Inland Revenue Commissioners* [1993] AC 70 (HL).

[87] In *Maskell v Horner* [1915] 3 KB 106, 118, Lord Reading CJ held obiter that if a person voluntarily and knowingly pays a disputed claim in order to close a transaction, this is to be treated as a gift. This should not, however, apply to payment under protest.

[88] Goff and Jones, 4–029 to 4–031 and 10–052 to 10–056.

mistake (assumption of risk) and partly within compulsion (submission to an honest claim).[89] This is less problematic for assumption of risk defeating a mistake, where it can be questioned how substantial the doubts have to be in order to have the same effect as a straightforward mistake.[90] In other words, it is logical to say 'you were not mistaken, because you only had a few doubts'.

Submission to an honest claim as defeating compulsion, though, makes as little sense as saying 'you were not compelled, because you submitted to the demand'. No compulsion is effective unless it ends in submission. Submission is a necessary element of compulsion. How can submission then at the same time give rise to a defence against compulsion? And how can an unjustified demand become just merely because the person making the claim honestly believed it to exist? Neither 'submission' nor 'honest claim' can justify why the recipient should be entitled to keep the enrichment.

That said, both assumption of risk and submission to an honest claim can prevent restitution if discussions between the parties have resulted in a contract of compromise, whereby the parties resolve their dispute somewhere in the middle ground. This compromise provides the basis for the enrichment, and parties cannot rely on mistake of law, or on compulsion, in order to reclaim what they have performed under the compromise[91]—unless, of course, mistake or compulsion makes that compromise void or voidable under the rules of contract law.[92]

Non-contractual submissions must be treated differently. If the payer eventually agrees to make full payment, there is no consideration, and

[89] However, in *Kleinwort Benson Ltd v Lincoln City Council* [1999] 2 AC 349, 382G, Lord Goff recognized, in addition to change of position, 'settlement of an honest claim (the scope of which is a matter of debate)' as a defence against unjust enrichment claims.

[90] This issue is not fully resolved. Lord Hope stated in *Kleinwort Benson Ltd v Lincoln City Council* [1999] 2 AC 349, 410, that a 'person who pays when in doubt takes the risk that he may be wrong' but, within a few months, recovery was allowed in such a case: *Nurdin & Peacock v D B Ramsden & Co Ltd* [1999] 1 All ER 941, an inconsistency pointed out by P Schlechtriem, *Restitution und Bereicherungsausgleich in Europa*, Vol. I, no. 141f n 429. It is submitted that *Nurdin & Peacock* is primarily a case of involuntary, rather than mistaken, payment.

[91] See *Brennan v Burdon and others* [2004] EWCA Civ 1017, [2005] QB 303: a compromise cannot be set aside on the ground that it was entered into under a mistake of law (that a claim was time-barred).

[92] Goff and Jones, 9–045.

hence no contract of settlement[93] (and even German law would not recognize such a 'gratuitous settlement').[94] Furthermore, there is often no agreement, simply reluctant payment.

For an absence of basis approach, these are straightforward cases of enrichments made without basis. Only if the claimant knowingly and voluntarily paid what was not due, will this give rise to a defence, as provided by § 814 BGB in German law.[95]

The most important practical difference between an English unjust factor approach, and a German absence of basis approach, concerns payments made under an express reservation. While reservations generally exclude the defence under § 814 BGB,[96] English law will give effect to a reservation only if the recipient has accepted it.[97] This effectively means that a contract is needed to justify recovery in unjust enrichment. This is diametrically opposed to an absence of basis approach, under which a contract (or other legal basis) is needed only to justify keeping the enrichment. There can be no hope of reconciliation. The acceptance requirement for reservations must therefore appear on the casualty list if English law shifts to an absence of basis approach.

The acceptance requirement is also extremely questionable from an economic viewpoint. In any of the above cases, it would have made sense for a party to pay first and continue to run the company (and in the private law cases: the business between the parties), and then to resolve the legal questions later. The present law, under which all overpayments will be lost, makes that impossible. It thus gives a strong incentive to discontinue a business relationship which is otherwise workable.

[93] See also Burrows, 139.

[94] Under § 779 BGB, a contract of compromise requires both parties to give in, whereas mere recognition of a debt under § 781 BGB can be claimed back in unjustified enrichment if the recognition is not supported by an existing claim. See above, Chapter 2, section 6.2.E.

[95] See above, Chapter 4, section 1. Cases such as BGH 17.2.1982, BGHZ 83, 278, 282 have extended this defence to involuntary performance. Voluntary and knowing payment of what is not due could also be understood as a gift, which would then provide a basis for the enrichment.

[96] Except for reservations made as standard procedure rather than under the circumstances of the individual case: OLG Koblenz 20.9.1983, NJW 1984, 135.

[97] *Nurdin & Peacock v D B Ramsden & Co Ltd* [1999] 1 All ER 941, 957f.

The problem could be resolved by giving compulsion the same autonomous unjust enrichment definition that mistake and failure of consideration have been given. But as this is unlikely to happen, cases of performance of an ill-founded disputed claim provide a good argument for switching to an absence of basis approach. If English courts are presently waiting for the right case to contemplate such a switch, this might well be the category within which such a case could fall.

4. Lessons for German law

Our comparison between German and English law of unjust(ified) enrichment has revealed some weaknesses in the German model. Some parts of the German law are unnecessarily complicated (below, sections 1 and 2). And German courts have over the last decades shown a tendency to shy away from developing the performance-based approach and retreat into loose good faith and policy-based considerations (below, section 3).

1. Reducing and consolidating models of restitutionary liability

We have seen above that unjustified enrichment competes with six other models of restitutionary liability. Their number is justified if they can produce refined solutions.

This is certainly true for the *cessio legis* model. It is easier to operate than its English equivalent, subrogation. Where provided by statute, *cessio legis* prevents unjustified enrichment and ensures in situations involving three or more parties that eventually the right party will have to pay or otherwise perform.

Good arguments can also be found for keeping the general substitution model under § 275 BGB.[98] This largely runs in tandem with substitution in unjustified enrichment under § 818 para. 1, which serves a useful function in defining when an initial object of enrichment is to

[98] Above, Chapter 1, section 4.5.

be replaced by another object, even if English lawyers would probably think that its scope is far too narrow.[99]

The *negotiorum gestio* model can be equally useful and allows for recovery of expenditure in situations in which it would be more difficult to argue why a claim should lie in unjustified enrichment, and why the measure should be based on the claimant's outlay rather than the defendant's gain.[100] However, the reverse claim which the party whose business has been conducted will have against the intervener—namely restitution of everything the intervener has obtained during the course of conducting the business—overlaps with unjustified enrichment. This claim is, however, important for the balance between the two parties. More precisely, it ensures that whenever an intervener can recover expenditure, the other party can claim the enrichment which the intervener has derived from the intervention. That link could easily be lost if the latter claim was confined to unjustified enrichment.

Nevertheless, there appears to be no particular reason why there should be separate rules for measuring this enrichment-based recovery in *negotiorum gestio* and in unjustified enrichment. The present reference which the BGB makes to mandate for this claim could be changed in favour of §§ 818–820 BGB.

Unjustified *negotiorum gestio* makes the law unnecessarily untidy. It is currently used mainly to allow gain-based recovery in situations where a claim lies in infringement-based unjustified enrichment.[101] We have seen above, though, that the wording of § 818 BGB, coupled with liability under § 816, will allow gain-based recovery in situations where courts currently use unjustified *negotiorum gestio*. Unjustified *negotiorum gestio* is therefore not primarily used for allowing gain-based recovery, but for disallowing such disgorgement where the defendant was not intentionally conducting someone else's business (i.e. not intentionally infringing the right of another party). However, as liability between unjustified *negotiorum gestio* and unjustified enrichment is concurrent,[102] this cannot exclude gain-based

[99] Above, Chapter 6, section 2.2.
[100] Above, Chapter 5, section 3.2.
[101] Above, Chapter 5, section 2.3, and Chapter 6, section 3.
[102] Above, Chapter 7, section 3.

recovery against an innocent or negligent infringer under unjustified enrichment. Therefore this problem has to be addressed in unjustified enrichment, and it is then possible to ask whether there is any need for rules on unjustified *negotiorum gestio*.

For anyone trained in the common law it is difficult to understand why German law should need a separate set of rules for claims between owners and possessors of property (the owner/possessor model). We have seen that the differences between the results achieved under the owner/possessor model on the one hand, and under the unjustified enrichment model on the other, are almost negligible. Verse has provided forceful arguments why there is really no justification for this separate regime, and he would like to see it abolished.[103] It is probably no coincidence that he based his findings on a comparative review of German and English (and also French) law.

It is equally possible to ask whether there really is a need for two separate restitutionary models for failed contracts, namely unjustified enrichment for all contracts which are, or have been, made void *ab initio*, and another under contract law for those contracts which have been terminated.[104] Hellwege has provided similarly forceful arguments why these two regimes should be reunited as one.[105] He also based his findings on a comparative review of German and English (and also Scots) law. It is also worth mentioning that both authors read restitution at Oxford University.

Some of the overlaps between tort and unjustified enrichment are also difficult to justify.[106] There appears to be no particular reason why 'restitutionary damages' should be available in tort only for violation of intellectual property rights, and why restitution for violation of other rights should be confined to unjustified enrichment. There is certainly no statutory basis for such a distinction. The tradition of German law to see 'restitution for wrongs' as part of unjustified enrichment is as strong as the scepticism for 'restitutionary damages'.

[103] Verse, *Verwendungen*, 157. See also Verse (1998) Rest L Rev 85.

[104] Above, Chapter 3, section 3.

[105] Hellwege, Ch. 3; similar Coen, 49f (comparing English and German law, the UN Convention on the International Sale of Goods, the UNIDROIT principles, and the Principles of European Contract Law).

[106] Above, Chapter 1, section 4.3.

Hence, the best solution would be to relocate the small and untidy corner of gain-based damages from the German law of tort to restitution under unjustified enrichment.

2. Reducing and consolidating types of unjustified enrichment claims

As discussed above, the performance/non-performance divide is a major strength of the German law of unjustified enrichment, and essential for carving out the largest number of unjustified enrichment situations in which 'absence of basis' or 'lack of legal ground' can be reduced to the simple inquiry whether any area of law outside unjustified enrichment allows the recipient to keep the enrichment. We have also seen that there are three types of unjustified enrichment claim that German courts and scholars see as operating under 'enrichment in another way', i.e. not based on performance. Two of these—the *Eingriffskondiktion* (based on infringement by the defendant) and the *Verwendungskondiktion* (based on expenditure by the claimant) fit that bill.

However, the comparative perspective has revealed that the same cannot be said for the third recognized 'non-performance' type, the *Rückgriffskondiktion* (based on the claimant's payment of the defendant's debt against a third party). This is clearly enrichment based on performance, defined as the intentional transfer of assets to another party with a particular obligation in mind. The difference to other cases is that within the *Rückgriffskondiktion* the notion of performance is not used in the usual way to define the correct defendant under the 'recipient perspective rule'.[107] The *Rückgriffskondiktion* allows leapfrogging to a different defendant, namely the debtor who was relieved of the obligation by the claimant's performance. It is really no more than an exception to the rule by which performance defines a defendant, and in some cases also an exception to the defence of 'no mistake' in § 814 BGB. We have seen that the very policy reasons that underlie the performance-based definition of the right defendant do not

[107] Under the 'recipient perspective rule', if there has been performance, it is the view of the enriched party that decides which of the various possible parties performed. See above, Chapter 3, section 2.

apply in situations where the *Rückgriffskondiktion* is allowed.[108] Consequently, German law would gain greatly in clarity and consistency if the *Rückgriffskondiktion* were relocated to its proper place within performance-based unjustified enrichment.

3. Developing rules rather than resorting to good faith

We have seen that over the last decades, German courts have time and again moved cases out of the sphere of application of defined rules and into the diffused sphere of good faith where each case is decided on its own merits. There may indeed be genuine cases that defy the general rules, and equitable considerations have some role to play in defining the liability which is based on unjustified enrichment. However, if we compare the attitude of German courts with that of their English counterparts, we cannot fail to notice that German courts have done considerably more to backtrack to a *Moses v Macferlan* type of equitable approach towards unjust(ified) enrichment.[109] German courts have often resorted to good faith or moved performance cases outside performance-based restitution when they could have better used those cases to develop the existing rules. For example, the case involving the fraudulent credit broker (case no. 16) could have been used to refine the 'recipient perspective rule' as operating for void, imperfect, or otherwise failed obligations, and not applying to purely imagined obligations.[110] We have seen that this rule protects a party against being sued by the wrong party in tri- or multipartite performance situations, and that it is justified where contracts are valid, void, voidable, or terminated, because it allows the recipient to rely on valid defences which arise out of this valid, void, or failed relationship. However, preference of the recipient is difficult to justify if the entire situation which could or could not provide a legal ground for keeping the enrichment is purely fictitious, because fictitious legal relationships cannot give rise to valid defences. By moving this case outside performance-based restitution, where it clearly belongs, the highest German court in civil

[108] Above, Chapter 5, section 4.4.

[109] Above, Chapter 8, sections 1.3.B and 2.2.

[110] BGH 5.11.2002, BGHZ 152, 307; below, Chapter 10, section 16 (translation); discussed above, Chapter 3, section 2.

law matters has missed the opportunity of a reasoned development of the law. Similar observations can be made about various other cases discussed above.[111]

5. Conclusions

We have seen above how German law could benefit from the English experience and perspective, in particular by trimming down the numerous competing models of restitutionary liability outside unjustified enrichment. Moreover, at times when English courts have rapidly developed unjust enrichment in a far more principled way, German courts have lost some of their focus and have tucked uncomfortable cases away inside ill-fitting categories or left them to good faith considerations on the merits of each case rather than use those cases profitably to develop the principles of unjustified enrichment.

We have also seen that English law is capable of switching to a German-style absence of basis approach towards unjust enrichment, as proposed by Birks. The necessary bases of enrichment could be developed (above, section 2). The remaining question is whether the benefits of such a switch would outweigh the disadvantages.

Perhaps the most important benefit is the simplicity and explanatory force which an absence of basis approach offers for restitution of performances. The unjust factor approach was a response to the artificiality of its predecessor, under which restitution in 'quasi-contract' was allowed on the fictitious promise to pay back money which the defendant had received at the expense of the claimant. Fictions may or may not be convenient (they usually are not), but they never can explain themselves. A fictitious promise is a means for constructing a claim, but does not inform us why the claim should be allowed. In contrast, the unjust factors each told their own story why a claimant should be allowed to recover. However, as the law of unjust enrichment unfolded and more and more time-honoured limitations to

[111] E.g. the prostitution advertisement case, BGH 5.5.1992, BGHZ 118, 182 and the black labour case BGH 31.5.1990, BGHZ 111, 308, 312, below, Chapter 10, section 12 (translation); both discussed above, Chapter 4, section 3.3.A.

enrichment claims were removed, the most prominent unjust factor, mistake, has lost most if not all of that explanatory power. The consecutive removal of two primary limitations—i.e. that the mistake must be a 'liability mistake' and not a mistake of law—meant that any mistake which was causally linked to enrichment and disenrichment would in principle allow a party to claim back the enrichment. Such a simple mistake will explain neither to the man on the Clapham omnibus[112] nor to trained lawyers why a particular claim in unjust enrichment should be allowed, in particular since simple causative mistakes are irrelevant in most other areas of law.

Moreover, there are a growing number of cases where a mistake-based claim in unjust enrichment was allowed, but where it was far from clear that the claimant had actually acted under a mistake.[113] In *Deutsche Morgan Grenfell*, Lord Hoffmann went as far as saying that the claimant was arguably 'deemed to have made a mistake'.[114] One might be forgiven for thinking that mistake is nowadays less used for explaining restitution and used more as a focal point for backward reasoning. A game of 'spot the mistake if you think the claimant should win' could easily become the unjust enrichment equivalent to a crossword. The explanatory force of a 'deemed mistake' does not exceed that of its predecessor, the fictitious promise, and can certainly not rival that of 'give this back to me, I did not owe it to you and you have no right to keep it', which is equally understandable to the man on the Clapham omnibus and the trained lawyer.[115]

It has also been argued above that the present unjust factor approach is too narrow in one area,[116] and perhaps too wide in another,[117]

[112] Above, Chapter 8, section 1.3.A.

[113] As e.g. in *Kleinwort Benson Ltd v Lincoln City Council* [1999] 2 AC 349 (HL); *Nurdin & Peacock v D B Ramsden & Co Ltd* [1999] 1 All ER 941.

[114] *Deutsche Morgan Grenfell Group plc v Her Majesty's Commissioners of Inland Revenue* [2006] UKHL 49. Lord Hoffmann referred to the claimant in *Kleinwort Benson Ltd v Lincoln City Council* [1999] 2 AC 349 (HL); see also Häcker, 180.

[115] In *Deutsche Morgan Grenfell*, Lord Hoffmann used the following words to justify the outcome in *Kleinwort Benson*: '[T]he money was not owing. It is therefore fair that he should recover it'.

[116] Section 3.2.C.

[117] Section 3.1.

and that a switch to an absence of basis approach would solve both problems.

Switching to an absence of basis approach also has disadvantages. The most important of these is the potential widening of the scope of unjust enrichment by creating additional claimants and defendants,[118] and also by including new situations which are presently only partially covered by unjust factors ('rising heat').[119] Both these increases are unwelcome as a matter of legal policy. A means would have to be found of excluding the additional unjust enrichment claims without resorting to an amorphous case law based on equitable consideration. We have seen that German law has eliminated this potential disadvantage by adopting the performance/non-performance divide, and that this could also operate to the advantage of English law.

Some writers are worried that a switch to an absence of basis approach could undermine the traditional English concern for security of receipts.[120] I fail to see, however, how an absence of basis approach, when combined with the performance/non-performance divide, could threaten people's reliance on keeping their lawful gains. The unjust factor 'mistake', in its present reduced form, is capable of wreaking greater havoc. It will even call for recovery in some situations of 'rising heat' which can be easily excluded by the performance/non-performance divide.[121]

It is submitted that a switch to an absence of basis approach would offer English law the chance to perform far more effectively than the present German law. Not only is the English legal system unhindered by the baggage of the BGB with its various inconsistencies, but it also currently has a judiciary which has demonstrated great skill and motivation to develop the law of unjust enrichment in accordance with principles and rules. They are much less tempted than their

[118] Section 3.2.B.

[119] Section 3.2.A.

[120] This concern has been expressed in particular by Virgo, 129; Kit Barker, 'Responsibility for Gain: Unjust Factors or Absence of Legal Ground? Starting Points in Unjust Enrichment Law', in: *Structure and Justification in Private Law*, 47, 73 (referring to the traditional position of English law that no justification is required if someone makes a gain at the expense of another person). See also above, Chapter 8, section 2.6.

[121] Section 3.2.A.

German colleagues to rest on their laurels and to move cases which bring fresh challenges out of the realm of principled reasoning and into the sphere of decisions made *ex aequo et bono*. At the end of the day, English lawyers may even teach German lawyers a thing or two about how to run a tight ship under an absence of basis approach towards unjust enrichment.

As time was ripe forty years ago for moving beyond fictitious promises, it may now be ripe for moving beyond deemed mistakes, preferably without resorting to fictitious gifts.[122]

122 Sections 3.2.A. and 2.3.C.

PART III
CASES AND STATUTES

10

Cases

This chapter contains 17 translations of key judgments by the *Bundesgerichtshof* which relate to unjustified enrichment and restitution. Fourteen of these are the author's own translations, of which twelve were published in 1997, both in the German Law Archive (<http://www.iuscomp.org/gla>) and in Basil Markesinis, Werner Lorenz, and Gerhard Dannemann, *The German Law of Obligations, Vol. I.* They have been nominally revised for the present text. The translations of case nos 6 (wrecked car), 13 (incapacity), and 15 (honorary consul) first appeared in 2003 in *Cases, Materials and Texts on Unjustified Enrichment*, ed. by Jack Beatson and Eltjo Schrage. They are reproduced below in unaltered form and by kind permission of Hart Publishing. The translations of case nos 16 and 17 have not been previously published. Permission to reproduce the translations of case nos 1–5, 7–12, 14, 16, and 17 can be obtained directly from the author.

These 17 cases include:

Case 1: BGH 21.12.1956, BGHZ 23, 61 (unwanted building)
Case 2: BGH 25.3.1963, BGHZ 39, 186 (bombed site)
Case 3: BGH 20.6.1963, BGHZ 40, 28 (fire brigade)
Case 4: BGH 31.10.1963, BGHZ 40, 272 (electrical appliances)
Case 5: BGH 11.1.1971, BGHZ 55, 176 (young bulls)
Case 6: BGH 14.10.1971, BGHZ 57, 137 (wrecked car)
Case 7: BGH 7.1.1971, NJW 1971, 609 (underage flyer)
Case 8: BGH 19.1.1984, BGHZ 89, 376 (standing order)
Case 9: BGH 15.5.1986, NJW 1986, 2700 (accident insurance)
Case 10: BGH 9.3.1989, BGHZ 107, 117 (toxicity research)
Case 11: BGH 23.2.1990, NJW-RR 1990, 827 (embezzlement)
Case 12: BGH 31.5.1990, BGHZ 111, 308 (black labour)
Case 13: BGH 20.6.1990, BGHZ 111, 382 (incapacity)

Case 14: BGH 17.6.1992, BGHZ 118, 383 (overpaid maintenance)
Case 15: BGH 5.10.1993, NJW 1994, 187 (honorary consul)
Case 16: BGH 5.11.2002, BGHZ 152, 307 (credit broker)
Case 17: BGH 9.7.2008, NJW 2008, 3277 (non-marital property)

The *Bundesgerichtshof* is Germany's highest court in civil and commercial matters. It hears in particular appeals from the *Oberlandesgerichte* (Higher Regional Courts, called *Kammergericht*, in Berlin). At first instance, cases are heard either by a *Landgericht* for higher value claims, or by an *Amtsgericht*.

1. BGH 21.12.1956, BGHZ 23, 61 (unwanted building)

Facts

The claimant leased from the defendant some six and a half acres (*Morgen*) of land for the purposes of cultivating agricultural products, and of breeding and keeping small animals. The lease was to run for nine years. The terms of the lease agreement specified that the leaseholder was entitled to erect such constructions on the site as were appropriate for the breeding and keeping of small animals. However, with the exception of a poultry coop, no solid constructions were to be erected without express written consent by the lessor. All of the small constructions were to remain on the property after the expiry of the lease. The lessor was to remunerate the leaseholder for the increase to the value of the property, the amount of which was to be determined by an expert opinion.

Soon after, the claimant erected a solid building. Differences of opinion arose between the parties as to the type of construction, the development, and the use of this building, resulting in an early termination of the lease. The property was handed back to the defendant.

In turn, the claimant claimed an adequate remuneration for the increase in value which had been caused to the property by the erection of this building.

The action remained without success throughout all instances.

Reasons

In agreement with a decision by this present Senate (acting as Senate for Agricultural Matters) of 5 May 1953, the Appeal Court assumed that the defendant became owner of the erected construction in accordance with §§ 94, 946 BGB, because the claimant intended the construction to be permanent rather than to serve temporary purposes. The appeal has raised no legal objections to this effect. . . .

The Appeal Court refused to grant a claim for compensation under § 951 BGB, which is based on the integration of chattels into real property (§ 946 BGB). On this point, the Appeal Court states that the defendant can require the construction to be removed, because it amounted to interference with his property (§ 1004 BGB), this proprietary claim taking precedence over the enrichment claim under §§ 951, 812, 818 BGB. Several trains of thought are raised by the appeal against this argument. They give rise to the following considerations:

(a) The lessor's demand that the construction be removed is not defeated by the terms of the lease agreement. They oblige the lessor to take over and pay for only such small constructions and installations which fall within the framework of the lease agreement. This does not apply to the construction which is presently under consideration.

(b) It is true that § 951 para. 1 sent. 2 BGB does exclude claims that the previous condition be restored. However, this provision relates to claims by the person who has combined objects under § 946 BGB. This person can therefore not require from the enriched party that the previous condition be restored, apart from a claim under § 951 para. 2 BGB. However, this does not imply that the enriched party cannot claim restoration, perhaps on some other legal grounds. . . . [BGH NJW 1954, 265 distinguished.]

(c) The Appeal Court takes the view that, where a building is constructed on somebody else's property, claims under § 951 para. 1 BGB are subject to the requirement that the enriched party had to tolerate the construction on its property. Consequently, the Appeal Court argues, the enriched party need not pay compensation if it can require that the building be removed, be it under a contract (§§ 556, 581 BGB), under torts provisions, or under property law (§ 1004). This view has been frequently favoured by scholars [references omitted]. As regards court decisions, it is apparently only the *Oberlandesgericht* Celle which has addressed this question, and decided in the same sense as the Appeal Court (MDR 1954, 294). This present Senate has already ruled in its decision of 17 September 1954 (Lindenmaier/Möhring zu § 1004 Nr 14) that the unauthorized construction of a building on somebody else's property can amount to interference with property rights. It can be left open whether the Appeal Court's view should be supported, and equally whether the appeal is right in arguing that any claim for the removal of the building would be barred by the defence of abuse of law. Yet another question which needs not be decided is whether any necessary permission by the building inspectorate for the demolition of the building [reference omitted] would influence the merits of the case or, as the Appeal Court believes, have a bearing only on the execution of the judgment. For no such application for demolition of the building has hitherto been made. Nevertheless, it should be mentioned that the 17 September 1954 decision of this Senate concerned a building which had created several residential flats, and these flats were already occupied. On the other hand, the present case concerns a building which, according to expert evidence, requires expenditure amounting to DM 8,000 in order to be converted to living quarters which are ready for occupation. . . . When addressing the question of abuse of law, consideration should also be given to the fact that the defendant had never granted consent to the construction of the building. It remains questionable whether this defence could, at the end of the day, serve to force the defendant to take over the unwanted building. However, all the questions raised above need not receive a final answer, because the claim under § 951 para. 1 BGB is refuted for the following legal considerations.

§ 951 para. 1 sent. 2 BGB is a provision which serves the interests of the enriched party. It protects this party against claims by the other party that the previous condition be restored. If due consideration is given to the interests involved, it becomes apparent that the enriched party can defeat an enrichment claim by referring to the possibility that the previous condition is restored. This is at least the case if a building would otherwise be imposed on the enriched party, which this party could put to profitable use only by incurring considerable expenditure. In such a case, an enriched party cannot be considered as acting against good faith if this party, instead of paying, itself restores the previous condition, or, if this cannot reasonably be expected of this party because of the considerable expenditure which the restoration of the previous condition would entail, leaves this to the party which has erected the building. Accordingly, and by analogy to § 1001 sent. 2 BGB, a person who would otherwise be liable for giving up the increased value of its property, must—at least under the conditions set out above—be allowed to substitute the payment by granting consent to the removal [of the object which has been connected with this property], and use this as a defence against an action [reference omitted]. During the present proceedings, the defendant has repeatedly required the claimant to remove the building. Thereby, the defendant has referred the claimant to the removal of the enrichment, and has thus used his right of substitution. Such a referral to the removal [of the object] is compatible with good faith, because the defendant never permitted the construction, because the building in its present state does not yield any profit, and because the building amounts to an interference with the defendant's property. Therefore, the claimant has no claim for payment against the defendant. It will now be upon the defendant to procure any necessary permission for the demolition of the building. On the other hand, by relying on his right to substitute [the enrichment claim], the defendant has bound himself to tolerate the demolition of the building.

2. BGH 25.3.1963, BGHZ 39, 186 (bombed site)

Facts

In 1955, the defendant constructed a business building for M, a merchant, in the city of F. In this context, the defendant used the claimant's adjacent bombed site for keeping a site hut and for storing building materials. The defendant did so in spite of the claimant having expressly refused permission, following a request which the defendant had made at the beginning of December 1954. The defendant had cleared part of the claimant's property of the debris in order to render it fit for the defendant's purposes.

By his action, the claimant claims from the defendant, *inter alia*, compensation for the value of the use of his property by the defendant amounting to DM 9,000 plus interest. The defendant argues that it does not owe anything to the claimant, because the defendant had to spend more on clearing the debris than the value of the use of the property as a storage site. Moreover, the partial clearing of the debris had increased the value of the claimant's property. The claimant denies this. He alleges that he sold the property on 23 December 1955 for less than he had paid for it in 1954. He states that the purchaser did not pay him more for the property than she would have paid in any event. In addition, the city of F would otherwise have cleared the site of debris without charging him. Therefore, the claimant argues, he is not enriched by the defendant having cleared part of the property of the debris.

The *Landgericht* allowed the action for payment of compensation for use amounting to DM 7,774.51 plus interest. The *Oberlandesgericht* disallowed the action in its entirety. The appeal leads to the judgment by the *Landgericht* being restored.

Reasons

According to the facts as established by the Appeal Court, the defendant took unlawful possession of the claimant's property for use as a storage site.

1. Therefore, the legal relationship between the parties is governed by §§ 987ff BGB.

(a) When acquiring possession, the defendant did not act *bona fide*. The defendant knew that the claimant had refused permission for the use of the property.

According to §§ 990, 987, 100 BGB, the defendant is therefore obliged to pay adequate compensation in money for the value of the use in lieu of such benefits from use of the property which cannot be directly surrendered in kind [references omitted]. For this purpose, it does not matter whether or not the claimant himself would have acquired any benefits from use of this property during the same time.

(b) The Appeal Court disallows the claimant's claim for compensation for value of the use on the ground that the expenditure incurred by the defendant for clearing the debris considerably exceeded the 'costs for storage' which the defendant saved; in doing so, the Appeal Court classifies the costs incurred by the defendant as useful expenditure which increased the value of the property.

The Appeal Court has overlooked § 996 BGB. According to this provision, the possessor cannot require compensation for other than necessary expenditure if the possessor is liable according to § 990 [reference omitted]. As has already been stated, this provision applies to the defendant. Clearing the site of the debris was not necessary expenditure on the property (§§ 994, 995 BGB). Therefore, the defendant cannot require the claimant to reimburse it for costs incurred for clearing the site of debris.

2. The defendant cannot base its claim on *negotiorum gestio*; in this context, it can be left open to which extent liability for *negotiorum gestio* can arise at all in a situation to which §§ 987ff BGB apply.

By using and by clearing the property of debris, the defendant conducted the claimant's (the owner's) business, although the defendant was aware that it was not entitled to do so (§ 687 para. 2 sent. 1 BGB).

In this situation, the defendant would have a restitutionary claim against the claimant for its expenditure on clearing the site only if the claimant himself had relied on claims against the defendant under §§ 677, 678, 681, 682; however, it is undisputed that this is not the case [references omitted].

3. Finally, the defendant cannot successfully rely directly on the provisions on unjustified enrichment. If the claimant's assets have been increased at all by the clearing of the property, such enrichment has not occurred without legal ground at the claimant's expense (§ 812).

As has been stated, in the present situation the defendant is prevented from claiming from the defendant reimbursement of the expenditure incurred in clearing the property of debris by the express provisions of §§ 996 and 687 para. 2 BGB. The defendant's aim, which is frowned upon by the law, can therefore not be achieved by means of § 812 BGB. This would amount to a circumvention of the statutory purpose. The purpose of these provisions is that no enrichment may be imposed on the owner against his will by a *mala fide* possessor, or on the person whose business is conducted by a *mala fide* person conducting such business. Expenditure which has been incurred in such a way is not to be reimbursed. Rather, the owner can keep any benefits which he may thus have received without providing compensation.

Therefore, §§ 997 and 687 para. 2 amount to specific regulations which exclude the application of § 812 BGB [references omitted].

For this reason, the owner or the person whose business has been conducted are, in such cases, not enriched *without legal ground.* Rather, the legal ground is to be found within §§ 996 and 687 para. 2 BGB.

4. From no legal aspect can the defendant therefore be entitled to claim from the claimant compensation for its expenditure on clearing the property of the debris.

3. BGH 20.6.1963, BGHZ 40, 28 (fire brigade)

Facts

In 1959, several forest fires occurred along the Federal Railway line between Sch. and G. as a result of sparks flying from passing train engines. These fires were combated, *inter alia*, by the volunteer fire service of the claimant, a local authority. The claimant claims compensation from the defendant, the Federal Railway, for expenditure incurred in this context.

The *Landgericht* disallowed the action. The *Oberlandesgericht* gave interlocutory judgment on the merits in favour of the claimant. The defendant's appeal was rejected.

Reasons

1. (No action in tort).

2. On the other hand, the *Oberlandesgericht* ruled that the action should succeed on the ground of unjustified enrichment. . . .

It is not necessary to dwell further on this question, because the action succeeds on the merits according to the provisions on *negotiorum gestio* (§§ 683, 670 BGB), as will be explained below.

The Appeal Court, though, denies such a claim. It argues as follows:

It is true that the action taken by the fire brigade concerned the defendant's sphere of interests and had beneficial effects on these interests, so that therefore the claimant had conducted the defendant's business. However, the claimant had failed to establish that it had the intention to carry out business for the defendant. In accordance with its duties under public law, the claimant, by combating the fire(s), had conducted its own business. Under these circumstances, it would have been up to the claimant to show that it also intended to act in favour of the 'arsonist'. There was nothing to show, and no facts had been pleaded or proven which could support the conclusion, that there had indeed been such an intention.

These arguments cannot be followed.

(a) The Appeal Court has chosen the correct starting point for its argument. It is indeed decisive whether or not the claimant had the intention to (also) conduct another person's business (cf. BGHZ 38, 270, 276). However, the considerations by which the *Oberlandesgericht* denies such an intention are not free from erroneous appreciation of the law.

It has been recognized by the courts that management within the meaning of § 677 BGB can also occur if the interests which a person is looking after by his actions are primarily his own and only secondarily those of another person. In particular, the mere fact that a party acts in pursuance of its duties under public law does not prevent the conclusion that this party, at the same time, conducts a third party's business of a private law nature (BGHZ 16, 12, at 16; 30, 162, at 167).

It may prove difficult to establish whether in such cases there has been the intention to conduct also someone else's business. If such a will has failed to manifest itself in any form to the outside, it will not be considered. Therefore, there always needs to be some clue which demonstrates to the outside world such an intention to conduct somebody else's business.

Such clues can also arise from the nature of the business. If this business is, by its very nature, entirely or partially at least *also* one which objectively is that of another party, an intention to conduct this other party's business must be presumed, and it falls on the party which denies such intention to prove the opposite. The situation is different for those actions which seem neutral to the outside, i.e. actions which in themselves allow no conclusion as to whether the party in question acts in its own interests or in those of another party. For those actions, it will fall on the person who relies on the intention to act in the interest of another party to plead and prove such intention (BGHZ 38, 270, 276; other references omitted).

These principles have generally been stated correctly by the Appeal Court. However, that Court has overlooked the fact that the same principles also apply if the business, in the way it appears to an outside observer, serves both the interests of the acting party and of a third party. This is presently the case. It is true that the fire brigade acted in fulfilment of the duties imposed on it by public law. However, the purpose and aim of its actions were, and always are, to come to the aid of third parties. All those who might suffer from the unhindered continuation and spreading of the fire could be considered as such third parties. It was therefore in their interests that the fire brigade jumped into action, and it was therefore their business which was conducted in this way.

In addition to the owners of the affected properties, it was also the Federal Railway who belonged to this circle of interested parties. According to § 1 SachschHG,[1] the Federal Railway is strictly liable to the owners for this damage. Therefore, as an objective analysis reveals beyond doubt, it must have been in the urgent interest of the Federal Railway to mitigate this damage [reference omitted]. According to what has been said above, it must therefore be presumed that the claimant, by bringing the fire brigade into action, also intended to help the defendant and that, therefore, the claimant had the intention to conduct another person's business as required by § 677 BGB.

It would have been up to the defendant to prove the opposite. No such evidence has been furnished, and, under the given circumstances, would indeed have been very difficult to furnish.

(b) There is, however, one restriction which must be added to the above considerations.

There are cases of conducting business whereby the law obliges a party to act gratuitously. If the necessary requirements are met, no claim for reimbursement of expenditure arises under §§ 683, 670 BGB, simply because the acting party is intended to shoulder these costs by virtue of this specific obligation.

In the present case, the Fire Protection Act of Hesse contains in § 14a provision which concerns the question to what extent the fire brigade can require third parties to pay compensation. This provision has the following wording:

> "If the owner or possessor of the building on fire has caused the fire wilfully or grossly negligently, the local authority can require him to pay compensation for those costs which the authority incurred by combating the fire. In other cases, fires are combated free of charge."

[1] This Act has since been replaced by the Haftpflichtgesetz (Liability Act).

In the interpretation which the *Oberlandesgericht* gives to this provision, the last sentence concerning the gratuitous action is intended to favour only those owners or possessors who have not caused the fire in a wilful or grossly negligent way, but not to favour third parties. According to §§ 549, 562 ZPO (Code of Civil Procedure), the present Court is bound by this interpretation.

There are no other provisions to indicate that the fire brigade must act gratuitously in favour of such third parties.

Therefore, as regards the relations between the claimant and the defendant, the defendant cannot rely on the claimant local authority to shoulder all the costs for putting out the fire(s).

4. BGH 31.10.1963, BGHZ 40, 272 (electrical appliances)

Facts

In 1958 and 1959, the claimant had several houses constructed on his real property in H-S. According to his allegations, he instructed a B firm to provide all electrical installation, including the delivery of electrical appliances.

The B firm ordered the required electric cookers and hot water tanks from the claimant.

On 20 January 1959, the claimant sent to the defendant via his architect a 'confirmation of order' for 22 electric cookers and an equal number of low pressure tanks. On 22 January 1959, the architect returned this letter to the claimant with a notification that this confirmation had to be a mistake. Neither he nor his client had instructed the claimant. If the claimant had received instructions from the B firm, then the claimant should contact this firm. The claimant did not reply to this communication and alleges that this failure was inadvertent. On 27 July 1959, the claimant delivered 20 hot water tanks to the defendant's construction site with a 'delivery note', which was addressed to the defendant via his architect, and the textual part of which contained the entry: 'Recipient new building H-S'. O, an electrician employed by the B firm, took delivery at the construction site and acknowledged receipt by signing the delivery note. By date of 29 July 1959, the claimant billed the defendant for 20 hot water tanks.

On 27 August 1959, the claimant sent the defendant a further bill for 20 electric cookers, ready for delivery on request. On 23 September 1959, the claimant delivered 19 electric cookers to the defendant's construction site. The attached delivery note contained the same description of the recipient as did the note issued for the hot water tanks. Again, the electrician O took delivery and signed the delivery note.

Soon after delivery, electricians employed by the B firm installed both hot water tanks and electric cookers into the defendant's new buildings.

The claimant alleges that the appliances were not to be delivered to the B firm on credit, but rather that this firm had agreed with the claimant to receive commission, and that the claimant was to deliver the appliances directly to the defendant, and to bill the defendant accordingly. The claimant believes that it has entered into a sales contract with the defendant. If this was not the case, the defendant was either to pay the claimant the value of the appliances, or to surrender the appliances, on the ground that the defendant was unjustifiedly enriched.

The claimant has moved that the defendant be ordered to pay DM 10,906.22. If this motion were to fail, the defendant should be ordered to surrender 20 hot water tanks and 19 electric cookers.

The defendant argues that he had instructed no one but the B firm, whom he had paid. Furthermore, he believes that he acquired *bona fide* title in the appliances from the B firm, and denies any liability in unjustified enrichment.

While the *Landgericht* refused the action, the *Oberlandesgericht* allowed it to essential parts.

On appeal by the defendant, the judgement by the *Landgericht* was restored.

Reasons

I.1. The Appeal Court states that no sales contract had been concluded between the parties. To this extent, the Appeal Court's considerations are without legal flaw. In the present appeal proceedings, the claimant no longer relies on contractual claims against the defendant.

2. The Appeal Court furthermore arrives at the conclusion that the defendant acquired title in the appliances by their installation into the defendant's property. The Appeal Court denies that the defendant

had already previously acquired *bona fide* title by agreement and by handing over (§§ 929, 932 BGB). In the Appeal Court's view, the B firm acquired possession in the appliances when they were delivered to the building site, and the B firm did not transfer possession to the defendant prior to the installation.

The appeal raises several complaints against this argument. This Senate believes all of them to be without foundation. However, they need not be discussed. For the claimant has no claim against the defendant, regardless of whether he acquired title in the appliances by agreement and handing over, or by installation. In either case, the claimant cannot rely on property for its claims, because the claimant is no longer the owner of the appliances. Neither does the claimant have a claim in unjustified enrichment. If the defendant acquired title according to §§ 929, 932 BGB, he would be liable in unjustified enrichment only if he gratuitously acquired property in the appliances from the B firm (§ 816 para. 1 sent. 1 BGB). This is not the case. Equally, and in contrast to the view taken by the Appeal Court, the claimant has no claim in unjustified enrichment under § 951 in conjunction with § 946 BGB, as will be explained under (II.).

II.1. The Appeal Court must be followed in its view that the claimant was owner of the appliances until the moment when they were installed in the defendant's building, so that the claimant lost title by this installation in accordance with § 946 BGB. As the Appeal Court explains, hot water tanks and electric cookers are chattels which are built in *for the purpose of constructing* a building. According to § 94 para. 2 BGB, they become essential components of the building, and therefore also, in accordance with § 94 para. 1 BGB, of the defendant's real property. The Appeal Court adduces the argument that modern residential properties are considered incomplete if they do not have hot water tanks; the same also applied to electric cookers since, according to the common view prevailing in northern Germany, buildings are only complete if there are cooking installations in the kitchen. The Appeal Court's considerations on this point are in line with the decision by this *Bundesgerichtshof* in NJW 1953, 1180, and are not attacked by either of the parties.

2. Whoever loses title in a chattel which he owns when this is integrated into real property belonging to another person, can claim

reimbursement in money under § 951 para. 1 sent. 1 BGB in accordance with the provisions on giving up an unjustified enrichment.

Today, it is nearly unanimously acknowledged that the loss of title does not in itself give rise to a claim under § 951 para. 1 sent. 1 BGB. Rather, the reference to the provisions on unjustified enrichment implies that a restitutionary claim does arise only under the requirements set forth in § 812 para. 1 BGB (BGHZ 35, 356, 359ff; Berg, *AcP* 160, 505f). This position is also shared by the Appeal Court. What matters therefore is whether the defendant received the enrichment, which consists of the installed appliances, by way of performance by the claimant, or in another way at the expense of the claimant, and without legal ground (§ 812 para. 1 sent. 1 BGB).

3. The installation of the appliances cannot be considered as performance by the claimant. It was carried out by the B firm, and this firm owed both installation and appliances to the defendant on the basis of the contract which this firm had concluded with the defendant, as the Appeal Court states.

Whenever a client instructs a building contractor or a craftsman to construct a building, or facilities within this building, this client will perceive any performance made by the building contractor or craftsman on the basis of a contract with the client as a performance by the party which he instructed. He will not perceive this as performance by any subcontractor which the contractor might have instructed in turn, or by the owner of any material which this owner supplied to the building contractor or craftsman. Such a client must be allowed to rely on his belief that he will have to pay for this performance no one but the person whom he instructed, even if this performance was to be effectuated entirely or partially by a third party on instruction from the client's contractual partner (von Caemmerer, *Festschrift für Rabel* p. 373, note 156).

By judgment of 5 October 1961 (VII ZR 207/60, BGHZ 36, 30), this present Senate denied a claim in unjustified enrichment against the client in a case which was similar to the present one. In this case, an owner of real property had instructed a company to construct a building for a certain price. This company had, in turn, instructed a building contractor to erect the building. This present Senate decided that the building contractor had no claim in unjustified enrichment against the owner of the real property, even if the building contractor's contract with the company was void for lack of agreement (*Dissens*), or if the company entered into the agreement in the name, but without authority, of the owner of the real property.

On this point, the Senate stated that the direct shift of wealth from the building contractor onto the owner of the real property, which was necessary for a restitutionary claim, was lacking. For the owner, the increased value of the property was not a transfer of assets by the building contractor, but by his contractual partner, the company.

This decision of 5 October 1961 has been attacked by academic writing (Flume, *JZ* 1962, 281; Berg, *NJW* 1962, 101). Berg, after all, does agree with the result in the case of *Dissens*, and so does Esser, *Fälle und Lösungen zum Schuldrecht*, pp. 124ff. The critics argue in particular that this Senate failed to consider sufficiently that this was a case of restitution of performance (*Leistungskondiktion*), where it did not matter whether or not the shift of wealth was immediate.

However, the decision of 5 October 1961 can equally be justified if considered solely under the aspect of *Leistungskondiktion*, as done by this new doctrine.

Recent academic writing considers a performance within the meaning of § 812 para. 1 BGB to be an intentional enlargement of another person's assets which has been brought about with a specific purpose in mind (*bewußte und zweckgerichtete Vermehrung fremden Vermögens*), see Esser, *Schuldrecht*, 2nd ed., § 189 no. 6; Berg, NJW 1962, 101). From this, Berg draws the following conclusion for the case decided by judgment of 5 October 1961: if the company had acted without the client's authority, the building contractor could claim restitution of performance against the client, provided that the building contractor had intended to perform towards this client.

This view cannot be followed. The outcome cannot depend one-sidedly on towards whom the performing party intended to effectuate performance. Rather, and in order to protect the client if his contractual partner involves third parties for the construction of the building, this must be the decisive point: who should be considered as having performed the contribution in an objective analysis undertaken from the perspective of the client? It is not the inner intention of the performing party which matters, but rather how the party which effectuates performance should be identified 'from the view of the recipient of the performance' (Esser, *Fälle und Lösungen zum Schuldrecht* p. 128, note 19; other references omitted). The same argument has found an expression in the decision of 5 October 1961, where it is stated that, for the owner of the real property, the increase in value was a contribution by the company he had instructed, and not by the building contractor.

If, however, it must be assumed that a contribution, seen from the decisive perspective of the recipient, presents itself as coming from his contractual partner, this recipient can be subjected to a *Leistungskondiktion* or indeed to any restitutionary claim only by his contractual partner, and only if the performance was made without legal ground in the relationship between these two parties, e.g., because the contract which they have entered into is void. Whoever has been employed by the contractual partner—e.g., as a sub-contractor—in order to effectuate performance, does not have any claim in unjustified enrichment against the recipient, neither under restitution for performance, nor for an enrichment which occurred 'in another way' within the meaning of § 812 para. 1 sent. 1 BGB. Rather, a claim for enrichment in another way—often called *Eingriffskondiktion* or restitution for interference (cf. Esser, *Schuldrecht* § 189, no. 1) can only accrue, according to recent academic writing, if the object of the enrichment was not performed to the recipient at all, i.e. not by anybody (Esser, *Fälle und Lösungen zum Schuldrecht* p. 127s).

From the viewpoint of this doctrine, therefore, the building contractor, in the case decided by judgment of 5 October 1961, was equally to be denied a restitutionary claim against the owner of the real property, i.e. because what this person had received had been 'performed' by his contractual partner, and this performance did not lack a legal ground. Consequently, it was not perceivable that the building contractor should have a restitutionary claim, e.g. on the ground that his contract with the company was void, or because the company had falsely and without the owner's knowledge pretended to be the owner's agent.

4. These principles governing restitutionary claims in situations involving sub-contractors are equally to be applied if a building contractor uses and installs materials which are not his own. If the client may reasonably, and does, perceive that performance by those craftsmen which he instructed extends to the material which they have built into his property, the owner of the material can have no

claim in restitution against the client, neither as a *Leistungskondiktion* (restitution of performance), nor as an *Eingriffskondiktion* (restitution for interference), cf. in particular Esser, *Fälle und Lösungen zum Schuldrecht* pp. 127ff; *Schuldrecht*, § 196 no. 2b sub aa. In such a case, the client must be protected in the same way as he would against restitutionary claims by a sub-contractor. If accordingly the question of who performed is to be answered from the client's viewpoint, it does no longer matter whether the client could be protected against restitutionary claims by the owner of the materials by an analogous application of the provisions on *bona fide* contractual acquisition of title (§§ 932ff BGB, § 366 HGB), as discussed, but rejected by the Appeal Court [references omitted].

5. After what has been said above, the decisive question is whether the defendant could consider delivery and installation of the appliances as performance by the B firm. According to the facts established by the Appeal Court, the answer must be positive.

In January 1959, the defendant had immediately returned to the claimant the confirmation of order which the claimant had sent to him and had added the remark that this must be a mistake. By the same act, he had expressed his view that the claimant had entered into a contract with the B firm for delivery to this firm. Since the claimant did not reply to this letter from the defendant, the defendant was allowed to presume that, when several months later the claimant delivered the appliance to the building site, this was done on the basis of a contract concluded between the claimant and the B firm (. . .).

Accordingly, the claimant has no claim for reimbursement under §§ 951 para. 1 sent. 1, 812 para. 1 sent. 1 BGB.

III. (No proprietary claim for surrender of the appliances.)

5. BGH 11.1.1971, BGHZ 55, 176 (young bulls)

Facts

A thief stole two young bulls from the claimant, a farmer, and sold them to the *bona fide* defendant for DM 1,701. The defendant processed the animals in his meat product factory. Both of the previous court instances allowed the claimant's action that the defendant should pay him compensation for value to the amount of DM 1,701. The defendant's appeal, while admitted, was without success.

Reasons

1. The defendant could not acquire title in the animals from the thief in accordance with § 935 para. 1 BGB. The claimant therefore remained owner of the animals when the defendant took possession of them. It was only after the animals had been slaughtered and when the meat was processed in the defendant's factory that the defendant acquired title in accordance with § 950 BGB. This is not disputed between the parties.

The claimant therefore lost property in the animals 'as a consequence of the provision' of § 950 BGB. According to § 951 para. 1 sent. 1 BGB, he can therefore require 'compensation in money in accordance with the provisions on the return of an unjustified enrichment'. It has been well settled by the courts (BGHZ 17, 236; BGHZ 35, 356, 359s; BGHZ 40, 272, 276 [case no. 4 above] that this reference to the provisions on unjustified enrichment not only relates to the measure, but also to the grounds of liability for unjustified enrichment (so-called *Rechtsgrundverweisung*, reference to the grounds of a claim). Therefore, the claimant can claim against the defendant under this provision only if the general requirements for a claim in unjustified enrichment are met, in particular if the defendant acquired property in the meat without legal ground vis-à-vis the claimant. This is presently the case.

2. In particular, the contract between the defendant and the thief cannot serve as a justifying cause, i.e. as a ground which could justify that the defendant should be allowed to keep the property, which he acquired through § 950 BGB, without paying compensation to the claimant. §§ 932ff BGB provide a final solution for the conflict of interests which arises when an unauthorized person disposes of somebody else's property to a third party. Such a third party, if it is not *mala fide*, is protected if the owner did not involuntarily lose possession in the chattels. In this situation, the third party acquires title under §§ 932ff BGB and may keep the property without having to compensate the previous owner. In this situation, the contract between the

unauthorized person and the third party is the cause which justifies this shift of wealth. However, in all other cases—including the present case, where the owner involuntarily lost possession in the chattels—the law solves this conflict of interest by favouring the owner. He keeps the property and therefore the claim for surrender under § 985 against the third party as possessor. If this third party later becomes owner as a consequence of §§ 946–8, 950 BGB, such acquisition of title is not justified by the previous contract for acquisition which the unauthorized party entered into with the third party. The third party's acquisition of title is not based on this contractual disposition. On the contrary, under § 935 BGB this contractual disposition is without any effect, and the third party acquires property only under §§ 946ff BGB. However, these provisions do not in themselves contain a justifying cause for this shift of wealth, as can be taken from § 951 para. 1 sent. 1 BGB.

3. The claim under § 951 para. 1 sent. 1 BGB is not excluded by the specific regulations in §§ 987–993 BGB (cf. § 993 para. 1 alt. 2 BGB). It is true that the claimant remained owner and the defendant unauthorized possessor of the animals until the moment when they were processed by the defendant. As a consequence of the processing by the defendant, the latter was no longer in a position to surrender the animals to the claimant. The defendant is liable in damages for such impossibility only under the requirements set out in §§ 989, 990 BGB (action pending, *mala fide*), which, however, have not been met in this case, as has not been disputed. However, this does not stand in the way of a claim under § 951 para. 1 sent. 1 BGB, because this is not a claim for damages, but a claim for restitution.

This Court has repeatedly ruled that other restitutionary claims are not excluded by the specific regulations in §§ 987–993. In BGHZ 14, 7ff, a previous owner was allowed a claim for restitution in a case where a *bona fide* possessor used up the goods (in this case: fuel) for his own purpose and thereby saved expenses. Courts have also constantly ruled that a previous owner can claim restitution in the case where a possessor sells property which is not his own and in this way acquires the value of this property. Under § 816 para. 1 sent. 1, the possessor is bound to give up what he acquired by way of the disposition [reference omitted]. The same also applies to the disposition of chattels in which the owner involuntarily had lost possession, once the owner ratifies the disposition, in particular when he claims against the person who made the unauthorized disposition under § 816 para. 1 sent. 1 BGB. In none of these cases is the previous owner's claim in restitution against the previous possessor barred by §§ 987–993 BGB. The reason for this is the same in all these cases. While a *bona fide* possessor should be protected by §§ 987-993 BGB—within certain limits—against what appears to be unreasonable claims for damages by the owner, the same possessor should not be allowed to keep the value of the object to the extent that he has acquired this value by what objectively is a wrongful interference with the owner's property rights. However, to this effect, all cases of *Eingriffskondiktion* (restitution for interference with another's right) must be treated in the same way. In particular, this also applies to the present case where the possessor, within the meaning of § 950 BGB, processes chattels of which the owner involuntarily lost possession and in this way strips the owner of his title in the chattels. The restitutionary claim under § 951 para. 1 sent. 1 BGB which then arises will no more be excluded by §§ 987–993 BGB than the other aforementioned restitutionary claims (this is also the view taken by academic writing: [references omitted]).

4. As regards the measure of the restitutionary claim, the same principles must apply to this case as to restitutionary claims against the possessor for unauthorized consumption or unauthorized disposition. It has been well settled (BGHZ 9, 333; BGHZ 14, 7) that the previous possessor who faces a claim under § 812 or § 816 BGB cannot under § 818 BGB deduct from this claim the performance which he made towards a third party in order to acquire the object in question. This is because the claim for restitution replaces the previous claim for surrender of the object under § 985 BGB. The possessor could not rely on performance made to a third party as a defence against this claim for surrender. No more can the possessor do the same against a claim for restitution (BGHZ 47, 128, 130ff). Rather, the possessor must rely on that third party to which he performed for claiming back his performance. The same applies to the situation governed by § 951 para. 1 sent. 1 BGB (in the same sense already RGZ 106, 1021). It is therefore only from the thief that the defendant can claim back the DM 1,701 which he paid that person. This payment does not amount to a defence under § 818 BGB against the claimant's restitutionary claim.

6. BGH 14.10.1971, BGHZ 57, 137 (wrecked car)[2]

Facts

The defendant sold the plaintiff a used car but did not disclose the fact that it had earlier been involved in two accidents. The car was destroyed in an accident due solely to the plaintiff's fault. Only following this did the plaintiff discover that he had been deceived when concluding the purchase. He therefore rescinded the contract of sale on account of mistake and fraud and demanded the purchase price rendered at the time be repaid.

Reasons

II. Claims on grounds of unjust enrichment:

The Appeal Court rules that the sale contract is void ab initio on the basis that it was entered into by reason of fraud perpetrated on the plaintiff by the defendant and owing to the plaintiff's rescission according to §§ 123, 142. The Court of Final Appeal must also proceed on the basis of this ruling. (. . .)

The Appeal Court rules (. . .) that an enrichment claim against the defendant company (in the following: "the defendant") has not been established to the extent that it would exceed the 800 DM awarded by the *Landgericht* (the depreciation in the automobile's value at the time of the sale to the plaintiff owing to the earlier accidents: first accident = 700 DM, the second = 100 DM).

The Appeal Court justifies its view by means of the *Saldotheorie*, according to which the vendor's enrichment resulting from payment of the purchase price did not exist in the full amount of the purchase price. When assessing this enrichment, regard is also to be had to the fact that the vendor, by executing the sale contract, reduced the object of sale and thereby the asset value due to the purchaser which it had at the point in time of the transfer. The Appeal Court assesses the enrichment of the defendant firm according to this, for (from an

[2] This translation first appeared in *Cases, Materials and Texts on Unjustified Enrichment*, ed. by Jack Beatson and Eltjo Schrage with the collaboration of Mindy Chen-Wishart, Martin Hogg, Barry Nicholas, Martin Schermaier, David Sellar, Dannie Visser, and Floor Gras (Hart Publishing, 2003). Reproduced with kind permission of the publisher.

economic viewpoint), it is no longer possible to return the automobile contemporaneously with the return of the purchase price due to the accident but only according to the amount by which the plaintiff, owing to his ignorance of the first two accidents, had paid too high a purchase price, i.e. by 800 DM.

This is not free from judicial error.

1. In BGHZ 53, 144, the Senate decided a case where, as with the facts presented here, the purchaser of an automobile had successfully rescinded the sale contract owing to fraud after the car driven by him had been destroyed in an accident. In contrast, however, there was no evidence in that case of the plaintiff having caused the accident by his own fault. That judgment of the Senate includes the following submissions: the *Saldotheorie* is ultimately a statutory correction which was undertaken by the courts for reasons of fairness, which takes the fact into account that a performance is made for the purpose of another which normally justifies regarding obligations to return arising in the case of a void contract as dependent on each other. However, in a case where the purchaser defrauds the seller, this does not exclude it being regarded as fair redress—in departure from the *Saldotheorie*—that the risk of the sale object being destroyed by the purchaser is to be borne by the seller where there is no evidence that the purchaser is at fault in the impossibility of returning the sale object undamaged.

Accordingly, the Senate in that judgment, following on from older case law, did not apply the *Saldotheorie* but rather the theory of two enrichment claims.

2. The Appeal Court's judgment, passed before the judgment BGHZ 53, 144, recognised and contemplated the problem completely, whether it should apply the theory of two enrichment claims or the *Saldotheorie* in this case. It sees no cause to disregard the application of the *Saldotheorie* considering the seller's fraud on the purchaser, at least not if (as here) the purchaser caused the sale object's destruction. The Appeal Court rules that in such a case there are no aspects of fairness which support burdening the vendor with the object's destruction rather than the purchaser who has caused its destruction, even if the former brought about the exchange of performances by his fraud.

The Senate is not able to follow the Appeal Court's view.

(a) Whosoever caused another to enter into such a disadvantageous contract commits fraud. As a rule, the defrauder is undeserving of protection. This can also have an effect in enrichment law.

In the present case too, the Senate believes that it would not correspond to the notion of fairness if a fraud perpetrated on the purchaser by sole reason of which this party was induced to conclude the sale contract and acquire the sale object, would, in view of the reversal of a transaction following the successful rescission of the sale contract, remain unconsidered from the outset in those cases where the purchaser is responsible for the impossibility of returning the sale object.

(b) In a number of most recent articles, the view is held that the *Saldotheorie* must be completely abandoned. Generally, this issue need not be decided here. Rather, the Senate restricts itself to deciding the case as presented, that namely, the purchaser has been led to conclude the contract owing to fraud. In these cases, and indeed, independently of the fact whether the subsequent destruction of the sale object by the purchaser occurred with or without fault, the *Saldotheorie* is inapplicable. Rather, the starting point is the theory of two enrichment claims according to which the seller's enrichment exists in the receipt of the purchase price without regard to the object of sale delivered by the seller to the purchaser and its future fate at the hands of the purchaser.

(c) The Senate's view corresponds to the notion of fairness in that the seller's fraudulent act is to be considered when reversing a contract where the purchaser is at fault in the loss of the sale object. This would not be the case were the *Saldotheorie* theory to be applied.

However, this view can also be justified by the cohesion of the provisions contained in §§ 818 and 819. Its judgment BGHZ 53, 144 the Senate had already raised the question (which it left open there) whether the application of the theory of two enrichment claims instead of the *Saldotheorie* results from § 819 where a fraud is perpetrated on the purchaser. The Senate affirms this question.

(aa) According to § 818 III the debtor is free from the obligation to give up the thing acquired or its value provided he is no longer enriched. Concerning the reversal of a void sale contract the *Saldotheorie* procures for the seller the advantages of this provision in as much as the sale object has depreciated in value or has been destroyed by the purchaser. In the reversal of a transaction, provided the purchaser cannot offer the object to the seller in its original condition, this party is also no longer regarded as enriched. If the purchaser was forced to pay the full purchase price to the purchaser despite the loss of the object, then the seller would be burdened to a greater degree than would be consistent with the basic principles underlying § 818 III. The *Saldotheorie* is therefore the logical application of the legal notion expressed in § 818 III to reciprocal contracts in which the performance and return performance lie in one relationship of exchange (synallagma), a factor which must also be considered when reversing void contracts according to the law on enrichment.

(bb) The basic principle of the *Saldotheorie* so described also illustrates the limits of its application. These limits exist in any event where § 818 III does not apply from the outset, the debtor is therefore by no means protected in the case of every lapse of enrichment according to the legislator's intention but rather is liable pursuant to §§ 818 IV, 819, 292, 987 ff 'according to the general provisions', i.e. to a large extent no longer under rules of unjust enrichment [references omitted].

Such is the case here. The defendant caused the purchaser to conclude the sale contract by fraud, which the plaintiff, as the defendant knew, had he known that the car purchased had been involved in an accident, would certainly not have concluded. It is therefore to be assumed that the defendant was already aware from the conclusion of the sale contract, that the plaintiff could rescind the contract on the basis of fraud. The defendant company must therefore allow itself to be treated as if it had known the invalidity of the sale contract from the outset (§ 142 II), i.e. as if it had already known when it received the purchase price and transferred the car to the plaintiff of the defect in the legal basis for the exchange of performances rendered by both parties. Thereby the requirements of § 819 I were fulfilled from the outset with respect to the defendant. Therefore, according to this provision, increased liability attaches to the defendant.

Thereby however, the internal justification for an application of the *Saldotheorie* in the present case lapses. The starting point for the judgment of the present case must rather be the two theory of two enrichment claims just as in the case decided in BGHZ 53, 144. Therefore, the subsequent fate of the car purchased by the plaintiff primarily does not initially come into consideration when calculating the defendant company's enrichment which occurred by its acquiring the purchase price.

3. This does not mean in the present case however, that the defendant would be bound under all circumstances to repay the full amount

of the purchase price to the plaintiff and that the fact that the latter had himself caused the destruction of the car in the accident would not play any role.

Similarly, the notion of fairness demands here as in the (above-mentioned) claim in delict that whereas the defendant's fraudulent act plays a role in the assessment of the plaintiff's enrichment claim, so the destruction of the car by the defendant's negligence also falls to be considered.

(a) However, this cannot happen by an application of § 254, in contrast to the claim discussed above arising from delict, because § 254 is not applicable [references omitted] within the framework of liability for enrichment.

(b) The applicability of § 254 to enrichment claims does not however exclude enrichment claims being subject to the general principle contained in § 242, of which § 254 is only an instance specially regulated in statute. The BGH has stated this repeatedly. It is also acknowledged in case law that the notion of compensation contained in § 254 is also to be considered for claims other than for damages [references omitted].

(c) The distinguishing feature of the present case lies in the fact that the plaintiff first declared rescission on account of fraud once he had completely destroyed the car by reason of his own negligence. Thereby, the fraud concerned a point which was not especially important under the circumstances. In this state of facts it is quite possible that—if the fault of the plaintiff in the destruction of the sale object is particularly gross—the plaintiff exercises claims, which have become available to him as a result of his rescission, excessively, i.e. in an illicit way, if he intends to shift the whole risk of the sale object to the defendant.

For this reason, a judicial balancing according to § 242 is to be undertaken in consideration of the defendant's fraudulent act on the one hand and the plaintiff's negligent act in causing the accident on the other. On the basis of this weighing up it is to be decided to what extent the loss of the car is to be attributed to the plaintiff or the defendant.

The Court of Final Appeal is not in the position to undertake such a weighing up because hitherto neither the defendant's fraudulent act (primarily only submitted by the Appeal Court) has been established nor the course of the accident upon which it possibly depends how much the plaintiff's causative actions weigh in the loss of the car. The plaintiff's fault in the accident can be very different. It can extend from recklessness bordering on contingent intent to a very minor act of negligence (in connection with a combination of unfortunate coincidences). In view of the complete uncertainty concerning the actual course of events up to now, it is not possible for the Senate to establish by itself whether the plaintiff's fault was so causal for the loss of the car, that in comparison, the defendant's contributory cause was so insignificant as to be left completely unconsidered and the appeal dismissed according to § 563 ZPO. That the trial judge under certain circumstances could come to such a result is a possibility which the Senate will not exclude by its submissions made here.

7. BGH 7.1.1971, NJW 1971, 609 (underage flyer)

Facts

On 27 August 1968, the defendant, who was born on 5 September 1950, took a scheduled flight operated by the claimant from Munich to Hamburg, after having purchased a ticket for this flight. At Hamburg, he managed to join the transit passengers and to re-enter the plane for a flight to New York, without being in possession of a valid ticket for this part of the journey. He was refused entry to the United States, because he did not have a visa. The claimant thereupon made the defendant sign a document according to which the defendant owed the claimant the sum of US$ 256, issued the defendant with a ticket for the return journey and, on the same day, took the defendant back to Munich on a scheduled flight operated by the claimant. The defendant's mother as his statutory agent refused to grant consent to legal transactions concluded between the defendant and the claimant.

By the present proceedings, the claimant requires the defendant to pay the fixed flight rates for the journeys from Hamburg to New York = DM 1,188, and from New York to Munich = DM 1,024, basing these claims alternatively on contract, tort, unjustified enrichment and *negotiorum gestio*.

The *Landgericht* disallowed the action, while the *Oberlandesgericht* ruled in favour of the claimant. The appeal by the defendant—leave to which having been granted by the *Oberlandesgericht*—was without success.

Reasons

I. . . . (No claim in contract.)

II. 1. . . . (No claim in tort.)

2. On the other hand, the Appeal Court believes that the claimant has a claim in unjustified enrichment against the defendant as regards the price for the journey from Hamburg to New York.

The Appeal Court argues that the defendant was enriched by the claimant‘s performance, which was effectuated without a legal ground, and that the defendant is to pay to the claimant the value of this performance in accordance with §§ 812, 818 para. 2 BGB. The defendant is enriched by the fact that he actually took advantage of a performance of monetary value, and thereby acquired an economic value, even if this value has not materialized in his overall assets. Since it is impossible to undo the actual use, any subsequent change of position under § 818 para. 3 BGB is excluded by definition. The value of the enrichment is to be measured according to the usual remuneration paid for the performance received. It is without consequence that the defendant was a minor: in the Appeal Court‘s view, the provisions on unjustified enrichment apply to minors without any limitations.

3. The appeal attacks these considerations, but ultimately without success. The appeal, however, is right in stating that the Appeal Court cannot rely on the jurisprudence of this present Senate for its view that the defendant is liable as the recipient of a performance which by its nature cannot be returned in kind, regardless of whether or not this performance has increased the defendant's assets or has saved him expenses. It is true that in the decisions mentioned by the Appeal Court (BGH, JZ 60, 603; BGHZ 36, 321, 323; BGHZ 37, 258, 264) the present Court did refer to the value of the services which had been conferred in each of those cases when determining the amount of the enrichment in question. Such value is to be measured according to the usual or reasonable remuneration for the service in question. However, by stating this, the present Senate did not express the view that it was without any importance in these cases whether or not the debtor of the restitution claim had saved any corresponding expenses.

On the contrary, those cases concerned the provision of legal services and the rationalization of works, and thereby services which the debtor of the restitution claim was in need of. It could therefore be assumed that the debtor would have obtained these services at any event from elsewhere and at the usual or at a reasonable rate, in particular since remunerated contracts for the provision of such services had already been entered into. It appears that these decisions by this Senate have generally not been interpreted in the way in which the Appeal Court understands them.

On the contrary, the courts have always taken the view that there is an enrichment within the meaning of §§ 812ff BGB only if, and to the extent that, the enriched party has experienced a true increase of assets, be it only by having saved expenses. . . .

One must adhere to this established court practice. It would otherwise become doubtful whether the generally recognized and supreme principle of the law of unjustified enrichment could remain recognized for all situations, namely that the enriched party's obligation to give up the enrichment must never lead to a diminution of this party's assets in excess of the amount by which this party is truly enriched (BGHZ 1, 75, at 81; other references omitted).

4. However, cases such as the present demonstrate that there can be a need for a modified and more differentiated view. For the peculiarities of this dispute consist in the circumstance that, *on the one hand*, the defendant argues that his assets were not at all increased by flying on the claimant's aircraft. The defendant argues that this journey was for him a luxury which he would never have obtained if he had had to pay for it. Besides, he would at any event have been unable to do so because he lacked the necessary financial means. Therefore, he had not saved anything, and the claimant's performance was used up at the moment when he received it. *On the other hand*, the defendant was aware from the beginning that he received the claimant's performance without a legal ground. (The fact that the claimant was a minor will be disregarded at this stage).

(a) Thus, several principal questions of the law of unjustified enrichment are entangled with each other. In the first instance, under § 818 para. 3 BGB, extraordinary expenditure which otherwise would not have been incurred can make an enrichment disappear which initially has accrued [reference omitted]. Therefore, if such expenditure immediately coincides with the receipt of the performance, this expenditure should be apt to prevent that there is even an initial enrichment. On the other hand, the recipient can generally not rely on change of position as a bar to, or as a measure of, enrichment if he knows on receipt or learns later that there is no legal ground for the performance [references omitted]. However, a party which from the outset is not enriched by receiving performance is, in principle, not liable at all under §§ 812ff BGB, even if this party, on receipt of performance, is aware of the lack of a legal ground [reference omitted].

In the present case, this would lead to the following consequences. If the defendant had received a ticket, or the money for the flight, from a third party without legal ground, he would be liable to this party to compensate for that value under § 818 para. 2 BGB. Under the same subjective circumstances, the mere fact that he obtained the performances which he desired directly from the claimant seems to imply that the defendant is not liable at all. These two results cannot be reconciled with each other. Therefore, the question as to what the defendant 'received' must rather be answered in the same way for both of these situations.

(b) The same inconsistency cannot be avoided—as the Appeal Court seems to have in mind—by applying separate and fundamentally different standards to the receipt of services which by their nature cannot be returned in kind, i.e. by considering the mere use of such services as an enrichment and entirely ignoring whether or not expenses have been saved which otherwise would have become necessary. Neither can it be considered an adequate solution if one continues to calculate the enrichment according to the expenses saved, but desists from measuring these savings according to the particular circumstances associated with the enriched party, and rather measures these according to what one generally would have paid for the performance received if matters had taken their proper course (cf. BGHZ 20, 345, 355; other references omitted). For both options would disadvantage a person who *bona fide* receives a performance and has every reason to trust that he may keep it, thereby receiving something which he would not otherwise have obtained, and without acquiring any other lasting financial advantages from the same act.

(c) What is instead required, in order to remove the inconsistency which has thus occurred, is to co-ordinate, in a sensible fashion, the separate provisions which are contained in §§ 818ff BGB. It is with justification that some of the academic writing (von Caemmerer, *Festschrift für Rabel*, Vol. I, p. 368; other references omitted) pay special attention to the circumstance that claims for unjustified enrichment in civil law are primarily geared towards 'what has been obtained' or its corresponding value. And indeed, apart from the heading, §§ 812ff BGB from the outset and up to § 818 paras. 1 and 2, invariably speak of 'what has been performed' or 'what has been obtained'. It is for the first time in § 818 para. 3 (and then again in §§ 820 para. 2, 822) BGB that the concept of 'enrichment' is used as a measure for limiting liability in accordance to the preceding provisions, to which this limitation is therefore quintessential. It is ultimately this concept on which the normal application of the so-called *Saldotheorie* (doctrine of the balance) is based.

The basic idea of the law of unjustified enrichment, i.e. that the duty of a *bona fide* enriched party to give up [an enrichment] must under no circumstances result in a reduction of the assets of this party in excess of the amount of the true enrichment, therefore finds its manifestation precisely in the provision of § 818 para. 3 BGB from which it has expressly been deduced by the jurisprudence (BGHZ 1, 75, 81; RGZ 118, 185, 187).

On this basis, however, it seems entirely appropriate, and even necessary, to transfer those principles which decide whether or not the enrichment has survived, and apply them to the question whether or not there has been an initial enrichment, provided the interests involved are the same. This is at least necessary if such a transfer can solve inconsistencies within the law of unjustified enrichment, which would arise if one were to apply different requirements to the survival of an enrichment on the one hand, and to the existence of an initial enrichment on the other, even if no convincing reasons can be found for such different treatment. In these situations, considerations of equity alone—which have a particularly strong influence on the law of unjustified enrichment (cf. BGHZ 36, 232, 235)—require that the necessary adjustments be made.

It has been set out above that an enriched party who is aware of the lack of a legal ground when receiving the enrichment, is generally not allowed to rely on a subsequent disappearance of this initial enrichment. In this situation, there seems to be no reason why the same person, under the same conditions, should be allowed to deny the very accrual of an enrichment. This should at least not be permitted if the enrichment in question—as in this case—consists in the saving of expenses for extraordinary matters, which the enriched party would or even could not otherwise have afforded. If the enriched person is aware of the lack of a legal ground, it cannot make any difference whether he first incorporates into his assets what he initially has received and spends it later, or whether it is the received performance which itself satisfies the extravagance. What is decisive is that the party in question, while knowing the legal ground is lacking, has actually *received* something for which this party, if this something is no longer present, must principally compensate in value according to § 818 para. 2 BGB.

It is with justification that von Caemmerer [ibid, further reference omitted] underlines that the regular measure of an unjustified enrichment claim is governed by §§ 818 paras. 1, 2 and 4, 891, 820 BGB, whereas the exceptional limitation to the changing amount of surviving enrichment under § 818 para. 3 BGB is intended to protect only a *bona fide* recipient. The same must already apply to the accrual of an enrichment if, as has been stated, there is no reason to treat the disappearance and the accrual of an enrichment in a different way. In such a case a *mala fide* recipient must accept being treated *as if* he had saved something and had in this way increased his assets [reference omitted]. The compensation for the value of the received performance, which he owes under §§ 818 para. 2, 819 BGB is—as in other cases (cf. BGHZ 37, 258, 264; BGHZ 36, 321, 323)—to be measured by the amount of the usual or reasonable remuneration.

5. (Defendant is to be considered *mala fide*.)

III. 1 The claim for payment of the fixed flight price for the *defendant's return journey from New York to Munich* is allowed by the Appeal Court under the provisions on *negotiorum gestio*. The Appeal Court argues that, by transporting the defendant to Germany, the claimant conducted a business which was objectively in his interest. The application of §§ 677ff BGB would not be precluded if the claimant believed it was acting under a valid transport contract concluded with the defendant. Nor would this application be prevented if the claimant, according to the legislation of the country of entry, was under a legal obligation to carry back the defendant. It was equally within the presumed will of his mother—her intention being decisive because she was the defendant's statutory agent—that the defendant be transported back. Again, the claimant could require as compensation for expenditure the usual remuneration for its business performance.

2. The appeal fails again to succeed in its attacks against these considerations.

(a) In principle, it was up to the defendant to make arrangements for his return to Germany after his unsuccessful attempt to enter the USA, so that in transporting the defendant back to Germany, the claimant conducted a business which objectively was not its own. By this, it is presumed that it was at least *also* for the defendant that the claimant intended to carry out this business (BGHZ 40, 28, 31 [case no. 3 above]). The defendant has not been able to rebut this presumption. If the claimant mistakenly believed it was obliged to the defendant to carry him back, this does not stand in the way of *negotiorum gestio* (BGHZ 39, 87, 90; BGHZ 37, 258, 263). Equally, the circumstance that the claimant acted in its own interests, or in fulfilment of its own duties under public law, or of other duties under private law, does not prevent the conclusion that the claimant also carried out the defendant's business (BGHZ 54, 157, 160; BGHZ 40, 28, 30 [case no. 3 above] with further references). The appeal has not argued against this.

(b) But the appeal argues, although without justification, that it was objectively not in the defendant's interest that the claimant took care of his immediate return to Germany in one of the claimant's planes. The Appeal Court has rightly stated that this saved the defendant from trouble which would otherwise have been unavoidable because of his attempted illegal entry into the USA, and from a possible enforced expulsion by the American immigration authorities. This shows sufficiently the objective interest which the defendant had in returning on a plane operated by the claimant.

(c) The Appeal Court was also right in ruling that it could be presumed that the defendant's mother would consent to the claimant providing his return. This is in accordance with the jurisdiction of the present Senate which, short of any evidence to the contrary, considers that the intention one must presume is the one which serves best the well-understood interests of the defendant (BGHZ 47, 370, 374).

On this point, the appeal argues that the claimant could not have presumed that the defendant's mother had a particular interest in having her son return on a scheduled flight. He could equally have returned by boat, which would have been cheaper.

This argument cannot be followed. The claimant was allowed to presume that the defendant's mother would intend to do what would be the best for her son in any given circumstances. The defendant was by no means in a position to embark at his pleasure on a return voyage to Germany by boat, but would have been exposed to all the dangers connected with him first being interned, if the claimant had not taken him instantly back to Germany. The latter was the solution which, under the given circumstances, served best his rightly understood well-being, even if the costs for the flight were relatively high, albeit not intolerable.

(d) It does therefore not matter whether the immediate return of the defendant was also within the public interest (§ 679 BGB).

(e) Rather, the defendant must compensate the claimant for its expenditure on his return flight under § 683 para. 1 BGB. Because the carrying out of this business constitutes an activity which the claimant undertakes within the framework of its business, the claimant is entitled to require that the usual remuneration be paid for the performance which it has made. This is the overwhelming majority opinion in jurisdiction and academic writing, to which this Senate accedes [references omitted].

8. BGH 19.1.1984, BGHZ 89, 376 (standing order)

Facts

In 1978, the defendants (a community of heirs) entered into a lease agreement for a public house with the H brewery. The claimant, a bank, transferred rent payments amounting to DM 1,000 per month to the defendants under a standing order issued by the H brewery. By letter of 22 February 1980, the H brewery informed the defendants that it would discontinue the lease payments due to alleged defects in the premises of the public house. At the same time, the brewery cancelled the standing order by a letter to the claimant dated 3 March 1980.

The claimant inadvertently continued to pay under the standing order for another thirteen months, and now claims from the defendant return of those DM 13,000 plus interest. *Landgericht* and *Oberlandesgericht* have disallowed the action. The appeal was admitted, but without success.

Reasons

The Appeal Court takes the view that the claimant has no direct enrichment claim against the defendants. In the Appeal Court's view, in cases involving payment orders, the payer always has a direct claim against the payee if a valid payment order has been lacking *ab initio*. However, if a standing order has been carried out in the past, but has meanwhile been cancelled, the recipient of the payment must be protected against an enrichment claim by the bank. By issuing the standing order, the debtor has created a situation on which the recipient of the payment is entitled to rely, following a legal policy expressed in §§ 170, 171 para. 2, 172 para. 2, 173 BGB. Such a reliance situation exists in the present case. From the view of the defendants, payments by the claimant were to be seen as continued performance by those who instructed the bank. In spite of the communication by the H brewery that they were to cancel payments due to defects in the leased object, the defendants were entitled to presume from the continuous receipt of payment that the lessee had refrained from acting upon its announcement to terminate payments, and had not cancelled the standing order. The mistake by which the bank ignored the [cancellation of the] standing order is rooted in the relationship between the bank and its customer, and for that reason the general rules for return of enrichment in triangular relationships are to apply.

The appeal does not succeed in its objections against these considerations.

1. The Appeal Court is right to assume that payments which a bank makes towards a third party under a standing order issued by a customer are a case of performance by order (*Leistung kraft Anweisung*). By its standing order, the H brewery instructed its bank (the claimant) to pay in monthly instalments to the defendants the rent which it owed. By this, a cover relationship (*Deckungsverhältnis*) was created between the H brewery and the claimant, according to which

the claimant rendered its own performance toward the H brewery, i.e. by transferring the rent to the defendants, at the expense of the H brewery. In addition, a value relationship (*Valutaverhältnis*) existed between the H brewery and the defendants, within which the H brewery effectuated its own performance towards the defendants (i.e. by having the claimant transfer the rent).

2. The Appeal Court is furthermore right to state that, in cases involving performance by order, return of the enrichment must, *as a principle*, occur within each relationship of performance. Therefore, if the cover relationship between the party which issues the order and the party which receives it is deficient, return of the enrichment must occur within this relationship. If, on the other hand, the value relationship between the party which issues the order and the party which receives the ordered performance is deficient, return of the enrichment must be carried out within that relationship (cf. BGHZ 40, 272 [case no. 4 above]; BGHZ 87, 393; other references omitted).

On the other hand, this Senate has, on several occasions, expressed the view that mechanical solutions must not be applied when sorting out unjustified enrichment in situations which involve more than two parties. Attention must be given to the specific circumstances of the individual case, which must be taken into account in order to find an adequate way of undoing the enrichment (BGHZ 87, 393; other references omitted).

One case before this Senate concerned an order which initially had been validly issued and made known to the recipient by handing over a cheque. Subsequently, the order was cancelled *without knowledge of the recipient*, before the recipient's account had been credited or the sum paid out. In this case, the Senate decided that the bank, which nevertheless honoured the cheque, had no direct enrichment claim against the holder of the cheque, and had to turn towards its client for any enrichment claim (BGHZ 61, 289). Likewise, the Second Civil Senate has held that a bank, which has inadvertently credited the account of a recipient with a certain transfer amount *after cancellation* of the transfer order, has no direct enrichment claim against the recipient, whereas the transfer was based on a claim which the recipient had against the person who ordered the transfer, this person had given advance notice of the transfer to the recipient, and the recipient *was unaware of the cancellation* (BGHZ 87, 246).

On the other hand, this Senate has decided that a bank, which mistakenly effectuates payment under a cancelled order, does have a direct enrichment claim against the recipient of the payment, if this person *knew of the cancellation of the order* when receiving the payment (BGHZ 87, 393).

Finally, this Senate has left open what the legal situation would be if a valid order is lacking *from the outset* (BGHZ 61, 289, 292; BGHZ 88, 232).

This jurisdiction has gained approval by academic writing, at least as far as the results are concerned [references omitted]. This Senate adheres to this jurisdiction. Accordingly, the claimant has no direct enrichment claim against the defendants, since the defendants had no knowledge that the H brewery had cancelled its standing order to the claimant. Additionally, where a standing order is cancelled, one cannot assume that a valid order had been lacking from the outset.

(a) The Appeal Court rightly assumes that the defendants were unaware that the H brewery had notified the claimant of its cancellation of the standing order. It is true that the H brewery had notified the defendants by letter of 22 February 1980 that it hoped the defendants could understand that 'due to those defects, for which we are not accountable, we will terminate payment of the rent, because we in turn cannot obtain any rental payments'. However—as the Appeal Court is right to point out—this letter was only to be understood as announcing a future termination of payment. As the rent continued to be transferred to the defendants' account regularly and for a year, the defendants were allowed to believe that the H brewery—for whatever reasons—would continue to make monthly payments to them, and would find another way of clarifying the differences in opinion which had arisen. While the defendants' knowledge of cancellation of a standing order could have given rise to a direct enrichment claim of the claimant against the defendants, no such knowledge can be imputed from the 22 February 1980 letter by the H brewery.

(b) Furthermore, it can still be left open whether a bank has a direct enrichment claim against the recipient of a payment if, from the outset, there was no valid order by the bank's client upon which the bank could have acted. For the legal situation which arises if a standing order is cancelled corresponds to the situation which exists if an order has initially been validly issued and notified to the recipient by handing over a cheque, but where the order has been cancelled in good time, i.e. before the amount is credited or paid out (BGHZ 61, 289).

It is true that in a situation such as the present (as well as where a cheque is cancelled) there is no valid order at the time when the third party receives payment. However, until the moment when the standing order is cancelled, such an order exists as between the person who has issued and the person who has received the order, and within an intact legal relationship. The relationships of performance, which are decisive for the way in which enrichment is returned, are determined by what initially were the concurrent intentions of all parties concerned. It is true that a person who has issued a standing order does express by its cancellation towards the instructed bank that he no longer wishes the bank to effectuate benefits to accrue to the recipient at his (the instructing person's) expense. If the bank still performs, because it has overlooked the cancellation of the standing order, the bank nevertheless intends to perform only towards its customer. The recipient, whose viewpoint is decisive (BGHZ 40, 272 [case no. 4 above]; other references omitted) will share this view, based on the purpose which the instructing party attributes to the issuing of the standing order. The recipient need not be concerned about whatever happens within the cover relationship, i.e. between his contractual partner and that party's bank. The mistake which occurs when the bank ignores the cancellation of the standing order finds its roots in the legal relationship between the bank and its customer. While the bank is not allowed to act under a customer's standing order once its cancellation has been validly declared, the reasons for this are to be found solely in the legal relationships which exist between the bank and its customer. It is, in principle, within these legal relationships that mistakes have to be sorted out (BGHZ 87, 393; other reference omitted). This Senate continues to see no reason to distinguish between a transfer from a current account and the issuing of a cheque, which is nothing but a specific case of an order (BGHZ 61, 289, 293; but see Lieb JZ 1983, 960, 962). Therefore, the claimant has no direct enrichment claim against the defendants.

The opposite view (cf. OLG Düsseldorf WM 1975, 875) treats a transfer under a standing order after it has been cancelled in the same way as a transfer for which there was no valid order from the outset. However, this fails to take into account the performance relationship as determined by the parties concerned when the standing order was issued. In particular, this view overlooks the fact that the bank, by effectuating the transfer, only wishes to perform towards its customer, and that the recipient understands the payment which he receives in the same way. Therefore, a cancelled standing order cannot be treated in the same way as an order which was lacking from the outset.

4. This result is also appropriate and conforms to the interests involved. It is true that the customer of a bank deserves protection for his interest not to be affected by benefits which his bank confers on third parties after he has cancelled an order which he initially has issued. For this reason, this Senate has decided that the bank which overlooks the cancellation of an order must bear the risk which stems from this mistake, at least in the case where the customer has notified the third party of the cancellation, and therefore has done everything to avert the consequences of a mistaken payment (BGHZ 87, 393). However, if the customer cancels a standing order and does not afterwards notify the recipient of the cancellation—as is presently the case—and tolerates without protest for thirteen months that deductions are made from his account, it is justified to refer the bank to its customer for the return of the amounts transferred. In contrast to the case where the recipient knows of the cancellation, in this case the recipient merits protection of his reliance. He relies on the continued existence of the standing order and does not know that the payments are based on a mistake by the bank [references omitted].

9. BGH 15.5.1986, NJW 1986, 2700 (accident insurance)

Facts

The claimant is an association of accident insurers, which insures school pupils against accidents by virtue of statutory provisions. The defendant's daughter, who was born on 25 January 1966, had a traffic accident on 10 November 1977 on her way to a music class, and the claimant covered the costs for her medical treatment. When the claimant learned that the accident occurred on the way to an independent music school operated by the city of E, rather than—as first assumed by the claimant—on her way to the local authority's secondary school, the claimant notified the defendant that the attendance at music school was not covered by the statutory accident insurance. Subsequently, the claimant repeatedly required the defendant to return the effectuated performances amounting to a total of DM 3,961.50.

The *Landgericht* allowed the action for payment of this sum with interest. The *Oberlandesgericht* dismissed the action. Leave to appeal was granted, and on the claimant's appeal, the judgment by the *Landgericht* is restored.

Reasons

I. The Appeal Court assumes that the claimant has no claim against the defendant in *negotiorum gestio*, as the claimant conducted exclusively its own business in the belief that it owed medical treatment to the defendant's daughter on the basis of statutory provisions. No flaws appear in this legal reasoning, which has not been attacked by the Appeal.

II. The Appeal Court states furthermore that the claimant cannot base its claim on unjustified enrichment.

In the Appeal Court's view, it was the daughter who was the recipient of the treatment which amounts to performance. Therefore, any relationship of performance existed solely between herself and the claimant. There was no statutory basis for any recourse by the claimant against the defendant. A direct restitutionary claim against the defendant could not arise because the claimant—for lack of any such intention—did not knowingly pay another person's debt, i.e. the defendant's maintenance obligations towards his daughter. Neither could the claimant be allowed to waive its restitutionary claim against the defendant's daughter—i.e. the creditor—and make a declaration that its performance, which initially was wrongly made, should retrospectively be made in respect of the obligation of the defendant, i.e. the real debtor. Such a 'right of choice', if bestowed on the mistaken party, would fail to meet the debtor's legitimate interests; neither would it take sufficient account of the interests of the creditor, and of third parties.

This reasoning is successfully attacked by the appeal. The claimant has a claim under § 812 para. 1 sent. 1 BGB against the defendant for reimbursement of the expenditure incurred for the medical treatment.

1. According to specific statutory regulations which govern accident insurance cover for school pupils, the claimant is not obliged to provide insurance cover for the accident which the defendant's daughter suffered. Thereby, the daughter was unjustifiedly enriched when the claimant paid the costs for her medical treatment. When the claimant required from the defendant reimbursement of its expenditure, the claimant expressed by this request that it waived its restitutionary claim against the defendant's daughter, and that its mistaken performance on its own account should now be considered as having been made on account of the defendant. Since, contrary to the view taken by the Appeal Court, it is possible to make such retrospective specification of the debt which is to be serviced (*Tilgungsbestimmung*), the claimant paid, under § 267 BGB, the costs of medical treatment on account of the claimant, who is liable for maintenance towards his daughter. In consequence, the claimant can take recourse against the defendant.

2. It is disputed whether the specification of the serviced debt can be altered retrospectively in cases of mistaken payment on one's own account, to the effect that the performance made can be specified as performance by the true debtor.

(a) Part of the academic writing adheres to the view that the performing party is allowed to change its specification of the serviced debt retrospectively in accordance with § 267 BGB [references omitted]. The opposite view denies such a retrospective right to specify the debt, on the ground that it overly favours the mistakenly performing party [references omitted]. There is a conciliatory view which does admit a retrospective right of choice by a mistakenly performing party, but denies any retroactive effects of such a declaration [references omitted].

(b) The *Bundesgerichtshof* repeatedly had to deal with this disputed question. In one case, two tortfeasors were liable, but not jointly and severally, and one of the tortfeasors, who was liable only up to a certain ceiling, had made payments to the victim which were in excess of this sum. In this case, the Court allowed the performing party to make a retrospective specification of the debt serviced, and thereby admitted a restitutionary claim between the tortfeasors. By this, the Court aimed to prevent the inequitable result that generous compensation for damages by one of the parties should turn into a windfall for the second tortfeasor who had deferred payments (BGH, NJW 1964, 1898, at 1899; see also LAG Düsseldorf, Betr. 1978, 1136). Similarly, this Court has argued in favour of a party who performs on the mistaken assumption of being itself liable, that this party should be allowed to clarify or declare retrospectively that restitutionary claims against the creditor are waived, and that performance was made on account of the debtor who was liable for compensation. However, until today this Senate has allowed a restitutionary claim under §§ 267, 812 BGB only in cases where the third party did *at least also* intend to perform for the true debtor. On the other hand, this Senate has always left it open whether such a retrospective specification of the debt serviced can also be allowed in cases where performance was mistakenly made on what is another person's debt (BGHZ 70, 389, at 397).

3. Considerations of equity have a particularly strong influence on the law of unjustified enrichment. The principle of good faith (§ 242 BGB) is therefore of particular importance for enrichment claims (BGHZ 36, 232, at 235; BGHZ 55, 128, at 134). On this basis, the Senate does allow for a retrospective specification of the debt serviced at least in the present case, with due consideration to the interests of the parties involved.

a) At the latest in March 1978—i.e. as early as some four months after the accident—the claimant realized that it was not liable under statutory provisions to perform towards the defendant's daughter. If the claimant in consequence waived the restitutionary claim which it had in principle against the then approximately twelve year old daughter, and rather took recourse against the defendant, who owed maintenance, for reimbursement of the costs of medical treatment, such recourse must not be refused, or at least cannot be refused in accordance with good faith. In this context, it is obviously not the claimant's aim to search for a 'better' debtor, or to avoid any 'risk of insolvency' it would otherwise have to shoulder. Rather, the claimant wants no more than to have recourse to the person who alone ultimately profited from performances which had been made by a statutory insurance, though without legal ground. Good faith requires that the claimant be allowed such recourse. It would be inequitable if disadvantage were to result to the claimant from the very fact that it first of all paid for the medical costs which accrued without first closely examining its liability as statutory accident insurer, thus making it possible that the necessary medical care was provided to the child as the victim of the accident. The defendant also profited from this conduct because, to this extent, he initially did not have to bother taking all those steps which otherwise would have been for him to take. For this reason, the claimant must be allowed to specify retrospectively under § 267 BGB the mistaken payment as a performance made on account of the defendant.

(b) There are no interests of the defendant worthy of protection which would oppose such a retrospective specification of the debt serviced. At the time of the accident, the defendant was liable for maintenance towards his daughter; he had to pay the costs for medical treatment. Since he as the person who owed maintenance could not have refused to pay the costs, no performance is imposed on him by the claimant who specifies this as the debt to be serviced. Neither is he placed into any worse position by the claimant being allowed to take recourse against him. For until now, he has made no performance towards his daughter; nor is there any set-off situation between himself and his daughter which might be affected by such recourse. On the other hand, it would be inequitable if, as a final result, precisely the defendant who owed maintenance was relieved by this mistaken performance which served the well-being of the child. This cannot be altered by the fact that the defendant may meanwhile be prevented from having recourse against the person who caused the accident, or against his medical insurers . . . , due to the time which has meanwhile elapsed. It was known to the defendant in March 1978 at the latest, that the defendant as the statutory accident insurance body was not liable to perform, and for this reason reclaimed the costs which had already been paid. He could therefore be reasonably expected to make known to the person who caused the accident, or to his medical insurers, any claims which might have arisen. . . . Nor was the defendant exposed to any unreasonably long period of uncertainty, as the claimant declared its specification of the debt serviced within a short time after performance had mistakenly been made. On the contrary, the claimant repeatedly reminded him of his obligation. For the same reason, no change of position can have occurred in the present case (§ 819 BGB).

(c) The defendant's daughter has no apparent interests worthy of protection which could raise equitable considerations against such a retrospective specification of the debt serviced. The daughter received medical treatment for which the claimant paid; no recourse was taken against the daughter. The daughter's interests are not immediately touched by the fact that it is ultimately the defendant as the person who owes maintenance who has to shoulder the expenditure incurred. For the daughter as the person entitled to maintenance could have required the defendant to pay the costs for medical treatment in any event.

10. BGH 9.3.1989, BGHZ 107, 117 (toxicity research)

Facts

The claimant is a German chemical business which develops and markets i.a. herbicides. For this purpose, the claimant operates large research and testing installations. The Federal Biological Office permitted the marketing of growth regulating products containing the agent chlormequat-choride, and of herbicides containing the agent choridazone. For this purpose, the claimant had submitted extensive research reports on the toxicological safety of both chemical agents. When deciding on the admission of similar products manufactured by the defendant, the Office in 1983 and 1984 relied on the claimant's toxicological research. The claimant believes that the defendant must bear part of the claimant's expenditure on research.

The *Landgericht* dismissed the action. The appeal was without success (OLG Köln, NJW-RR 1986, 1117). The further appeal against this decision was, ultimately, without success.

Reasons

II.1 Contrary to the view taken by the appeal, the defendant is not liable under the principles governing the *Eingriffskondiktion* (enrichment claim based on interference) under § 812 para. 1 sent. 1 alt. 2 BGB. According to this provision, the debtor must give up to the creditor what the debtor has received in another way and without legal ground. Non-performance based unjustified enrichment operates if a person has obtained something without legal ground and at the expense of another person. Generally, restitution does not depend on the way in which this acquisition has occurred. Liability in restitution can even arise from acquisition by virtue of a statutory provision, but without legal ground, or by virtue of (lawful) conduct of third parties, including public authorities excercising governmental powers. The fact that there was a legal ground for acquiring something from a third party cannot replace lack of legal ground within the legal relationship within which restitution is to occur.

(a) Therefore, whether or not there is restitutionary liability in the present case does not depend on whether the Federal Biological Office acted lawfully when it used scientific findings on the ecological safety of the agents chlormequat-chloride and chloridazone, which had previously been presented in the course of the claimant's admission proceedings, for the purpose of admitting crop treatment products manufactured by the defendants in accordance with § 8 *Pflanzenschutzgesetz* (Protection of Plants Act, PflSchG; BGBl I, 2591). . . .

When considering the balancing of enrichment between the parties to this action, again no consideration can be given to the following circumstance. The legislature, after intensive discussion on this situation, i.e. where the authority continues to use application documents of the first applicant without compensation being paid—[references omitted], created a new regulation in § 13 of the amended *Pflanzenschutzgesetz* of 15 September 1986 which safeguards a situation of equal competition conditions between those concerned, by blocking the use of the first applicant's documents and/or by providing for compensation by the second applicant. Under § 13 para. 3 PflSchG, which entered into force on 1 January 1987, under certain circumstances an independent liability of the later applicant for compensating the earlier applicant will arise in the future. When looking at restitutionary liability within the time frame of the present case, this provision cannot serve to either confirm or exclude such liability. Mere considerations of equity cannot support a balancing of enrichment via the principles of *Eingriffskondiktion*, not even when coupled with the realization that regulation has become necessary for the safeguarding of diverging economic interests.

(b) Balancing enrichments via the *Eingriffskondiktion* occurs only if the debtor uses as his own a protected legal position which belongs to the creditor, and which the debtor could not lawfully use without permission by the owner of this legal position. In the area of non-corporeal (including intellectual) property law, restitution is granted if there has been interference with the content of attribution (*Zuweisungsgehalt*) of a right, the economic use of which has been reserved for the creditor (BGHZ 68, 90, at 98—concerning a registered design; other references concerning business names and trademarks omitted]. The starting point for liability for enrichment 'in another way' is the infringement of a legal position which, according to the intention of the legal order, has been attributed to the authorized party for its exclusive disposition and use [references omitted]. Liability for enrichment 'in another way' arises only if a pecuniary advantage has been obtained in disregard of the content of attribution of the right which has been violated. Scholars widely agree on this requirement for liability (Wilburg, *Die Lehre von der ungerechtfertigten Bereicherung nach österreichischem und deutschem Recht*, 1934, p. 34; von Caemmerer, in: *Festschrift für E. Rabel*, 1954, p. 353; further references omitted).

As regards the restitution of an enrichment 'in another way', this content of attribution of a legal position replaces the requirement which exists for restitution for performance, i.e. that the enrichment must result from a performance by the creditor of the restitutionary claim (BGHZ 82, 229, at 306). In order to balance enrichments via the *Eingriffskondiktion*, a legal position must have been infringed upon which deserves protection, and which the law envisages for economic use. The content of attribution of the protected legal position corresponds to a prohibitory claim by the owner of the right; it is in the gift of this person to allow the economic exploitation of this right by a third party who would otherwise be excluded from its use. Accordingly, the object of an *Eingriffskondiktion* is only such an advantage which the law perceives as pecuniary asset, and which the enriched party could acquire only by violating a protected legal position and by infringing the owner's exclusive right of exploiting his legal position.

On the other hand, the mere interference with a chance of exploitation is not sanctioned by liability in unjustified enrichment. Rather, the protected legal position must enable the creditor to prevent its exploitation by third parties without his consent [references omitted]. Mere chances of acquisition and profit do not fall within the content of attribution of a right in a restitutionary sense, not even if these chances are attached to a right which enjoys protection by the law of torts, as does the right to an established and operating business (BGHZ 71, 86, at 98). Contrary to the appeal's view, it is therefore not sufficient for the purposes of a restitutionary analysis that first applicants will often sell their admission procedure documents to subsequent applicants, if they are not in a legal position to prevent the marketing of similar products.

(c) The defendant can therefore not be liable in unjustified enrichment. He has reaped a pecuniary advantage which stemmed from the authority's permission to market the crop treatment products without previous and cost-intensive tests for their ecological safety. However, this does not amount to an interference with any protected right of the claimant's by which the claimant could enjoin the defendant. The defendant markets ecological crop treatment products, and the claimant cannot in its own right prevent their commercial use. The defendant has made use of the knowledge of established facts, not of secret documents or of a secret procedure for obtaining this knowledge. His gainful advantage does not flow from the employment of any secret know-how to which his access would have been barred. Neither does his conduct amount to an infringement upon the claimant's right to an established and operating business, as part of which secret know-how can enjoy protection under § 823 para. 1 BGB [references omitted]. It is advantageous to the defendant that, according to the state of knowledge of the admission authority, there is no need for any series of tests in order to prove ecological safety. This knowledge, which serves to his advantage, and its use cannot, however, be barred by the claimant, since the safety of these products is now common knowledge, as is demonstrated by the permitted use of these products. It is open to anybody to make use of such public technical knowledge which is not protected by specific trade rights. By themselves, even considerable intellectual and financial efforts do not lead to the protection of the resulting achievements [references omitted].

11. BGH 23.2.1990, NJW-RR 1990, 827 (embezzlement)

Facts

The claimant's wife was employed by the defendant. After it had become known that she had embezzled more than DM 200,000, the claimant and his wife, by notarial deed, recognized that they owed the defendant the sum of DM 177,122.91 (the remaining sum having already been paid back) and submitted to immediate execution of this document against their assets. As a security for this recognition, the claimant created a mortgage on his real property in favour of the defendant for the sum of DM 175,000. By a written contract of the same date, the wife promised the defendant to submit until 31 July 1986 a proposal on how the amount should be paid back. She failed to keep this promise. At the beginning of August 1986, the defendant reported the wife to the police. The claimant declared rescission of the recognition of debt, based on mistake and deceit. The claimant moved that the execution of the notarized deed should, as far as it concerned him, be declared inadmissible, and that the defendant be ordered to agree that the mortgage entry be cancelled from the land register. The action was successful.

Reasons

The Appeal Court is right in its view that, in accordance with § 812 para. 2 sent. 2 alt. 2 BGB, the purpose has not been achieved which the claimant intended by his performance. According to the facts as established by the lower courts—this establishment not being disputed—the debt was recognized and the mortgage created in order to prevent the defendant from reporting the claimant's wife to the police. It has also been established that the parties have actually agreed on this purpose, which is a requirement for the application of this provision (BGHZ 44, 321, 323; judgment of 23 September 1983 by this Senate, . . . NJW 1984, 233). The Appeal Court has, without mistake, deduced such an agreement from the circumstance that the defendant had required the claimant's wife to provide securities precisely in order to avoid being reported to the police, and that the claimant subsequently did provide such securities. The defendant nevertheless did report the wife to the police.

The appeal complains that the Appeal Court failed to consider the full content of the meeting of minds, as it appears from the defendant's pleadings—to which the description of facts in the judgment refers—as well as from the evidence. It was not only towards the wife, the appeal argues, but also towards the claimant himself that the defendant declared that it would only refrain from reporting the wife to the police under the additional condition that an acceptable proposal for repayment be made until the end of July 1986. However, this is irrelevant for the application of the aforementioned unjustified enrichment provision. It is true that the claimant would then have known that it would take more than the recognition of debt and the creation of the mortgage in order to prevent a report to the police. But this does nothing to change the fact that he made these performances only in order to prevent a report to the police, that there was agreement as to this envisaged purpose, and that this purpose has not been achieved. It does not matter for the application of § 812 para. 2 sent. 2 alt. 2 BGB for which reason the intended purpose has not been achieved.

If the purpose of the performance is not achieved because the performance has not been made in full, or because—as is presently the case—an additional act is stipulated but not carried out, a defense under § 815 may arise against the claim for restitution, namely that the person who performed has prevented the occurrence of the result in a manner which offends good faith. The Appeal Court has failed to examine the case from this particular aspect. This does, however, not affect the outcome of the attacked judgment. According to the parties' submissions, the claimant and his wife had entrusted a credit broker with arranging the loan which they would have needed for paying off their debts. These efforts were undisputedly hindered when a member of the defendant's staff disclosed the criminal offence to this credit broker. This does not imply that this staff member ought to have submitted false information. But it must equally be said that the claimant was not responsible for the situation which resulted from the truthful information, because it was not the claimant who had committed a criminal offence. Neither was he responsible for what was undisputedly the consequence, namely that a proposal for repayment could not be submitted in time. Therefore, the claimant cannot be reproached for dishonest behaviour within the meaning of § 815 BGB. Therefore, the action is justified.

12. BGH 31.5.1990, BGHZ 111, 308 (black labour)

Facts

The claimant raises against the defendant an assigned claim for remaining payments under a works contract amounting to DM 20,505 plus interest. In 1985 and 1986, S, the claimant's husband, carried out works for the defendant, without having been entered in the crafts register, and without having his trade registered. Both facts were known to the defendant. The defendant paid at least DM 4,500 to S for his work. S failed to pay either tax or social insurance contributions on this amount. S then assigned the remainder of his alleged claim for payment under a works contract to the claimant.

The *Landgericht* ordered the defendant to pay DM 11,880 plus interest, and dismissed the remainder of the claim. The *Oberlandesgericht* (NJW-RR 1990, 251) dismissed the action in its entirety. On appeal, this judgment was quashed and the case referred back.

Reasons

1. The Appeal Court assumes that not only the defendant, but also S as his contractual partner have violated the *Gesetz zur Bekämpfung der Schwarzarbeit* (Act to Combat Illicit Work, SchwArbG).

In the Appeal Court's view, S did exercise a craft profession without being registered in the crafts register (§ 11 Nr. 3 SchwArbG). S did this in order to gain considerable economic advantages. His endeavour was therefore covered by the aforementioned provision. In consequence, S had neither contractual nor non-contractual claims which he could have assigned to the claimant.

2. The first part of these considerations is correct.

...

3. The contracts concluded between S and the defendant were therefore void under § 134 BGB. As has been set forth in more detail by the present Senate [reference omitted], by imposing fines on both the contractor and the client, the Act to Combat Illicit Labour intends to prohibit illicit labour jobs as such, and to prevent any exchange

of performances between the 'parties to the contract'. This already strongly indicates that the legal order wants to deprive of any effect a contract which contravenes the prohibition on illicit labour jobs. In particular, as has been said elsewhere by this Senate [reference omitted]—the purpose of the Act to Combat Illicit Labour can be achieved only if such contracts are considered to have no legal effect. This is at least the case if—as presently—both parties have violated the provisions of the Act to Combat Illicit Labour. Even so, in individual cases it may nevertheless offend good faith if one party relies on a contract being void for violation of a statutory provision [reference omitted].

4. The contracts under consideration being void, the claimant can at best raise claims for the return of performances made. According to the jurisdiction of the present Senate, §§ 677ff (*negotiorum gestio*) do, in principle, apply to such cases (BGHZ 37, 258 (263), remainder of reference omitted]. However, in the present case, the 'expenditure' incurred by S consisted in an activity which was prohibited by law. Therefore, S could not consider this 'expenditure' to be 'necessary according to the circumstances'; for this reason alone, claims for remuneration under §§ 683, 670 cannot succeed.

5. However, contrary to the opinion of the Appeal Court, the claimant can rely on the provisions on unjustified enrichment. Such a claim under § 812 para. 1 sent. 1 BGB is, ultimately, not excluded by the provision of § 817 sent. 2 BGB. It is true that this provision does, in principle, apply to situations such as the present. This defence can also be raised against somebody who succeeds the original creditor as a new claimant [reference omitted].

Through his exercise of a craft, S, the assignor, has violated the Act to Combat Illicit Labour. According to the findings by the Appeal Court, both parties wanted their contracts to be carried out precisely as illicit labour jobs. Therefore, there can be no doubt that S was conscious of the violation, and nevertheless decided to carry on.

6. Enrichment claims, however, form part of the law which is governed by equitable considerations, and are therefore particularly influenced by the principle of good faith [reference omitted]. It would be irreconcilable with this principle if the defendant were not to pay for the value of what he obtained without legal ground, but were rather entitled to keep it for free.

In a case which involved the sale of a brothel, and where the vendor had already performed, the *Reichsgericht* ruled that it amounts to deceitful conduct if the buyer refuses to pay, and at the same time refuses to return the house in reliance on § 817 sent. 2 BGB. Such conduct is not protected by the legal order (RGZ 71, 432). The present case is similar. § 817 sent. 2 BGB, which prevents the creditor from reclaiming the enrichment, comes as a severe blow to that party [reference omitted]. Whenever this rule is applied, one must not lose sight of the purpose which the prohibitory norm intends to serve [reference omitted]. In individual cases, it can be necessary to opt for a restrictive interpretation of § 817 sent. 2 BGB, a provision which is problematic as a matter of legal policy, and disputed as concerns its scope of application. The Act to Combat Illicit Labour does not primarily intend to protect one or both parties to the contract; above all, it serves public interests. When the Act was passed, concerns for the labour market were to the fore. According to the Official Reasons for the draft legislation, illicit labour leads to increased unemployment in many professions, causes loss of tax revenue, and damages the social insurance bodies; it also threatens self-employed business owners, who cannot work as cheaply as those engaged in illicit labour. It is only second to these concerns that the client should also be protected against his loss of remedies for defective works (BT-Drucksache 2/1111 and 9/192). The Act was designed as a protective norm within the meaning of § 134 BGB, because the purposes which it intended could only be achieved by rendering the prohibited transactions void [reference omitted]. Given the fact that the Act pursues mainly political aims of a general nature, these aims are, on the other hand, mostly served by excluding all contractual claims. In order to fulfil the aims of the Act, it is not absolutely necessary that a client who orders an illicit labour job be allowed to keep the advance performance for free and at the expense of the contractor. For the general deterrent effect, which the legislator was aiming for, is already achieved by the exclusion of contractual claims, combined with the threat of criminal prosecution and liability for outstanding tax and social insurance contributions once the illicit labour job becomes known. This Senate does not believe that this general deterrent effect would be undermined by allowing an enrichment claim (which, as will be shown below, must at any rate be subject to certain restrictions). The client, who is normally in a stronger economic position, should, in the legislator's view, on no account be treated more favourably than the contractor, who is economically in the weaker position (BT-Drucksache 2/1111, p. 10). Under these circumstances, a viewpoint based on good faith will gain the upper hand, namely that it would be inequitable if the client, who has benefitted from an advance performance, is allowed to keep this benefit for free [references omitted].

According to § 818 para. 2 BGB, the enrichment claim should compensate for the value which has accrued to the defendant without legal ground. When assessing what has been obtained by an illicit labour job, one must first consider that the contractor, by way of an enrichment claim, is on no account allowed to recover for amounts in excess of those stipulated by his void agreement with the client [reference omitted]. As a rule, very considerable deductions will have to be made from this amount to cover the risks which are connected with illicit labour jobs. In particular, the value is much reduced by the fact that the client can have no contractual claims for defective works from the outset, since the contract is void. If any defects have emerged, these must be additionally considered when calculating the balance of the enrichment.

13. BGH 20.6.1990, BGHZ 111, 382 (incapacity)[3]

Facts

The plaintiff had raised 20,000 DM as credit from a bank (BTB). At the plaintiff's direct instruction, part of the credit amount (7,000 DM) was paid out to another bank (N-B). To repay the loan and accrued interest the plaintiff had paid almost 34,000 DM to the BTB. However, the plaintiff had been incompetent to transact at the point in time the loan agreement was concluded. He therefore demanded the bank repay the 34,000 DM minus the amount of the loan he had received (13,000 DM). The defendant was prepared to satisfy any

[3] This translation first appeared in *Cases, Materials and Texts on Unjustified Enrichment*, ed. by Jack Beatson and Eltjo Schrage with the collaboration of Mindy Chen-Wishart, Martin Hogg, Barry Nicholas, Martin Schermaier, David Sellar, Dannie Visser, and Floor Gras (Hart Publishing, 2003). Reproduced with kind permission of the publisher.

possible claims of the plaintiff against the BTB. It argued however, that the plaintiff had to subtract the 7,000 DM which it paid to N-B from his repayment claim. In any event, this amount would have been paid out on the plaintiff's instruction.

Reasons

2. (. . .) The outcome of the legal dispute depends on whether the defendant may raise as a defence to the plaintiff's enrichment claim that the BTB by paying 7,000 DM to the N-B rendered a performance to him [= the plaintiff], which he is bound to repay as unjustified enrichment. The *Oberlandesgericht* [Regional Appeal Court, OLG] argued at this point that the BTB rendered payment in acceptance of the plaintiff's instruction. Concerning an instruction relationship, the actual payment by the party instructed to the third party was legally a performance of the instructed party to the instructor and a performance of the instructor to the third party. Therefore there would exist a cover ratio between the plaintiff as the instructor and the BTB as the party instructed as well as an underlying debt transaction between the plaintiff and the N-B as the recipient of the payment. Basically, reverse transactions would take place exclusively within the relevant relationship. However, something different would then have to apply if, from the outset, an effective instruction as well as an effective determination of the instructor's purpose were absent. Then there would be no 'performance' of the instructor to the recipient of the payment. Since no satisfaction would occur owing to the lack of an agreed purpose it would be unimportant whether the recipient of the payment has a claim against the bank's client. The reversed transaction should then take place exclusively between the recipient of payment and the bank.

Such should the case be here: the plaintiff had certainly given an instruction. However this instruction was void owing to his incompetence to transact. The void act of an incompetent person is not attributed to this person at all. The act was therefore equivalent to the absence of an instruction.

The appeal against these submissions is unsuccessful.

The Federal Supreme Court has hitherto left open the question how compensation for enrichment is to be dealt with if a valid instruction is absent from the outset.

(a) The Appeal Court [= *Oberlandesgericht*] correctly proceeds from the fact that compensation for enrichment in cases of performance following an instruction is basically enforced within the relevant performance relationship. In the case of defects in the cover ratio between the instructor and the party instructed compensation for enrichment is therefore to be dealt with within this relationship. If, in contrast, the underlying debt transaction between the instructor and the recipient of the instructions displays defects, then compensation for the enrichment is to be settled in this relationship.

Nevertheless, the Federal Supreme Court has repeatedly stated that when dealing with events which involve more than two persons under enrichment law, any schematic solution is excluded. The question always concerns the peculiarities of the individual case, which are to be regarded in the appropriate settlement of such events under enrichment law. (. . .)

(b) If a valid instruction together with a valid determination of purpose are absent from the outset owing to the instructor's incompetence to transact then the instructor has not effectuated a 'performance' because the payment of the instructed party cannot be attributed to him. According to the settled case law of the *Bundesgerichtshof* (Federal Supreme Court), a performance pursuant to § 812 I BGB is to be understood as an increase in the assets of another made consciously and with specific purpose (BGHZ 58, 184,188 with further arguments). If this increase in another's assets is effected by transferring money, then the competence of the instructor is required, owning to the character of the instruction as a legal transaction and the character of the determination of purpose which is at least similar to a legal transaction. If this is absent, then the payment by the party instructed to the third party does not represent the instructor's performance. Therefore by payment, the instructor cannot be enriched either by the satisfaction of the obligation existing against him in the underlying debt transaction nor can he acquire a claim under unjust enrichment against a third party. Rather, in this case, compensation for enrichment is to be found in the relationship between the party instructed and the recipient of the payment.

This view is also shared in literature [references omitted]. The Senate cannot accept the different view, viz. that even where there is no competence to transact, compensation is only to be found in the relationship between the instructor and the instructed party [reference omitted]. This view cannot be reconciled with the protection of the incompetent party provided by statute. For the same reason, such cases cannot turn upon the recipient's point of view. Protection of the incompetent party must take precedence over possible protection for *bona fide* acts by the recipient of the payment.

Since the plaintiff was incompetent when he issued the instruction to pay 7,000 DM to the N-B he was not enriched by the instruction being performed in light of the legal situation described.

Therefore, the defendant cannot rely on a counterclaim of unjust enrichment against the plaintiff 's claim for restitution (. . .).

14. BGH 17.6.1992, BGHZ 118, 383 (overpaid maintenance)

Facts

The marriage between the claimant and the defendant was dissolved by decree absolute. The claimant demands from the defendant repayment of excess amounts of maintenance paid to her, and bases the action on unjustified enrichment. By an in-court settlement of 8 November 1985, the claimant had agreed to pay maintenance amounting to DM 1,800 per month. He then sued for adjustment of the settlement and reduction of his maintenance obligations to DM 850 per month with effect from 1 September 1986, on the ground that income stemming from his haulage business had dropped considerably.[4] The *Amtsgericht* refused the action. On his appeal, the *Oberlandesgericht*, by judgment of 19 December 1988, reduced the maintenance payments to DM 1,620 per month for the time from 1 September 1986 until . . . [31 August 1987], DM 1,351 per month for the time from 1 September 1987 until 31 July 1988, and DM 1,546 with effect from 1 August 1988. While the *Oberlandesgericht* established that the defendant's maintenance need exceeds DM 1,800 per month, it held that the defendant, who was looking after the parties' common child,

[4] Titles for maintenance or for other periodic payments can be adjusted under § 323 ZPO (Zivilprozeßordnung, Code of Civil Procedure) if there has been a material change of those circumstances which determine whether, and the amount to which, such payments are owed. In its judgment, the court can adjust the payments due with retroactive effect, but only for the time after the adjustment action has become pending.

could have taken up some part-time employment, and therefore deducted a fictitious salary from the maintenance to be paid. . . . [Execution of the in-court settlement was reduced to DM 1,000 per month for some five months.] The claimant calculated his overpayment as amounting to DM 8,189 . . . Declaring set-off against a claim by the defendant for costs, he sued the defendant for DM 7,130.40. The defendant does not dispute that this amount has been overpaid, but relies on change of position.

The *Amtsgericht*, while considering an alternative set-off against a further claim for costs amounting to DM 499.48, delivered judgment against the defendant for payment of DM 6,630.92 with interest, and dismissed the remainder of the action. On appeal by the defendant, the *Oberlandesgericht* dismissed the action in its entirety. Leave to appeal was granted, by which the claimant petitions for the restoration of the judgment by the *Amtsgericht*. . . . The claimant's appeal was without success.

Reasons

I. The Appeal Court was right to assume that there has been an enrichment within the sense of § 812 para. 1 sent. 2 alt. 1 BGB. When maintenance has been paid without being due, balancing will generally occur under the rules on unjustified enrichment. This view has been taken by the present Senate *inter alia* as regards maintenance payments made under interim relief orders in divorce proceedings, if such payments are not due, or not to this amount, as a matter of substantive law [references omitted]. The same view has also been applied to maintenance payments made by an apparent father to the child: once a final decision has been reached that the child is illegitimate, the result is that the maintenance obligation, which previously existed, has lapsed with retroactive effect [references omitted]. The same is true for maintenance payments which have been made under an in-court settlement. To the effect that such a settlement is adjusted with retroactive effect in favour of the maintenance debtor, the legal ground for the maintenance paid so far lapses (§ 812 para. 1 sent. 2 alt. 1 BGB). In this situation, the maintenance debtor can, in principle, claim return of what has been obtained, or respectively compensation for value under § 818 para. 2 BGB. Since the claimant has paid more to the defendant during the aforementioned time than he was obliged to under the adjustment judgment by the *Oberlandesgericht*, he is principally entitled to claim repayment of what has been performed without legal ground.

II. However, the claim fails on the ground that the defendant is no longer enriched (§ 818 para. 3 BGB), without being subject to increased liability under §§ 818 para. 4, 819, 820 BGB.

1. As regards the loss of enrichment, the Appeal Court, having looked at the account statements and credit documents supplied by the defendant, established that the claimant's maintenance payments were used up by the defendant in their entirety for covering her ongoing living expenses; the only exception being those amounts which she used for paying back debts in instalments. There was no evidence of any account transfers which could indicate that any savings were accumulated. During the time in question, the defendant did not dispose of any other means which she could have saved by using up those maintenance payments. The amount of money which she had received under a credit agreement dating from 1980, which had been increased in May 1986, had already been used up by June 1986 (i.e. before September 1986) for the purchase of a used car. No continuing enrichment flowed from the ownership in this car, since there was nothing to indicate that the defendant would have sold this car to cover her living expenses if she had received less maintenance from the claimant. It was true that the defendant, since 1980 and also during the time under consideration, had continually paid DM 267 per month towards this loan. She was nevertheless, and from the start, not enriched by the value of the repaid loan. For she continued to pay these instalments, at the expense of restricting her other needs, even during the time when she received less maintenance when the execution [of the in-court settlement] was temporarily stayed. It was therefore not the overpayment which the defendant had used for paying back the loan, but rather the basic amount of maintenance. The defendant had used up for a more elaborate lifestyle the amounts which had been overpaid without a legal ground. Therefore, the necessary causal link between overpayment and reduction of debt was lacking.

These considerations withstand legal examination.

(a) According to § 818 para. 3 BGB, the obligation to give up what has been obtained, or to compensate for its value, is excluded to the extent that the recipient is no longer enriched. This provision serves to protect a *'bona fide'* enriched party who has used up what has been obtained without legal ground, in reliance on the (continued) existence of a legal ground. Such a party should not be obliged to give up or to compensate for value over and above the amount of a true (surviving) enrichment (BGHZ 55, 128, at 134; other references omitted). What matters therefore in cases of overpayment of maintenance, is whether the recipient has used up the amounts in their entirety to cover his ongoing living expenses, or whether they were used to acquire values or advantages which have survived in his assets (BGH NJW 1984, 2095; other references omitted). However, the payment which was made without legal ground must have caused just such a pecuniary advantage [reference omitted]. This becomes particularly apparent if the payment itself has relieved the recipient from a liability, e.g. because the enrichment debtor keeps a debit account which has been filled up by an erroneous bank transfer, or because the enrichment debtor himself has used the amount received to pay off debts which he would not have paid off otherwise. For in these situations, the amount which was received without legal ground persists, as it were, as surviving relief from a liability. On the other hand, the enrichment debtor can rely on the lapse of the enrichment if he pays off those debts using means other than those received without legal ground, e.g. money which a third party gave to him as a gift, and, without obtaining any replacement, uses up what he has received. For an enrichment debtor who pays off liabilities by using other means which are at his disposal, must not be in any worse position than an enrichment debtor who disposes of no more than, and thus exhausts, the enrichment.

(b) It appears that the appeal does not argue against this requirement of a causal link between the enrichment and the resulting surviving pecuniary advantage for the enrichment debtor.

However, the appeal argues that it cannot be assumed that any maintenance payments have been exhausted for covering ongoing living expenses. Such an assumption must rather be limited to maintenance payments which remain within the same area of what the maintenance debtor must be allowed to keep for his own subsistence. On the other hand, as regards maintenance payments which exceed this amount, stricter requirements should be placed on the maintenance creditor for his proof of how he used these payments. In order to achieve a solution which adequately reflects the interests involved, a presumption should operate in favour of the maintenance debtor that the maintenance creditor used amounts derived from such overpayments in order to acquire surviving assets, or to pay off his own debts. Such a presumption could be rebutted only by concrete evidence to the contrary. There is, in the appeal's view, no empirical rule that loan debtors will instantly default on their payments once their income is reduced. Without such a presumption, an enrichment debtor could always argue against the enrichment creditor that he (the debtor) would at any event have acquired a certain asset or paid off debts, regardless of the amount of the maintenance paid.

However, the appeal does not succeed with this argument.

It is the enriched party which must prove the lapse of the enrichment, as this is a defence which destroys the claim (BGH NJW 1958, 1725 = *LM* § 134 BGB Nr. 30). Court practice has created alleviations for this proof as regards overpayment of salaries and benefits owed to civil servants, which, by their nature and purpose, are similar to maintenance allowances. These alleviations operate if the overpayment has not been used during the time in question to build up specific savings, or other pecuniary advantages. Experience of life will argue in favour of recipients, in particular those on a low or average income, i.e. that they have spent the overpayment on improving their standard of life, without having to show specifically how this money was actually spent (RGZ 83, 161, at 163; BVerwGE 13, 107; other references omitted).

But even if a lasting pecuniary advantage has been created, this does not necessarily exclude such alleviations. The *Bundesverwaltungsgericht* (BVerwGE 15, 15, at 18) has also assumed a lapse of enrichment under § 818 para. 3 BGB in a case where a civil servant used the overpaid amount for paying off debts which, by restricting his standard of life, he would equally have paid off without the overpayment. In that case, the Court argued that the overpayment had resulted in no more than that the civil servant, by adapting to the extra amount which was at his disposal, restricted his lifestyle less than he would have done if he had paid off his debts on the lower income to which he was entitled. According to these principles, to which this Senate subscribes, it does not matter for the purpose of proving lapse of enrichment whether the surviving pecuniary advantage has been acquired by using the excess amount which was paid without legal ground, or by using the basic sum which was paid with legal ground. In most cases, it will be impossible to establish which of the two amounts was used to pay off the debt, because usually the amount owed and the amount not owed are paid in one total sum, and because the recipient will not distinguish between the partial amounts he uses in order to cover his ongoing living expenses on the one hand, and to pay off debts or to acquire objects which become part of his assets on the other (Lieb, in: *Münchener Kommentar*, 2nd ed. 1986, § 818 no. 83). What is decisive is rather the proof that the enriched party would at any event, and without the overpayment, have acquired the pecuniary advantage in question, if necessary by restricting its lifestyle, with the result that the overpayment has not caused this pecuniary advantage to the enriched party.

It is without success that the appeal argues that stricter rules of evidence should operate for the protection of the maintenance debtor as regards overpayment of maintenance above the amount the maintenance debtor must be allowed to keep for his own subsistence. Rather, the rules on evidence which have been developed for the civil servants cases are also to be applied to wage or maintenance payments under private law. For this situation is comparable to that involving salaries for civil servants [reference omitted]. This is in particular true for the present case. With DM 1,800 per month, the maintenance which the defendant received is within the area of a lower to middle civil servants' salary. There is nothing to show that civil servants demonstrate spending patterns which differ from those of a maintenance creditor. Equally, there are no other reasons which could justify a distinction. Nor do the interests of the enrichment creditor necessitate a presumption to the effect that any pecuniary advantage left with the enrichment debtor has been financed using the amount of the overpayment, with the consequence that such a presumption can be rebutted only by concrete proof that the amount in dispute has been spent otherwise. On the contrary, such a presumption would create too onerous a burden of proof, and contradict the statutory purpose which ties the duty of the enrichment debtor to provide compensation to a true increase of assets which stems from his having received something without legal ground (BGHZ 55, 128, at 134). This is even more so true because, in the income areas under consideration, larger acquisitions, e.g. of household goods or of a car, will, as a rule, be financed on a loan basis, whereby the necessary instalments for capital repayment and interests are paid by making sacrifices on other expenditure. Otherwise, reliance on change of position would be excluded in nearly all of these cases. It is therefore sufficient for the defendant to prove that she would have repaid her debts even without the overpayment.

The defendant has proved this point. It is not disputed that she has continued to pay monthly instalments of DM 267 since 1980 until very recently. This does include payments made by restricting her ongoing living expenses during those months in which, due to the temporary stay of execution, she had no more at her disposal than maintenance payments amounting to DM 1,000 per month. In addition, the Appeal Court has stated, without being challenged, that the defendant has not debited her accounts for any larger sums which could indicate any other savings she might have made. Likewise, the Appeal Court has stated that the defendant did not dispose of any other means which she could have used for her own subsistence. The Appeal Court was allowed to conclude from the above that the defendant had already previously planned the repayment of her loan as a fixed part of her monthly outgoings to be met in advance, and that any means which exceeded these outgoings, such as the overpayments, were used to improve her standard of living.

As regards the car itself, the defendant can equally rely on lapse of enrichment, for this car had previously been acquired by different means, i.e. by use of a loan.

2. The Appeal Court, without any erroneous appreciation of the law, has denied any increased liability under §§ 818 para. 4, 819 para. 1, 820 para. 1 BGB.

(a) Under § 818 para. 4 BGB, the recipient of a performance which was made without legal ground can no longer rely on a lapse of the enrichment once an action is pending; rather, the recipient will be liable in accordance with the general provisions. As the present Senate has decided elsewhere, this increased liability is not triggered by any pending proceedings in which the grounds and the amount of the performance in question are disputed, but rather once an action becomes pending for restitution of what has been received (§ 812 BGB), or for compensation of value (§ 818 para. 2 BGB). This Senate has seen no room for a more extensive interpretation of this provision, regardless of whether this concerned a declaratory action against a maintenance debtor following an injuctive order (BGHZ 93, 183ff), or an action for adjustment of maintenance payments under § 323 ZPO (Code of Civil Procedure; BGH NJW 1986, 2057). This is so because the provision of § 818 para. 4 BGB needs to be narrowly construed as an exception to the principle that the enriched party is liable for compensation only up to the limit of surviving enrichment, and also because the maintenance debtor is not without protection, since it is possible to stay the execution.

The appeal argues against this, that it is only in rare cases that execution is stayed in practice. Thereby, the risk of the enrichment lapsing is shifted entirely onto the maintenance debtor.

This objection does not provide a cause for the present Senate to change its established practice. Whenever a party petitions for the stay of an execution, the court will have to examine whether the reasons which support the underlying action for adjustment can justify a stay. The court will have to balance the interests of maintenance creditor and maintenance debtor, in particular in view of the difficulties which may prevent that maintenance paid in excess can be claimed back in a case where the maintenance title is adjusted with retroactive effect (BGH NJW 1984, 2057). If the practice of the courts fails to do justice to this in each and every case, such practice cannot change the legal position itself. It must also be argued against the claimant that his first instance petitions for a stay of execution have repeatedly failed on the ground that he has been unable to show the fall in his income which he had alleged. There were various ways in which he could have met the danger of the defendant relying on change of position. Nothing would have prevented the claimant from bringing an enrichment action soon after he paid maintenance, and without first waiting for an adjustment of the maintenance title. By this, he could have prevented the effects of § 818 para. 4, at least as concerns payments which had not already been used up (BGHZ 93, 183, at 189). Another option would have been to combine, by way of *Klagehäufung* (joinder of actions, § 258 ZPO), the action for adjustment with an action for future repayment of all maintenance paid in excess for the duration of the adjustment proceedings. He could have avoided the risk of costs by bringing such an action alternatively, i.e. conditional on his petition for adjustment being successful. § 260 ZPO does not prevent such an action. Finally, the defendant could have offered to grant the overpaid amounts as an interest free loan not requiring capital repayment, combined with an undertaking to waive any claims for repayment in case he lost his action for adjustment. Such a grant of maintenance on a loan basis has been perceived by the present Senate as a viable option in cases where maintenance is due, but where the maintenance debtor has separately applied for pension payments: if the pension is granted retroactively to the maintenance creditor, the maintenance debtor has secured a claim for repayment. Good faith will then require the person who is entitled to maintenance to accept a loan which has been offered in such a way (BGH NJW 1983, 1481; other references omitted). This also appears to be an option in a case such as the present.

(b) Under § 819 para. 1 in conjunction with § 818 para. 4 BGB, the recipient of the enrichment becomes subject to increased liability already from the time when he learns of the lack of legal ground. For this purpose, the recipient of the enrichment must have known the lack of the legal ground itself and the legal consequences which flow from such lack; on the other hand, mere knowledge of facts on which the lack of legal ground is based, are not sufficient (Lieb, in: *Münchener Kommentar*, 2nd ed. 1986, § 819 no. 2; other references omitted). It is true that the Appeal Court has left open whether or not the defendant had knowledge of those factual circumstances which provided the basis for the adjustment of the settlement on the maintenance claim. Therefore, for the purposes of this appeal it must be assumed in favour of the claimant that the defendant had such knowledge. However, the Appeal Court denied that the defendant was *mala fide*, for lack of knowledge of the legal consequences: as petitions by the claimant for a stay of the execution were repeatedly rejected, and as the action itself was defeated in the first instance, the defendant was allowed to rely until the appeal judgment of 19 December 1988 on her belief that she was entitled to DM 1,800 per month. No objections can be raised against this. What speaks in favour of the defendant is the uncertainty of the outcome of the legal proceedings. The appeal argues, on the contrary, that a maintenance creditor is no longer worthy of protection in his reliance once an action for adjustment is filed, and is therefore to be considered as *mala fide*. But such argument fails to see that such a result would undermine the protection of the recipient of the enrichment as it has found its expression in § 818 para. 4 BGB (see above at II 2a). For the maintenance creditor would be forced to save the maintenance for repayment claims from this time, even though

§ 818 para. 4 requires him to do so only from the time when the maintenance debtor confronts him with an enrichment action.

(c) Neither is this a case of increased liability under § 820 para. 1 sent. 2 BGB (it is presently only the second alternative of this provision which can be considered). This would require that performance was made for a legal ground, the lapse of which was considered as possible according to the content of the legal transaction, and which does in fact lapse later on. The purpose of this provision is that a recipient, who reckons from the beginning with an restitutionary obligation, must make his arrangements as if he had to return the performance which he received. In this situation, it must transpire from the very content of the legal transaction that the parties have realized the possibility of a lapse of the legal ground not just incidentally, but specifically (BGH NJW 1984, 2095; other references omitted).

The appeal likes to believe that these requirements have been met, because the maintenance which was agreed by the in-court settlement was based on the claimant's profits in 1984, so that the defendant had to reckon that there was such a particular likelihood that economic losses suffered by the claimant would lead to a reduction of her maintenance. In doing so, however, the appeal wanders into the area of an appreciation of facts from which it is barred. . . .

It can therefore be left open whether increased liability under § 820 BGB, according to the purpose of this provision, can apply at all to maintenance agreements, which are always subject to a reservation that there is no fundamental change to the basis of the transaction (*Vorbehalt des Wegfalls der Geschäftsgrundlage*).

15. BGH 5.10.1993, NJW 1994, 187 (honorary consul)[5]

Facts

The defendant was to have procured for the plaintiff the title of 'Honorary Counsel of Sierra Leone in Hungary' in return for payment

[5] This translation first appeared in *Cases, Materials and Texts on Unjustified Enrichment*, ed. by Jack Beatson and Eltjo Schrage with the collaboration of Mindy Chen-Wishart, Martin Hogg, Barry Nicholas, Martin Schermaier, David Sellar, Dannie Visser, and Floor Gras (Hart Publishing, 2003). Reproduced with kind permission of the publisher.

of $125,000. The plaintiff paid a deposit of $50,000. The defendant promised to return this payment should he not procure the title within a certain period. In order to guarantee his promise of repayment he made out a promissory note for $50,000 to the plaintiff. The plaintiff is now suing the defendant on the basis of this promissory note. The defendant refuses to pay, claiming that the transaction concluded is contrary to good morals and for this reason invalid.

Reasons

II. 1. (. . .)

2. Judicial error exists (. . .) in the Appeal Court's view that the defence to enrichment according to Article 17 WG, §§ 821, 812 II BGB does not oppose the plaintiff's bill-based claim according to Article 28 (1) WG even where the title purchase is immoral because § 817 (2) BGB prevents the bill being claimed from the defendant as enrichment. This view cannot be reconciled with the wording and the purpose of the statute.

Admittedly, the first half of § 817 (2) BGB generally excludes claims for recovery arising from claims of enrichment by performance where statute or good morals have been violated because no legal protection should be granted where claims are derived from transactions which violate statute or good morals. However, the second half of the subsection left unconsidered by the Appeal Court makes an exception where the performance consisted of entering into the obligation. The statute does not regard an immoral asset transfer to be concluded until the obligation has been fulfilled and intends to prevent it from taking effect.

In a case of dispute, this exceptional regulation intervenes if it is assumed that the title purchase is invalid owing to immorality. The entering into an obligation pursuant to the second clause of § 817 (2) BGB then lies in the acceptance of the defendant's promissory note given for the purpose of security, which is recoverable until the bill is satisfied or transferred to a third party (leading opinion); cf. Staudinger/Lorenz, BGB 12th edition § 817 marginal note 25; . . . Reuter/Martinek, *Ungerechtfertigte Bereicherung* S. 227; Koppensteiner/Kramer *loc. cit.* p. 63; other comments, Erman/HP Westermann, *BGB* 9th edition § 817 marginal note 24 for promissory notes given for the purpose of satisfaction; undecided in RG JW 1921, 461; (further references omitted). This view corresponds to the motives behind the BGB, in which the submission of a promissory note is cited as an example for entering into an obligation, (Mugdan, *Die gesamten Materialien zum Bürgerlichen Gesetzbuch für das Deutsche Reich,* Vol. II p. 475) and above all, behind the purpose of the law. For, by admitting the recovery of the acceptance of the promissory note, the plaintiff's secured claim is prevented from taking effect, for his claim should not be legally protected where the title purchase is immoral. That is, the first half of § 817 (2) BGB bars the plaintiff's claims in enrichment for recovery of the DM 50,000 paid as deposit. That the parties have reached a contractual agreement to the effect that this amount is to be repaid should the plaintiff not be elected to the honorary general counsel within a certain period, is of no consequence. § 817 (2) BGB cannot be altered by reciprocal agreement, nor can it be avoided by replacing the barred claim of enrichment by another claim.

As a result, and contrary to the Appeal Court's opinion, where the purchase of title is immoral § 817 (2) BGB operates to the disadvantage of the plaintiff and not the defendant.

III. The judgment challenged is therefore to be set aside (. . .). The defendant's defence to enrichment takes overriding effect against the bill-based claim (Art. 17 WG, §§ 821, 812 II BGB), because the causal agreement concluded by the parties, *viz.* that appointment to the honorary general counsel be procured for valuable consideration, is void owing to violation of good morals (§ 138 I BGB). According to—as far as can be ascertained—unanimous opinion in case law and literature with which the Senate agrees, transactions for valuable consideration relating to the procurement of official offices and titles violate the sense of decency of all just and right-thinking people (RGZ 86, 98 sq.; RG JW 1919, 447 sq.; RG JW 1931, 1924 sq.; further references omitted). Trading in offices and titles is largely disapproved of by respectable people, who obtain offices and titles by hard work and service and not by purchasing them. The reprehensibility results from associating the endowment of official offices and titles with pecuniary consideration which contradicts immaterial, ethical principles. Venality would debase titles and considerably damage the ability of public offices to function properly.

This cannot be tolerated, particularly in the case of offices which are associated with national tasks or special rights. The honourable office of an honorary counsel concerns such an office. (. . .)

The immorality of the agreement to procure the defendant's appointment as honorary general counsel of Sierra Leone in Hungary in return for $125,000 is just as unaffected by the plaintiff's claim that the state of Sierra Leone grants such offices in return for valuable consideration as his submission that the trade in titles has developed into an autonomous business field enjoying a respectable turnover. Abusive practices which have developed in certain circles are unpersuasive within the framework of § 138 I BGB. Nor is its application opposed by the fact that the plaintiff denies being aware of the immorality of the transaction. According to the settled case law of the Federal Supreme Court it is sufficient that the parties were aware of the circumstances from which the immorality arose, as is the case here.

16. BGH 5.11.2002, BGHZ 152, 307 (credit broker)

Facts

1. The claimant, a local council, has sued the defendant, a county council, for repayment of a sum of money which the claimant had transferred to the defendant in the following situation:

2. The parties, as had many other local councils, local corporations, and county councils who either had money to invest or were in need of credit, had been using the services of credit broker K. K brokered short-term credit agreements between local authorities. Interest rates were above those which banks offered for investment, and below what they charged for credit. K would approach local authorities independently of each other, so that there would be no direct contact between them. He succeeded in deceiving some local authorities into making payments directly to him in person, and thus to sideline many millions of Deutschmarks without at first anyone noticing. He covered up those gaps by pretending to local authorities who wished to lend money that a credit contract was to be concluded on named terms, with the other party being a named local authority who was allegedly interested in obtaining credit. In some cases, K indicated that the loan was to be paid not to the alleged borrower but, on instruction of that party, directly to a third party to which the borrower allegedly owed money.

3. During the summer of 1996, K caused the defendant in this way to grant a credit of DM 3.5 million at 3.45% interest p.a. to an alleged borrower, the city of P. By letter of 19 November 1996, K announced to the defendant that the 'time deposit' due on 21 November 1996 would now be paid back timely and with the accrued interest. The claimant paid the precise amount—DM 3,529,194.55—on that very date to the defendant's account, indicating 'Redemption City of P' as purpose for which the money was to be used. The claimant did this on the strength of a letter by K, also dated 19 November 1996, in which K had told the following to the claimant (but without having actually consulted the representatives of the city of P.):

4. '. . . as agreed, you will make a time deposit on the following terms:
Borrower: City of P.
Amount: DM 3,529,194.55
Duration: 56 days bearing interest, from 21.11. 1996 until 17.1.1997
Interest rate: 3.2% p.a.
Please make the payment to the benefit of: County council W.
Purpose of use: Redemption City of P.'

5. The claimant argues that the defendant must return to the claimant the DM 3,529,194.55 credited to its account under unjustified enrichment for lack of instruction or of a specification by the city of P. as to the debt to be serviced. Furthermore, the defendant should surrender any benefit, or other advantages as savings made on interest, which the defendant derived from having been granted this capital without legal ground.

6. The *Landgericht* has accordingly held that the defendant must pay to the claimant DM 3,429,194.55 plus default interest since 3 May 2000, and must furthermore give a breakdown of the benefits which the defendant has derived from having used the principal amount, respectively of the amount of interest saved in this way. . . .

Reasons

7. Only a small part of the defendant's leapfrog appeal is well-founded [the part which relates to giving a breakdown of benefits].

8. The *Landgericht* held that a claim lies in unjustified enrichment, and has essentially given the following reasons:

9. The transfer of DM 3,529,194.55 was a performance made by the claimant in the sense of § 812 para. 1 sent. 1 alt. 1 BGB. The claimant had solely its own purpose in mind, namely paying out a short-term credit which it thought to have agreed with the city of P, by transferring the money to the defendant which had been named as recipient of the payment. This is not altered by the view which the defendant took of this payment, namely that this represented the redemption of a credit contract which the defendant believed to have entered into with the city of P. The *Landgericht* recognizes that in certain cases of triangular relationships it is the recipient's perspective which decides, when in doubt, which party has made a particular performance. However, the recipient perspective cannot be relevant if in reality there is no such multi-party relationship within which different performances are made. The *Landgericht* distinguished the present case from cases in which a bank had made an unauthorized payment to a recipient who was unaware of the lack of authorization and from whose perspective the payment looked like a performance (in the sense of § 812 para. 1 sent. 1 alt. 1) made by the account holder. In these cases, the *Bundesgerichtshof* exceptionally limits recovery to the relationship between bank and account holder. What makes the present case different in the view of the *Landgericht* is that the representations made by K cannot be attributed to the city of P. When brokering credit contracts, K never appeared as agent of the parties to the contract, but invariably as an independent credit broker. The defendant could therefore not rely on the impression that it was the city of P which was performing. It is a general principle of the doctrine of ostensible legal relationships (*Rechtsscheinlehre*) that even a *bona fide* party is not protected if the creation of an impression that a particular legal relationship exists cannot be attributed to the other party. Contrary to the position held by the defendant, the claimant can also not be considered as third party in the sense of § 267 BGB, because the claimant was performing what it thought to be its own obligation, rather than that of a third party.

11. The *Landgericht* also rejected another argument made by the defendant, namely that the claimant could not rely on disenrichment

because the claimant subsequently received repayment of other loans it had given to other local authorities under invalid credit contracts. This does not alter the fact that the transfer of assets from claimant to defendant was immediate. Moreover, loss is not a requirement for a claim in unjustified enrichment.

12. (Claims for information and breakdown of benefits).

13. The reasons given by the *Landgericht* withhold legal scrutiny . . . [except for those which relate to the breakdown of benefits].

14. The *Landgericht* was right to decide that the claimant has a right to repayment under unjustified enrichment. This is, however, not a case of performance-based unjustified enrichment (*Leistungskondiktion*) under § 812 para. 1 sent. 1 alt. 1, but a case of enrichment in another way (*Nichtleistungskondiktion*) under § 812 para. 1, sent. 1 alt. 2 BGB.

15. In cases involving three parties where performance is made on an instruction, unjustified enrichment claims are generally confined to performance relationships between the parties, namely the cover relationship (*Deckungsverhältnis*) between the instructing party and the instructed party, and the value relationship (*Valutaverhältnis*) between the instructing party and the recipient. On a performance-based analysis of unjustified enrichment, when the instructed party transfers assets to the recipient, all three parties understand this correctly as the instructing party effectuating two separate performances, namely a performance by the instructed party towards the instructing party, and a performance by the instructing party towards the recipient (established position of the courts, see BGH 31.10.1963, BGHZ 40, 272 [case no. 4 above]; nine other references omitted).

16. There are, however, exceptions to this principle. It is also established jurisdiction of the *Bundesgerichtshof* that the instructed party may recover directly from the recipient under § 812 para. 1 sent. 1 alt. 2 (enrichment in another way) if the recipient is aware of the lack of instruction at the time of receipt, and thus of the fact that the debt to be served has not been specified effectively (cf. BGHZ 66, 362, at 364, four other references omitted). But even if the recipient was not aware at the time of receipt that a valid instruction was lacking, the supposedly instructed party has a direct claim against the recipient under § 812 para. 1 sent. 1 alt. 2 (BGHZ 111, 382, at 386f [case no. 13 above]; judgment of this Senate in BGHZ 147, 145, at 151; see also

BGHZ 147, 269, at 274). Without a valid instruction, the payment cannot be attributed to the supposedly instructing party as this party's performance. As the *Landgericht* has rightly argued, any other decision would ignore the principle which is generally recognized for the doctrine of ostensible legal relationships, namely that a *bona fide* contract party will be protected only if the other party to the contract can be attributed with having created the impression of the existence of a legal relationship. The so-called recipient perspective rule cannot replace a lack of determination of purpose (or lack of determination of the obligation to be discharged) by the supposedly instructed party, not even if the supposedly instructing party actually owed the full amount which was paid to the recipient. Furthermore, a recipient who trusts that a valid instruction exists and that a specification of the debt to be serviced have been validly made is normally sufficiently protected by the rules on disenrichment in § 813 para. 3 against the legal consequences of a direct claim in unjustified enrichment by the (supposedly) instructed party (judgment of this Senate in BGHZ 147, 145, at 151 with further references). These principles also apply in the present case.

17. According to the facts established by the *Landgericht*, when transferring DM 3,529,194.55 to the defendant, the claimant intended to perform the credit contract which it thought to have concluded with the city of P, and thought to be acting on an instruction by the city of P to pay to the defendant, a party it thought to be entitled to receive this sum. The claimant thus intended to perform towards the city of P. This is therefore a case of payment without instruction in the sense of unjustified enrichment law, with the effect that the claimant as supposedly instructed party has a direct claim against the defendant under § 812 para. 1 sent. 1 alt. 2 BGB (enrichment in another way). The perspective of the defendant as recipient is not relevant at all, because no specification of the debt to be discharged has been made by the city of P as the supposedly instructing party. Only where such a specification has actually been made will the ground be set for using the reasonable perspective of the recipient for deciding which of different existing views should prevail as to which party has performed. The defendant's mere imagination that the defendant was the recipient of the payment is not sufficient for creating a performance relationship, nor for creating a legal ground. The defendant cannot rely on K having created the

impression of a legal relationship in the form of a performance by the city of P. Neither claimant nor the city of P can be attributed with the creation of such a ostensible legal relationship.

18. The appeal argues that the claimant performed as a third party in the sense of § 267 para. 1 BGB in order to discharge the city of P of an obligation to return a payment to the defendant. While there was admittedly no such obligation under a credit contract, the city of P was nevertheless liable to return payment to the defendant under the law of unjustified enrichment. This view cannot be reconciled with the facts established by the *Landgericht*. The claimant thought that it was performing its own obligation under an imaginary credit contract with the city of P. The claimant was thus lacking the will to discharge the debt of a third party, as is required under § 267 para. 1 BGB (see BGHZ 75, 299, at 303; BGHZ 137, 89, at 95). It is true that this provision is not looking at the subjective perception of the third party but rather at how the recipient of the payment should have reasonably understood the third party's behaviour (established jurisdiction, see e.g. BGHZ 72, 246, at 248f, BGHZ 137, 89, at 95; BGH 22.9.1994, II UR 166/93, WM 1994, 2286). However, that does not affect the outcome in the present case. As the purpose of the payment was indicated to be 'Redemption City of P', there is nothing to show that when receiving the payment the defendant believed, or was allowed to believe, that this payment had been made by a third party in the sense of § 267 para. 1 BGB, rather than by a party who had been instructed by the city of P.

(19.–21. No apparent authority of K to instruct the claimant to pay to the defendant on behalf of the city of P; no other attribution of K's behaviour to the claimant.)

22. Contrary to the view taken by the appeal, there are no other obstacles to the claimant's direct entitlement to repayment against the defendant in unjustified enrichment under § 812 para. 1, sent. 1, 2nd alt. BGB.

23. The defendant's reliance is not protected within the framework of unjustified enrichment rules. Moreover, the defendant is not much more worthy of protection than the claimant, the city of P, or other local and county councils involved. Having trusted blindly the representations made by K, they all have failed to contact their imagined

contract partners. They all have transferred or received millions of DM without valid contracts. Nothing would therefore rally for the defendant to be relieved of this obligation towards the claimant, in particular since the defendant remains free to take recourse against the city of P. The defendant has a performance-based claim under § 812 para. 1 sent. 1 alt. 1 BGB against the city of P as concerns the DM 3.5 million which the defendant transferred on 21 August 1996—the same 3.5 million which, together with accrued interest, were supposedly paid back by the claimant. When transferring the DM 3.5 million, the claimant intended to discharge a claim of the city of P under a credit contract which in fact did not exist.

24. This claim of the defendant against the city of P under § 812 para. 1 sent. 1 alt. 1 BGB is not defeated by the fact that the city of P understood this to be the repayment of a credit which the city of P had allegedly given to the O hospital and the cities of D and E. As has been explained above, the mere imagination of the recipient is sufficient neither for creating a performance relationship, nor for creating a legal ground. The opposite view would lead to the result that—depending on the arbitrary behaviour of credit broker K—a local authority which in fact had neither shifted any assets nor had specified which debt was to be served could nevertheless be perceived as having provided performance. The City of P cannot rely on K having created the impression of a legal relationship in the form of performances made by the O hospital and the cities of D and E, because the defendant has not caused this impression in any attributable fashion.

(25. Illegality defence in § 817 does not apply to non-performance-based unjustified enrichment; alleged violation of a statutory provision would not make a credit contract illegal.)

26. Contrary to the view taken by the appeal, the *Landgericht* has not erred in its treatment of what the appeal sees as disenrichment of the claimant. It is not necessary for a claim in unjustified enrichment to demonstrate a loss, which, on a 'but for' approach, can be eliminated through collateral benefits which are directly connected with the loss-causing event (see BGHZ 36, 232, at 233; BGH 28.6.1967, NJW 1968, 197). From the outset, there is accordingly no room for taking into account payments which other county councils have made towards the claimant under other imaginary credit contracts.

17. BGH 9.7.2008, NJW 2008, 3277 (non-marital property)

Facts

3. The parties met in 1990 and subsequently entered into a long-term non-marital relationship whereby the parties would keep separate homes and visit each other regularly. In 1999, the claimant acquired a property on which a house for one family with an additional self-contained flat was erected. This property was to serve the parties as their common home. They also planned that the claimant's daughter should move in, and that the defendant, who was working for a building society, would have his office in the house. Both parties contributed, both financially and through their own work, to this property development, which was projected to cost DM 320,000. They moved into the house in February 2000. After the relationship between the parties took a downturn in the beginning of 2003, the claimant had the request issued to the defendant that he should clear and surrender the property by the end of 2003. The defendant acceded to this request after the present action became pending.

4. By his counter-claim, the defendant seeks to be recompensed for the money which he invested in the development of the property, and also for his work. He claims . . . to have contributed DM 163,910.77 (= €83,806.25) in money and at least 1,000 hours of work, for which he claims an hourly rate of €10. The claimant states that he used his savings and pension investments for the building after the claimant had promised him a lifelong right to live in the property.

5. The claimant defends the counter-claim. She argues that what the defendant gave was to be seen as his contribution to the long-term non-marital relationship. She disputes any promise of a lifelong right to live in the property.

6. The *Landgericht* rejected the counterclaim. The defendant's appeal was without success. The present Senate has given leave to further appeal by the defendant to the amount of €93,806.25 plus interest.

Reasons

7. The appeal is well-founded and allowed [for most of the counter-claim]. The case is referred back to the Appeal Court.

8. The Appeal Court has taken the view that the defendant cannot claim payment under any legal aspect, and gives essentially the following reasons:

9. (No claim associated with a civil law partnership (*Gesellschaft bürgerlichen Rechts*).)

10. (No claim for revocation of a gift.)

11. The Appeal Court has held that the defendant has no claim under § 812 para. 1 BGB. Innominate contributions made within non-marital long-term partnerships can generally not be claimed back. Such a claim can exceptionally lie if only one of the partners is enriched by either a performance which exceeds what is usual within a long-term non-marital partnership, or a joint use of assets. These conditions are not fulfilled in the present case. Instead, both parties have contributed about equally, through their money and work, to what normally must be invested for erecting a jointly used family home. The defendant has valued the home at between DM 400,000 and DM 450,000. As he claims to have contributed some €100,000 [some DM 200,000], the remainder must have been invested by the claimant, or her parents or siblings. Furthermore, an enrichment can consist only in such an increase in the value of the house which is due to the performance of the defendant. Such an increase has not been pleaded. Any expenditure which the claimant has saved can become relevant only if the initial enrichment has lapsed. Finally, the long-term non-marital relationship cannot be considered to be a legal ground in the meaning of § 812 BGB, and must rather be understood as factual, extra-legal occurrence. The present parties have not performed in view of a legal ground which in reality does not exist, or which later lapses. This leaves only claims under § 812 para. 1 sent. 1 alt. 2 BGB. The Appeal Court recognises that the *Bundesgerichtshof* has thought it possible that a home which partners have built together but which on a formal property law view belongs to only one of the parties, can, on an economic view, nevertheless constitute a common added value for both parties. On the required case by case analysis, however, in the present case one cannot assume that the parties intended to create such a common added value for both parties. It is not disputed that the claimant did not intend to make the defendant co-proprietor. The parties wanted to prevent the defendant's children from his divorced marriage from taking hold of the house after the defendant's death. In this situation, it is contrary to the

interests of the parties if the defendant is awarded recompense in unjustified enrichment.

12. The Appeal Court has furthermore held that the defendant cannot not base any claims on a lapse of the basis of transaction (*Wegfall der Geschäftsgrundlage*). It is characteristic for non-marital partnerships that parties can split up at any time. Such a partnership therefore offers no basis on which parties could rely. As a rule, therefore, performances which one partner makes on a house in which the parties are to live together do not call for recompense. It would be different if the parties had entered into an agreement which, however, cannot be established in the present case. The defendant has pleaded no more than that the claimant was ready to grant him a right to live in the property, but not that he has accepted this offer and demanded its execution. According to his submissions, the creation of a proprietary right to live in the property was foiled when the claimant time and again postponed the signing of a notarial draft made in 1999. Furthermore, the fact that the defendant paid a monthly rent of DM 500 to the claimant by standing order speaks against the view that the claimant created a mere right *in personam* of the defendant to live in the property in consideration of his contribution to the house.

13. These considerations of the Appeal Court do not withstand legal scrutiny and the attacks of the appeal in all points.

14.–17. (No revocation of a gift.)

18.–23. (No civil law partnership, in particular since parties did not intend to create common assets.)

24.–31. (The court reviews its previous position, whereby long-term non-marital partnerships are to be considered as purely factual occurrences which do not give rise to a legal relationship (e.g., BGH 8.7.1996, FamRZ 1996, 1141, 1142), and the criticism of some scholars, such as Gernhuber and Coester-Waltjen, *Familienrecht*, 5th ed. 2006, § 44 no. 20; Lüderitz and Dethloff, *Familienrecht*, 28th ed. 2006, § 8 no 35.)

31. Within a marriage, the personal relationship stands also at the fore and determines how spouses deal with their assets. It has hitherto not been concluded that that performances made beyond what was owed are made outside of a legal relationship. These are rather considered to be contributions related to the marriage which on divorce can lead to claims under the rules on the basis of the transaction

(*Geschäftsgrundlage*), in particular if spouses have kept their assets separate [reference omitted]. An argument previously made for this view has since ceased to carry force, namely that a non-marital partner who makes a performance knowingly accepts the risk of failure and thus cannot be allowed to rely on the continuation of the relationship. While such a partner knows that the long-term relationship can be ended at any time, the contribution will nevertheless be made in the expectation that the relationship will continue. If one partner has actually relied on this expectation in a way which was recognizable for the other partner, i.e. the recipient of the performance, this reliance appears worthy of protection. The fact that, as a matter of law, only spouses are allowed to rely on the expectation that their relationship is for life, can no longer justify different treatment if one considers the prevalent high divorce rate [references omitted].

33. For this reason, the Senate no longer adheres to the view that claims under the rules on the lapse of the basis of transaction or under unjustified enrichment for failure of purpose are excluded between former partners to a long-term non-marital relationship. As concerns performances which exceed what is needed to live together day by day, one needs to examine case by case whether a claim for recompense may be justified under those legal aspects. This incidentally applies not only to non-marital relationships but also to other forms of living and running a household together, as one could imagine e.g. for widowed siblings, or other relatives or friends; a sexual connotation is irrelevant.

34. According to § 812 para. 1 sent. 2 alt. 2 BGB, the recipient must return a performance if the result has not been achieved which was intended with this performance in accordance with the legal transaction. A claim in unjustified enrichment for failure of this expectation requires that the recipient has consented to this expectation; one-sided expectations are not sufficient. However, a tacit agreement in this sense can be assumed if one party intends its performance to achieve a particular result, and if the other party recognises this and accepts this performance without objection (judgment by this Senate, BGHZ 115, 261 . . .).

35. Within a long-term non-marital relationship or any other long-term relationship, it is only for such contributions or work performances which go well beyond what this partnership requires on a day

to day basis that it will be possible to establish that such performance fulfils the requirement that it was aimed at a non-enforceable result. Merely living with the partner at present will not suffice. What is required is a specific agreement of purpose, as may for instance exist if partners do not intend to create commonly held assets, but if one increases the assets of the other while expecting to be able to participate in the acquired object on a long-term basis [references omitted].

36. The Appeal Court has not established any such agreement of purpose. (Repetition of the argument made above, no. 11, last two sentences). This, however, does not exhaust the facts which the defendant has pleaded.

37. According to the judgment of the *Landgericht*, to which the Appeal Court refers, the defendant has asserted that the claimant gave him a lifelong right to live in the house, and that for this reason he invested considerable assets in this property development, liquidated savings made for his old age, and furthermore made considerable contributions through work. The Appeal Court has considered these assertions in a different context, namely as being insufficient for establishing a right to live in the property, because the defendant did not state whether he accepted the offer. The Appeal Court also views the defendant's payment of a monthly rent of DM 500 as providing an argument against such a right.

However, these arguments cannot defeat the asserted agreement of purpose. For this, it is not necessary that a promise of a right to live in the property was executed. It is rather sufficient that the contribution which the defendant made served this purpose, that this was recognizable to the claimant, and furthermore that the contribution was accepted by the claimant without objecting to the purpose. Moreover, the appeal is right to complain that the defendant's rent payments were, as the claimant herself has stated, considered between the parties as contribution towards the living expenses. This implies that these payments provide no argument against the defendant's position.

39. When stating that the defendant has not sufficiently pleaded that the value of the house was increased by the defendant's contributions, the Appeal Court has overstretched the burden of pleading. It is not disputed that the property development was projected to cost DM 320,000. The alleged performances made by the defendant can be related to this value. As, according to his statement, the house has

a value of DM 400,000 to 450,000, there is nothing to support the view that the defendant's performances have not contributed to the value. A claim in unjustified enrichment cannot be rejected on those reasons.

40. Additionally, recompense may be awarded according to the principles on the lapse of the basis of transaction (§ 313 BGB), to the extent that the contribution made for the common purpose was based on the assumption or expectation that the relationship which this project served to arrange would last for good. Such an unwinding can for example occur in cases, in which recompense under partnership rules is excluded because no common assets were created, or in which an agreement of purpose in the sense of § 812 para. 1 sent. 2 alt. 2 BGB cannot be established.

40.–46. (The court refers to its jurisdiction on unwinding marital property after divorce in cases where parties had agreed to, but failed to keep their assets separate. A cooperation contract (*Kooperationsvertrag*) under family law may be implied if assets have been shifted well beyond what was due in terms of maintenance or in general contribution to marital life, and the basis of this transaction may lapse on divorce. This can be extended to other long-term relationships, but claims are limited to exceptional situations where the performing party cannot be expected, in good faith, to suffer a loss to lie where it has fallen.)

47. For these reasons, the appeal must be allowed in full. The matter is referred back to the Appeal Court, which must establish the missing facts, including those relating to the amount of the contributions in question.

48. For the purpose of the further proceedings, the Senate adds the following observations.

49. If a claim in unjustified enrichment is found to exist, it should not be excluded by § 815. It was not impossible from the outset that this long-term non-marital relationship would be, and was intended to be, for life. If this provision applies at all, it is only where the disenriched party has terminated the relationship contrary to good faith. Likewise, increased liability under § 820 para. 1 should be ruled out. The continuation of the long-term non-marital relationship was not an intended result the occurrence of which was uncertain. It is true that the partners are aware that their relationship can be dissolved at

any time, and that they thus might have been able to foresee the ending of their common use [of the property]. As a rule, however, it will only be a remote possibility from the perspective of the recipient that everything will turn out differently from what had been expected. That, however, is not an uncertainty in the sense of § 820 para. 1 sent. 1 BGB.

Furthermore, the doctrine of the balance (*Saldotheorie*) should not apply to claims such as those in the present case [references omitted].

11

Selected Provisions of the German Civil Code

The following translations of provisions of the German Civil Code which relate to restitution and unjustified enrichment in a wider sense have been partially adapted from two sources. A smaller selection, translated by myself, first appeared 1997 in the German Law Archive (<http://www.iuscomp.org/gla>). Provisions which were amended during the 2002 reform (§§ 214–215, 275, 285, 346–354) have been taken from the translation of the Reform Act by Geoffrey Thomas and Gerhard Dannemann, *German Civil Code—Bürgerliches Gesetzbuch*, published in 2002, also in the German Law Archive. The author has made some small revisions, and has also added a few extra translations of his own (§§ 100, 185, 267–268, 291–292, 426, 774, 779) which have not been previously published. Permission to reproduce these translations can be obtained directly from the author.

Book I (General Part), Section 2 (Things and animals)

§ 100 Benefits

Benefits are the fruits of a thing or of a right, as well as the advantages produced by the use of the thing or the right.

Book I, Section 3 (Legal transactions), Title 1 (Capacity to enter into transactions)

§ 104 Incapacity to enter into transactions

A person lacks the capacity to enter into transactions if he

1. has not completed the seventh year of life

2. is in a medical condition which, by disturbing his mental activity, prevents the free exercise of will, unless this condition, by its nature, is of a temporary kind.

§ 105 Void declaration of intention
(1) A declaration of intention made by a person without capacity to enter into transactions is void.
(2) A declaration of intention which has been made during a condition of unconsciousness or during a temporary disturbance of mental activity is equally void.

Book I, Section 3, Title 2 (Declaration of intention)

§ 119 Voidability based on mistake
(1) A person who, when making a declaration of intention, was mistaken about its content or had no intention to make a declaration with this content, can avoid this declaration if it can be assumed that he would not have made this declaration in knowledge of the facts and with a sensible appreciation of the case.
(2) Any mistake about such characteristics of a person or an object which are considered substantial is also considered a mistake about the content of the declaration.

§ 123 Voidability based on deceit or duress
(1) A person who has been caused to make a declaration of intention by deceit or duress can avoid this declaration.
(2) If a third party committed this deceit, a declaration which was to be made towards another party can be avoided only if this other party knew of ought to have known of the deceit. If a party other than the person towards whom the declaration was to be made acquired a right immediately by the declaration, this declaration can be avoided against this person if he knew or ought to have known of the deceit.

§ 134 Statutory prohibition
A legal transaction which violates a statutory prohibition is void, unless a different intention can be taken from the statute.

§ 138 Immoral transaction; usury
(1) A legal transaction which offends good morals is void.
(2) In particular, a legal transaction is void by which somebody, by exploiting the predicament, inexperience, lack of judgment or considerable weakness of will of another party, causes pecuniary advantages to be promised or conferred onto him or onto a third party in exchange for a performance, whereby these pecuniary advantages are clearly disproportionate to this performance.

Book I, Section 3, Title 6 (Consent and ratification)

§ 185 Disposition made by an unauthorized person
(1) If an unauthorized person disposes of an object, such a disposition is effective if made with the consent of the authorized party.
(2) The disposition becomes effective once it is ratified by the authorized party, or if the disposing party acquires the object, or if the authorized party becomes the heir of the disposing party with unlimited liability for the liabilities of the estate. In the last two situations, only the earlier disposition becomes effective if several dispositions have been made of the object which cannot be reconciled with each other.

Book I, Section 5 (Limitation), Title 3 (Legal consequences of limitation)

§ 214 Effect of limitation
(1) When limitation occurs, the debtor is entitled to refuse to perform his obligation.
(2) Performance made in satisfaction of a claim that has become time-barred may not be reclaimed, even if made without knowledge of the time-bar. The same applies to an acknowledgement made in accordance with a contract and to a security given by the debtor.

§ 215 Set-off and right of retention after limitation has occurred
The fact that a claim is time-barred does not preclude set-off and assertion of a right of retention if the claim was not time-barred at the moment when set-off could first have been made or performance refused.

Book II (Law of obligations), Section 1 (Subject matter of obligations), Title 1 (Obligation to perform)

§ 267 Performance by third parties

(1) If the debtor is not required to perform in person, a third party may also effectuate performance. Consent of the debtor is not required.
(2) The creditor may refuse the performance if the debtor objects.

§ 268 Right of redemption of third party

(1) If the creditor seeks judicial execution in an object belonging to the debtor, any party who risks losing a right in this object in the course of judicial execution is entitle to satisfy the creditor. The possessor of a thing has the same right if he risks losing possession in the course of judicial execution.
(2) Such satisfaction may also occur by payment into court, or by way of set-off.
(3) To the degree that a third party satisfies the creditor, the claim is transferred to this third party. Such transfer cannot be invoked to the detriment of the creditor.

§ 275 Exclusion of the obligation to perform

(1) A claim for performance cannot be made in so far as it is impossible for the debtor or for anyone else to perform.
(2) The debtor may refuse to perform in so far as performance requires expenditure which, having regard to the subject matter of the obligation and the principle of good faith, is manifestly disproportionate to the creditor's interest in performance. When determining what may reasonably be required of the debtor, regard must also be had to whether he is responsible for the impediment.
(3) Moreover, the debtor may refuse to perform if he is to effect the performance in person and, after weighing up the creditor's interest in performance and the impediment to performance, performance cannot be reasonably required of the debtor.
(4) The creditor's rights are determined by §§ 280, 283 to 285, 311a and 326.

§ 285 Surrender of substitute

(1) If, as a result of a circumstance under which § 275 paras. (1) to (3) relieves the debtor of the obligation to perform, the debtor obtains a

substitute or a substitute claim for the object owed, the creditor may demand surrender of what has been received as substitute or an assignment of the substitute claim.
(2) If the creditor may demand compensation in lieu of performance, then, if he uses the right laid down in para. (1) above, the compensation is reduced by the value of the substitute or substitute claim he has obtained.

§ 291 Interest during legal proceedings
A money debt carries interest from the time when the claim becomes pending, even if the debtor is not in delay. If the debt becomes due only after that date, it carries interest from the time it becomes due. The provisions of § 288 para. (1) sent. 2, para. (2), para. (3) and of § 289 sent. 1 apply accordingly.

§ 292 Liability in case of obligation to surrender
(1) If the debtor must surrender a particular object, once the claim becomes pending, any claims of the creditor for damages based on the deterioration, destruction or on the impossibility to surrender the object due to another cause are governed by the provisions which apply to the relationship between the owner and the possessor before the proprietary claim becomes pending, unless rules which are more favourable to the creditor arise from the obligation or from the delay of the debtor.
(2) The same applies to the creditor's claim for surrender or remuneration for benefits, and to the debtor's claim for reimbursement of expenditure.

Book II, Section 3 (Contractual obligations), Title 1 (Creation, subject matter and cessation), Sub-title 3 (Adaptation and cessation of contracts)

§ 313 Disturbance in the basis of the contract
(1) If circumstances upon which a contract was based have materially changed after conclusion of the contract and if the parties would not have concluded the contract or would have done so upon different terms if they had foreseen that change, adaptation of the contract may be claimed in so far as, having regard to all the circumstances of the specific case, in particular the contractual or statutory allocation of

risk, it cannot reasonably be expected that a party should continue to be bound by the contract in its unaltered form.

(2) If material assumptions that have become the basis of the contract subsequently turn out to be incorrect, they are treated in the same way as a change in circumstances.

(3) If adaptation of the contract is not possible or cannot reasonably be imposed on one party, the disadvantaged party may terminate the contract. In the case of a contract for the performance of a recurring obligation, the right to terminate [with effect for the past] is replaced by the right to terminate on notice [with effect for the future].

Book II, Section 3, Title 5 (Termination and right of revocation and of return in consumer contracts), Sub-title 1 (Termination)

§ 346 Effects of termination

(1) If one party to a contract has reserved a right to terminate the contract or if he has a statutory right of termination, then, if termination occurs, any performance received is to be returned, as are benefits derived from such performance.

(2) The debtor must pay compensation for value rather than effect a return, where

1. the return or surrender is excluded because of the nature of what has been acquired,
2. he has consumed, transferred, encumbered, processed or transformed the object received,
3. the object received has deteriorated or has been destroyed; any deterioration resulting from the proper use of the object for its intended purpose is, however, disregarded.

If the contract specifies a counter-performance, such counter-performance is to be taken as a basis for calculation of the compensation for value.

(3) There is no duty to pay compensation for value

1. if the defect which gives the right to termination became apparent only during the processing or transformation of the item,

2. in so far as the creditor is responsible for the deterioration or destruction or the damage would also have occurred in his hands,
3. if, in the case of a statutory right of termination, the deterioration or destruction has occurred in the hands of the person entitled even though he has taken the care which he usually takes in his own affairs.

Any remaining enrichment must be given up.
(4) The creditor may demand compensation, in accordance with §§ 280 to 283, for infringement of a duty under subsection (1) above.

§ 347 Benefits and expenditure after termination
(1) If, contrary to the rules of proper management, the debtor has failed to derive benefits even though it would have been possible to do so, he must compensate the creditor for their value. In the case of termination based on a statutory right, the person entitled must display with regard to the benefits only the standard of care which he usually takes in his own affairs.
(2) If the debtor returns the object, compensates the creditor for value, or if his duty to compensate for value is excluded pursuant to § 346 (3), Nos. 1 or 2, he must be reimbursed for necessary expenditure. Other expenditure is to be reimbursed in as much as the creditor is enriched by it.

§ 348 Concurrent performance
The obligations of the parties arising out of termination are to be performed concurrently. The provisions of §§ 320 and 322 apply *mutatis mutandis*.

§ 349 Declaration of termination
Termination is effected by declaration to the other party.

§ 350 Expiry of the right of termination after a period of time has been set
If a period has not been agreed for exercise of a contractual right of termination, the other party may fix a reasonable period within which the party entitled to terminate must exercise that right.

If termination is not declared before the end of that period, the right of termination expires.

§ 351 Indivisibility of the right of termination
If one or the other party to the contract consists of more than one person, the right to termination can be exercised only by all and against all persons. If the right to termination expires for one of the persons entitled, it also expires for the others.

§ 352 Set-off after failure to perform
Termination for failure to perform an obligation is ineffective if the debtor could free himself from the commitment by means of a set-off and declares a set-off immediately after the termination.

§ 353 Termination on payment of a forfeit
If a right to terminate on payment of a forfeit has been reserved, termination is ineffective if the forfeit is not paid before or when the declaration is made and the other party immediately rejects the declaration on this ground. The declaration is nevertheless effective if the forfeit is paid immediately after the rejection.

§ 354 Forfeiture clause
If a contract has been concluded with the reservation that the debtor will forfeit his rights under the contract if he does not fulfil his obligation, the creditor is entitled to terminate the contract if that case arises.

Book II, Section 7 (Plurality of debtors and creditors)

§ 426 Duty to recompense, cessio legis
(1) As towards each other, joint debtors are liable in equal shares, unless provided otherwise. If the amount due cannot be obtained from one of the joint debtors, this loss must be born by the other debtors who are obliged to recompense.
(2) To the degree that one joint debtor satisfies the creditor and can require the other debtors to provide recompense, the creditor's claim against the other debtors is transferred to this joint debtor. This transfer cannot be invoked to the detriment of the creditor.

Book II, Section 8 (Particular kinds of obligations), Title 12 (Mandate and contract to look after another person's business), Sub-title 1 (Mandate)

§ 667 Mandatee's obligation to provide restitution
The mandatee is obliged to give up to the mandator anything which he receives for carrying out the mandate, and anything he obtains from managing the business.

§ 670 Recovery of expenditure
If the mandatee, for the purpose of carrying out the mandate, incurs expenditure which, according to the circumstances, he was allowed to consider as necessary, the mandator is obliged to provide reimbursement.

Book II, Section 8 (Particular kinds of obligations), Title 13 (Negotiorum gestio)

§ 677 Duties of the intervener
Whoever manages a business for another person without having been instructed by this party, or without being otherwise entitled to do so towards this party, must carry out this business in such a way as is necessary to serve the interest of the master of the business and with regard to this party's actual or presumed will.

§ 678 Management against the will of the master of the business
If the intervener, by taking on the management of the business, acts against the actual or presumed will of the master of the business, and if the intervener ought to have realized this, he is liable towards the master of the business for compensation of the damage which results from the management of the business, even if he cannot be blamed for any other culpable conduct.

§ 679 Opposing will of master of business irrelevant
If the master of the business is opposed to the management of the business, this will is irrelevant if, without the management of the business, a duty which falls on the master of the business cannot be fulfilled in time, provided that the fulfilment of this duty is in

the pubic interest or concerns a statutory obligation to provide maintenance.

§ 680 Management of business in order to avert danger
If the management of the business is aimed at averting an urgent and impeding danger for the master of the business, the intervener is responsible only for wilful and grossly negligent conduct.

§ 681 Secondary duties of the intervener
The intervener must communicate his taking over the management of the business to the master of the business as soon as this is expedient and must wait for his decision, unless this postponing entails danger. Otherwise, the provisions in §§ 666 to 668 relating to the mandatee apply to the obligations of the intervener.

§ 682 Intervener's lack of capacity
If the intervener lacks capacity to enter into transactions, or is limited in such capacity, he is liable only under the provisions on damages for tort and on giving up an unjustified enrichment.

§ 683 Recovery of expenditure
If taking over the management of the business corresponds to the interest and the actual or presumed will of the master of the business, the intervener can claim compensation for his expenditure in the same way as a mandatee. In the cases of § 679 the intervener has this claim even if taking over the management of the business conflicts with the will of the master of the business.

§ 684 Giving up of enrichment
If the requirements of § 683 are not met, the intervener is obliged to give up to the master of the business anything which he obtains by managing the business, in accordance with the provisions on giving up an unjustified enrichment. If the master of the business ratifies the management of the business, the intervener is entitled to the claim set forth in § 683.

§ 685 Donative intent
(1) The intervener has no claim if he did not have the intention to claim compensation from the master of the business.

(2) If parents or other ancestors provide maintenance to their offspring, or vice versa, it is to be presumed when in doubt that there was no intention to demand compensation from the recipient.

§ 686 Mistake about identity of master of the business
If the intervener is mistaken about the identity of the master of the business, rights and duties arising from the management of the business accrue to the true master of the business.

§ 687 False management of business
(1) The provisions of §§ 677 to 686 do not apply if somebody conducts another party's business in the belief that this is his own business.
(2) If somebody treats another party's business as his own although he knows that he is not entitled to do so, the master of the business can rely on the claims arising from §§ 677, 678, 681, 682. If he relies on these claims, he becomes obliged towards the intervener under § 684 sent. 1.

Book II, Section 8, Title 19 (Incomplete obligations)

§ 762 Gaming and Betting
(1) Gaming and Betting do not create obligations. What has been performed on the basis of the game or the bet cannot be claimed back on the ground that the obligation did not exist.
(2) These provisions apply equally to any agreement by which the other party, for the purpose of fulfilling a gaming or betting debt, enters into an obligation towards the winning party, and in particular to a recognition of debt.

Book II, Section 8, Title 20 (Guarantee)

§ 774 Cessio legis
(1) To the extent that the guarantor satisfies the creditor, the creditor's claim against the main debtor is transferred to the guarantor. This transfer cannot be invoked to the detriment of the creditor. Defenses which the main creditor has under a legal relationship with the guarantor remain unaffected.
(2) Co-guarantors are liable towards each other only under § 426.

Book II, Section 8, Title 21 (Compromise)

§ 779 Notion of compromise; mistake as to basis of compromise
(1) A contract whereby parties give in reciprocally in order to settle a disagreement or uncertainty about a legal relationship (compromise) is invalid if the facts which are assumed to exist under the content of the contract in reality do not exist, and if the disagreement or the uncertainty would not have arisen if parties had known the true facts.
(2) If it is uncertain whether a claim can be realized, this is to be treated in the same way as an uncertainty about a legal relationship.

Book II, Section 8, Title 22 (Promise of obligation and recognition of obligation)

§ 781 Recognition of obligation
A contract whereby the existence of an obligation is recognized (recognition of obligation) is valid only if the declaration by which the obligation is recognized is made in writing. Writing may not be substituted by electronic form. If the creation of the obligation whose existence is recognized is subject to another form requirement, the recognition contract must be made in the same form.

Book II, Section 8, Title 26 (Unjustified enrichment)

§ 812 Obligation to provide restitution
(1) A person who obtains something by performance by another person or in another way at the expense of this person without legal ground is bound to give it up to him. The same obligation exists if the legal ground later lapses or if the result does not occur which the performance had been aimed at to produce according to the content of the legal transaction. (2) The recognition or denial of the existence of an obligation by way of contract is also considered as performance.

§ 813 Performance in spite of defence
(1) What has been performed for the purpose of fulfilling an obligation can also be claimed back if the claim was barred by a defence which

permanently excluded the claim from being raised. This is without prejudice to the provision of § 214 para. (2).
(2) If an obligation is performed before the fixed time, restitution is excluded; interest cannot be claimed for the time until performance would have been due.

§ 814 Knowledge of lack of obligation
What has been performed for the purpose of fulfilling an obligation cannot be claimed back if the person who performed knew that he was not obliged to perform, or if performance corresponded with a moral duty or with respect to decency.

§ 815 Result fails to occcur
Restitution for lack of occurrence of the result which the performance was aimed at is excluded if it was impossible from the beginning to achieve the result and if the person who performed was aware of this, or if the person who performed has prevented the occurrence of the result in a manner which offends good faith.

§ 816 Disposition by unauthorized person
(1) If an unauthorized person disposes of an object and this disposition is effective towards the entitled person, the unauthorized person is obliged to give up to the entitled person what he obtained by the disposition. If the disposition was gratuitous, the same obligation lies on the person who obtained a legal advantage immediately by the disposition.
(2) If performance is made towards an unauthorized person, and this performance is effective towards the entitled person, the unauthorized person is obliged to give up to the entitled person what has been performed.

§ 817 Violation of statutory prohibition or good morals
If the purpose of a performance was defined in such a way that by his acceptance the recipient violated a statutory prohibition or offended good morals, the recipient is obliged to provide restitution. Restitution is excluded if the person who performed is also to blame for such a violation, unless the performance consisted in the undertaking of

an obligation; what has been performed in order to discharge such an obligation cannot be claimed back.

§ 818 Measure of enrichment claim

(1) The obligation to provide restitution extends to benefits which have been obtained, as well as to anything which the recipient acquires on the basis of on obtained right, or in replacement for the destruction, damage to or deprivation of the obtained object.
(2) If, due to the nature of what has been obtained, return is impossible, or if the recipient for another reason is not in the position to return what he has obtained, he must compensate for the value.
(3) The obligation to provide return or compensation for the value is excluded to the extent that the recipient is no longer enriched.
(4) Once an action is pending against the recipient, he becomes liable under the general provisions.

§ 819 Increased liability: mala fide debtor, violation of statute or good morals

(1) If the recipient knows of the lack of a legal ground at the time of the receipt, or if he later learns of this lack, he is obliged to provide restitution from the time of the receipt or from the time when he obtains this knowledge as if an action for restitution had been pending at that time.
(2) If the recipient, by accepting performance, violates a statutory prohibition or offends good morals, the same obligation falls on him from the time when he receives performance.

§ 820 Increased liability: occurrence of result uncertain

(1) If a result was aimed at by the performance, the occurrence of which was considered uncertain according to the content of the legal transaction, and if this result fails to occur, the recipient is obliged to provide restitution as if an action for restitution had been pending at the time of the receipt. This also applies if performance occurred for a legal ground, the lapse of which was deemed possible according to the content of the legal transaction, and if the legal ground then lapses.
(2) The recipient is obliged to pay interest only from the time when he learns that the result has not been obtained or that the legal ground has

lapsed; he is not obliged to provide restitution of benefits to the extent that he is no longer enriched at this time.

§ 821 Enrichment as defence
A person who undertakes an obligation without legal ground can refuse performance even if the claim for release from this obligation is time-barred.

§ 822 Restitution by third parties
If the recipient gratuitously passes on what he has obtained to a third party, this third party must provide restitution as if the creditor had made the transfer onto him without a legal ground, to the extent that the recipient's disposition excludes the recipient's obligation to give up his enrichment.

Book 3 (Property law), Section 3 (Ownership), Title 4 (Claims arising from ownership)

§ 985 Claim for surrender
The owner can require the possessor to surrender the thing.

§ 986 Defences of the possessor
(1) The possessor can refuse to surrender the thing if he, or an indirect possessor from whom he derives his right to possess, has a right to possession against the owner. . . .
(2) . . .

§ 987 Benefits after action is pending
(1) The possessor must give up to the owner any benefits which he reaps after the action is pending.
(2) If the possessor, after an action is pending, fails to reap benefits which he could have reaped according to the rules of orderly business, he becomes liable towards the owner for compensation, to the extent that his conduct is culpable.

§ 988 Benefits reaped by gratuitous possessor
If a possessor has gratuitously acquired possession and possesses the thing in the belief that it is his own, or in order to exercise a right

to use the corporeal object whereas in reality he has no such right, he is obliged to give up to the owner benefits which he reaps before the action becomes pending, according to the rules on giving up an unjustified enrichment.

§ 989 Damages after action is pending
Once the action is pending, the possessor becomes liable towards the owner for the damage which occurs because, due to the possessor's culpability, the thing deteriorates, perishes, or cannot be surrendered by him for another reason.

§ 990 Liability in case of knowledge
(1) If the possessor, when acquiring possession, was not *bona fide*, he is liable towards the possessor from the time of this acquisition in accordance with §§ 987, 989. If the possessor later learns that he is not entitled to possession, he becomes liable in the same way, from the time when he gains this knowledge.
(2) Any additional liability of the possessor for delay remains unaffected.

§ 991 Liability of indirect possessor
(1) If the possessor derives the right for possession from an indirect possessor, the provisions in § 990, as regards secondary benefits, apply only if the requirements set forth in § 990 are also met in the person of the indirect possessor, or if the action has become pending against him.
(2) If the possessor was *bona fide* when acquiring possession, he nevertheless is responsible towards the owner for damage as described in § 989 from the time of this acquisition, to the extent that the possessor is responsible towards the indirect possessor.

§ 992 Liability of tortious possessor
If the possessor has acquired possession by unlawful interference, or by a criminal offence, he is liable towards the owner under the provisions on damages for tort.

§ 993 Liability of *bona fide* possessor for value
(1) If the requirements set forth in §§ 987 to 992 are not met, the possessor must give up any fruits which, according to the rules on orderly

business, are not considered as yield of the thing, under the rules on giving up an unjustified enrichment; otherwise, he is not liable for giving up benefits, or for damages.
(2) The provisions in § 101 apply to the possessor for that period of time for which he keeps the benefits.

§ 994 Necessary expenditure
(1) The possessor can claim from the owner reimbursement for necessary expenditure incurred on the corporeal object. However, the usual costs for upkeep are not to be reimbursed for that period of time for which the possessor keeps the benefits.
(2) If the possessor incurs necessary expenditure after the action is pending, or after liability as described in § 990 has set in, the owner's obligation to reimburse is governed by the provisions on *negotiorum gestio.*

§ 996 Useful expenditure
For other than necessary expenditures, the possessor can claim reimbursement only to the extent that they were incurred before the action was pending, and before liability as described in § 990 has set in, and to the extent that the value of the thing is still increased at the time when the owner regains the thing.

Select Bibliography

These works are cited in the text in abbreviated form.

Birks, Peter, *An Introduction to the Law of Restitution* (1985; reprinted 1989)

—— *Unjust Enrichment*, 2nd edn (2005)

Burrows, Andrew, *The Law of Restitution*, 2nd edn (2002)

—— *et al*, 'The New Birkisan Approach to Unjust Enrichment' *(2004) Rest L Rev 260–298*

von Caemmerer, Ernst, 'Bereicherung und unerlaubte Handlung', in: *Festschrift für Ernst Rabel*, Vol. I, ed. by Hans Dölle, Max Rheinstein, and Konrad Zweigert (1954), 333–401

Canaris, Claus-Wilhelm, 'Der Bereicherungsausgleich im Dreipersonenverhältnis', in: *Festschrift für Karl Larenz zum 70. Geburtstag*, ed. by Gotthard Paulus, Uwe Diederichsen, and Claus-Wilhelm Canaris (1973), 799–865

Cases, Materials and Texts on Unjustified Enrichment, ed. by Jack Beatson and Eltjo Schrage with the collaboration of Mindy Chen-Wishart, Martin Hogg, Barry Nicholas, Martin Schermaier, David Sellar, Dannie Visser, and Floor Gras (2003)

Chambers, Robert, *Resulting Trusts* (1997)

Chitty on Contracts, Hugh Beale (gen. ed.), 29th edn (2004)

Coen, Christoph, *Vertragsscheitern und Rückabwicklung. Eine rechtsvergleichende Untersuchung zum englischen und deutschen Recht, zum UN-Kaufrecht sowie zu den Unidroit Principles und den Principles of European Contract Law* (2003)

Dannemann, Gerhard, 'Restitution for Termination of Contract in German Law', in: *Failure of Contracts: Contractual, Restitutionary and Proprietary Consequences*, ed. by Francis Rose (1997), 129–153

—— 'Illegality as a Defence' *(2000) Oxford U Comparative Law Forum 4*

—— 'Unjust Enrichment by Transfer: Some Comparative Remarks' *79 Texas Law Review 1837–1867 (2001)*

Dawson, John P, *Unjust Enrichment: A Comparative Analysis* (1951; quoted from the 1999 reprint)

Draft Common Frame of Reference: see *Principles, Definitions and Model Rules*

Edelman, James, *Gain-based Damages* (2002)

English Private Law, ed. by Andrew Burrows, 2nd edn (2007), Ch. IV.18 on 'Unjust Enrichment' (Charles Mitchell)

Evans, Sir William, *An Essay on the Action for Money Had and Received* (1802), re-edited by Peter Birks, Francis Rose, and Lionel Smith and reprinted in (1998) Rest L Rev 1–33; quoted with reference to the original pagination

Fikentscher, Wolfgang and Heinemann, Andreas, *Schuldrecht*, 10th edn (2006)

Friedmann, Daniel, 'Restitution of Benefits Obtained Through the Appropriation of Property or the Commission of a Wrong' *80 Columbia L Rev 504–558 (1980)*

Friedmann, Wolfgang, 'The Principle of Unjust Enrichment in English Law' *(1938) 16 Canadian Bar Rev 243–267 and 365–386*

Giglio, Francesco, 'Restitution for Wrongs' *(2001) Oxford U Comparative L Forum 6*

—— 'A Systematic Approach to "Unjust" and "Unjustified" Enrichment' *(2003) 23 OJLS 455*

Goff of Chieveley, Lord and Jones, Gareth, *The Law of Restitution*, 7th edn by Gareth Jones (2007)

Grundstrukturen eines europäischen Bereicherungsrechts: Tagung der privatrechtlichen Sektion der Deutschen Gesellschaft für Rechtsvergleichung in Dresden, September 2003, ed. by Reinhard Zimmermann (2005)

Gutteridge, Harold and David, René, 'The Doctrine of Unjustified Enrichment' *(1935) 5 Camb LJ 204*

Häcker, Birke, 'Still at the Crossroads' *(2007) LQR 177*

Hedley, Steve, *A Critical Introduction to Restitution* (2001)

Hellwege, Phillip, *Die Rückabwicklung gegenseitiger Verträge als einheitliches Problem* (2004)

International Encyclopedia of Comparative Law, Vol. 10: 'Restitution/Unjust Enrichment and Negotiorum Gestio', ed. by Ernst von Caemmerer and Peter Schlechtriem (2007)

König, Detlef, 'Empfiehlt es sich, das Bereicherungsrecht im Hinblick auf seine Weiterentwicklung in Rechtsprechung und Lehre durch den Gesetzgebern neu zu ordnen?', in: *Gutachten und Vorschläge zur Überarbeitung des Schuldrechts*, ed. by Bundesministerium der Justiz, Vol. II (1981), 1515–1590

Kortmann, Jeroen, *Altruism in Private Law: Liability for Nonfeasance and Negotiorum Gestio* (2005)

Krebs, Thomas, *Restitution at the Crossroads: A Comparative Study* (2001)

Kuhlmann, Jens, *Rückgriffsgrundlagen bei Gesamtschuld, Bürgschaft und Schadensversicherung in Deutschland, England und Schweden* (2005)

Larenz, Karl and Canaris, Claus-Wilhelm, *Lehrbuch des Schuldrechts, Besonderer Teil, 2. Halbband*, 13th edn (1994)

The Limits of Restitutionary Claims: A Comparative Analysis, ed. by William Swadling (1997)

MacQueen, Hector, *Unjustified Enrichment* (2004)

Mapping the Law: Essays in Honour of Peter Birks, ed. by Andrew Burrows and Alan Rodger (2006)

Meier, Sonja, *Irrtum und Zweckverfehlung* (1999)

Mitchell, Charles, 'Claims in Unjustified Enrichment to Recover Money Paid Pursuant to a Common Liability' *(2001) 5 ELR 186*

Münchener Kommentar zum Bürgerlichen Gesetzbuch, Band 5: Schuldrecht, Besonderer Teil III, ed. by Peter Ulmer, 4th edn (2004)

Principles, Definitions and Model Rules of European Private Law: Draft Common Frame of Reference (DCFR), Outline Edition, prepared by the Study Group on a European Civil Code and the Research Group on EC Private Law (Acquis Group) (2009)

Reuter, Dieter and Martinek, Michael, *Ungerechtfertigte Bereicherung (Handbuch des Schuldrechts, Band 4)* (1983)

Rusch, Konrad, *Gewinnhaftung bei Verletzung von Treuepflichten: Eine rechtsvergleichende Untersuchung zum englischen und deutschen Recht* (2003)

Schäfer, Frank, *Das Bereicherungsrecht in Europa: Einheits- und Trennungslehren im gemeinen, deutschen und englischen Recht* (2001)

Schall, Alexander, *Leistungskondiktion und 'Sonstige Kondiktion' auf der Grundlage des einheitlichen gesetzlichen Kondiktionsprinzips* (2003)

—— 'Three-party situations in unjust enrichment epitomised by mistaken bank transfers', 12 Rest L Rev 110–131 (2004)

Schindler, Thomas, *Rechtsgeschäftliche Entscheidungsfreiheit und Drohung: die englische duress-Lehre in rechtsvergleichender Perspektive* (2005)

Schlechtriem, Peter, *Restitution und Bereicherungsausgleich in Europa: Eine rechtsvergleichende Darstellung*, Vol. 1 (2000), Vol. 2 (2001)

—— *Schuldrecht Besonderer Teil*, 6th edn (2003)

Schrage, Eltjo, *Unjust Enrichment: The Comparative Legal History of the Law of Restitution*, 2nd edn (1999)

Scott, Helen, *Unjust Enrichment by Transfer in South African Law: Unjust Factors or Absence of Legal Ground?*, PhD thesis, Oxford (2005)

Sheehan, Duncan, 'Natural Obligations in English Law' (2004) LMCLQ 172ff

—— 'Unjust Factors or Restitution of Transfers *Sine Causa*' (2008) Oxford U Comparative L Forum 1

Smith, Lionel, 'Demystifying Juristic Reason' *(2007) 45 Can Bus Law J 281ff*

Solomon, Dennis, *Der Bereicherungsausgleich in Anweisungsfällen* (2004)

J von Staudinger's Kommentar zum Bürgerlichen Gesetzbuch, §§ 812–22, Neubearbeitung by Stephan Lorenz (2007)

Structure and Justification in Private Law. Essays for Peter Birks, ed. by Charles Rickett and Ross Brantham (2008)

Tettenborn, Andrew, *Law of Restitution in England and Ireland*, 3rd edn (2002)

Unjustified Enrichment: Key Issues in Comparative Perspective, ed. by David Johnston and Reinhard Zimmermann (2002)

Verse, Dirk, *'Improvements and Enrichment: A Comparative Analysis' (1998) Restitution L Rev 85*

—— *Verwendungen im Eigentümer-Besitzer-Verhältnis* (1999)

Visser, Daniel, 'Unjustified Enrichment in Comparative Perspective', in: Mathias Reimann and Reinhard Zimmermann (eds), *The Oxford Handbook of Comparative Law* (2006), 969–1002

Wendehorst, Christiane, 'No Headaches over Unjust Enrichment: A Response to Daniel Friedmann', in: *The Draft Civil Code for Israel in Comparative Perspective*, ed. by Kurt Siehr and Reinhard Zimmermann (2008)

Wilburg, Walter, *Die Lehre von der ungerechtfertigten Bereicherung nach österreichischem und deutschem Recht* (1934)

Zimmermann, Reinhard, *The Law of Obligations: Roman Foundations of the Civilian Tradition* (1990; quoted from the 1996 paperback edn)

—— and Jacques du Plessis, 'Basic Features of the German Law of Unjustified Enrichment' *(1994) Rest L Rev 14–43*

Zweigert, Konrad and Kötz, Hein, *An Introduction to Comparative Law*, transl. by T Weir, 3rd edn (1998)

Glossary of German Legal Terms

Amtsgericht	local court of first instance
arglistige Täuschung	deceit, fraudulent misrepresentation
Auftrag	mandate, a contract governed by §§ 667ff BGB
Bereicherung	enrichment
– aufgedrängte –	imposed enrichment
– ungerechtfertigte –	unjustified enrichment
Bundesgerichtshof	Federal Court of Justice (Germany's highest court in civil and criminal matters)
Bürgerliches Gesetzbuch	German Civil Code
causa	(the underlying) cause (of an obligation)
cessio legis	assignment by operation of the law
condictio, pl. *condictiones*	enrichment claim
– *causa data causa non secuta*	enrichment claim based on failure of purpose
– *indebiti*	enrichment claim based on lack of obligation
– *ob causam finitam*	enrichment claim based on subsequent lapse of an obligation
– *ob rem*	(used synonymously for → *condictio causa data causa non secuta*)
– *ob turpem vel iniustam causam*	enrichment claim based on illegality
– *possessionis*	enrichment claim against a (mere) possessor
Darlehen	loan
Deckungsverhältnis	cover relationship: in tripartite relationships this denounces the two parties whose relationship is used for procuring the value to be shifted to a third party within the → Valutaverhältnis
diligentia quam in suis	standard of care based on the level which a given party usually takes in its own affairs

Doppelkondiktion	dual enrichment claim: in a chain of failed contracts between A and B and B and C, B's enrichment claim against C amounts to an unjustified enrichment which A can claim from B, thus allowing A to ultimately sue C
Eigentümer-Besitzer-Verhältnis	legal relationship between the owner of property and a possessor who has no right to possession, governed by §§ 985ff BGB
Eingriff	interference
Eingriffskondiktion	enrichment claim based on interference with a right of the claimant
Gegenleistung	counter-performance
Geschäftsführung ohne Auftrag	*negotiorum gestio*, literally: management of affairs without mandate
Geschäftsgrundlage	basis of transaction, an element within the doctrine of → Wegfall der Geschäftsgrundlage
in pari turpitudine (*melior est causa possidentis*)	German Latin for the English Latin *in pari delicto* (*potior est conditio defendentis*)—or the defence of illegality
Kondiktion	→ *condictio*
Landgericht	Regional court of first instance, in some situations Appeal Court for cases first heard by an → Amtsgericht
Leihe	a contract whereby one party gratuitously borrows an object from another, governed by §§ 598ff BGB
Leistung	performance
Leistungskondiktion	enrichment claim based on performance
Naturalrestitution	restitution in kind
Nichtleistungskondiktion	enrichment claim not based on performance
Nutzungen	benefits derived from property or a right, as defined in § 100 BGB

Oberlandesgericht	Higher Regional Court, usually acting as Appeal Court
Rechtsgeschäft	legal transaction, including contract, offer, acceptance, their revocation, rescission, or termination
Rechtsschein	appearance that a legal relationship exists (which in fact does not)
Reichsgericht	Imperial Court, until 1945 Germany's highest court in civil and criminal matters
Rückgriff	recourse
Rückgriffskondiktion	enrichment claim under which a claimant is allowed to take recourse against a third party
Saldotheorie	doctrine of the balance, whereby after the failure of contracts a claimant who obtains restitution for performance may not rely on disenrichment for the defendant's counterclaim; the opposite view is taken by the → Zweikondiktionenlehre
Schenkung	gift or donation, a contract governed by §§ 516ff BGB
Schuldanerkenntnis	recognition of debt, a contract governed by § 781 BGB
Surrogat	an object which has replaced the initial enrichment under § 818 para. 1 BGB
Tilgungsbestimmung	specification which debt is to be serviced by a payment or other performance
Valutaverhältnis	value relationship, in tripartite relationships this denounces the relationship between those parties where the value is to flow, as is the case e.g. for sending account holder and recipient account holder in a payment; to be distinguished from the → Deckungsverhältnis (cover relationship) used to procure this value, e.g. between sending account holder and this party's bank

Vergleich	compromise or settlement, a contract governed by § 779 BGB
Verwendung, pl. Verwendungen	expenditure
– nützliche ~	useful expenditure under § 996 BGB
– notwendige ~	necessary expenditure under § 994 BGB
Verwendungskondiktion	enrichment claim based on the claimant's expenditure on the defendant's property
vindicatio	proprietary claim of the owner against the possessor for surrender of the property (§ 985 BGB)
Wegfall	lapse
– der Bereicherung	disenrichment, change of position
– der Geschäftsgrundlage	lapse of the basis of transaction, a doctrine under which a contract can be adapted or terminated if circumstances have changed dramatically, now regulated in § 313 BGB and called Störung (disturbance) der Geschäfsgrundlage
Zuweisungstheorie	doctrine of attribution, whereby wrongs-based restitution is limited to the infringement of rights for which the law attributes the gain in question to the owner of the right
Zweckbestimmung	determination of the purpose of a performance (in particular, which obligation this performance is to serve)
Zweikondiktionenlehre	doctrine of the two enrichment claims whereby, after a contract has failed, enrichment claims by one party against the other are not affected by disenrichment in the counterclaim; the opposite view is taken by the → Saldotheorie

Index

Entries in *italics* are explained in the glossary of German legal terms on pp. 319–322.

The manufacturer's authorised representative in the EU for product safety is Oxford University Press España S.A. of el Parque Empresarial San Fernando de Henares, Avenida de Castilla, 2 – 28830 Madrid (www.oup.es/en or product.safety@oup.com). OUP España S.A. also acts as importer into Spain of products made by the manufacturer.

www.ingramcontent.com/pod-product-compliance
Lightning Source LLC
LaVergne TN
LVHW101443200926
848483LV00001B/35

* 9 7 8 0 1 9 9 5 3 3 1 1 4 *